Cooperatives across Clusters

LESSONS FROM THE CRANBERRY INDUSTRY

Anil Hira, Paul Gottlieb, Neil Reid,
Stephan Goetz, and Elizabeth Dobis

Oregon State University Press   Corvallis

Library of Congress Cataloging-in-Publication Data

Names: Hira, Anil, author. | Gottlieb, Paul David, 1959- author. | Reid, Neil, 1963 July 7- author. | Goetz, Stephan J. (Stephan Juergen), author. | Dobis, Elizabeth A., author.
Title: Cooperatives across clusters : lessons from the cranberry industry / Anil Hira, Paul Gottlieb, Neil Reid, Stephan Goetz, and Elizabeth Dobis
Description: Corvallis : Oregon State University Press, [2024] | Includes bibliographical references and index
Identifiers: LCCN 2024000989 | ISBN 9781962645010 (trade paperback) | ISBN 9781962645027 (ebook)
Subjects: LCSH: Ocean Spray Cranberries, Inc. | Agriculture, Cooperative—North America—History. | Agriculture—Economic aspects—North America. | Cranberry industry—North America—History.
Classification: LCC HD1491.A6 H57 2024 | DDC 334/.683476097—dc23/eng/202402033
LC record available at https://lccn.loc.gov/2024000989

∞ This paper meets the requirements of ANSI/NISO Z39.48-1992 (Permanence of Paper).
© 2024 Anil Hira, Paul Gottlieb, Neil Reid, Stephan Goetz, Elizabeth Dobis
All rights reserved.
First published in 2024 by Oregon State University Press
Printed in the United States of America

Oregon State University Press
121 The Valley Library
Corvallis OR 97331-4501
541-737-3166 • fax 541-737-3170
www.osupress.oregonstate.edu

Oregon State University Press in Corvallis, Oregon, is located within the traditional homelands of the Mary's River or Ampinefu Band of Kalapuya. Following the Willamette Valley Treaty of 1855, Kalapuya people were forcibly removed to reservations in Western Oregon. Today, living descendants of these people are a part of the Confederated Tribes of Grand Ronde Community of Oregon (grandronde.org) and the Confederated Tribes of the Siletz Indians (ctsi.nsn.us).

Dedicated to the hardworking and sometimes cantankerous cranberry growers of North America, whose dedication, enterprising spirit, and sense of mission are unmatchable.

Contents

List of Illustrations ix
List of Acronyms xi
Acknowledgments and Methods of Study xiii
List of Interviewees xv

1 Cluster Theory and the Challenge of Agricultural Cooperation 1
2 Why Do Cranberries Cluster? 31
3 The History of Cranberries:
   Escaping the Commodity Trap via Cooperatives 58
4 Market Forces Threaten Cooperation 77
5 The Emerging Giant in Québec—
   A Challenge to Ocean Spray Leadership? 107
6 Comparing Ocean Spray to Other Large Agricultural Cooperatives .. 130
7 Conclusion, Recommendations, and Implications
   for Agricultural Industry Organization 147

   References 177
   Appendixes
      A: Survey 191
      B: Ethics (Confidentiality) Forms 201
      C: Notes on GIS Maps 208
   About the Authors 209
   Index 213

Illustrations

FIGURES

1.1. Triple Helix. 11
1.2. Vernon's Product Cycle—A Revised Version. 14
2.1. Cranberry Processing Stations in Key Growing Clusters 43
2.2. Processing Stations in New England and Québec. 43
2.3. Processing Stations on the West Coast 44
2.4. Processing Stations in the Great Lakes 44
4.1. US per Capita Consumption of Cranberries, 1980–2016 (lb./person). . 79
4.2a. US per Capita Juice Consumption, 1980–2017 80
4.2b. US Total Cranberry Juice Consumption, 1988–2020 80
4.2c. US Cranberry Juice Consumption as a Percentage of Total Fruit Juice Consumption, 1988–2020. 81
4.3. US Fresh Cranberry Exports: Significant Markets, 1989–2018, Percent of World Total 85
4.4. Top US Export Markets: Prepared/Preserved Cranberries, 2012–2018 85
4.5. Acres Harvested and Production in Barrels in the US, 1900–2016 91
4.6. US Yield per Acre, 1900–2015 91
4.7. Value of Production in the US ($1000s), 1934–2017 91
4.8. US Processed Cranberry Price per Barrel, 1934–2017 vs. Ocean Spray Pool Price from 1975 to 2018 92
4.9. Acres Harvested by State, 1900–2017. 94
4.10. Total Production (Barrels) by State, 1900–2017. 94
4.11. Yield per Acre (barrels/acre) by State, 1900–2015 95
4.12. Yield per Acre (lb./acre), 1990–2020, Québec and Wisconsin vs. Other US States and BC 95
4.13. Price per Barrel by State Converges, 1900–2015 95
4.14. Canadian Cranberry Production, 1960–2018 97

4.15. Impressive Growth of Québec Production 98
4.16. Exports as Share of Total Canadian Production, 1996–2018 99
4.17. Top Destinations for Exports of BC Cranberries, 2018 99
4.18. Top Cranberry Export Destinations for Québec, 2018 99

TABLES

2.1. Basic Supply Chain Inputs for Cranberries 37
4.1. Global Cranberry Consumption 78
4.2. Global Production of Cranberries by Country, 2019 82
4.3. Global Cranberry Production: Major Increases
 in the United States, Canada, and Chile, 2011–2018 83
4.4. Total Chinese Cranberry Imports, 2014–2019 86
4.5. Chinese Market Prices for Different Types of Cranberries, 2018 89
4.6. Total Acres/Farm by State, 1997–2017. 96
5.1. Growth in B.C./Québec Production, 2006–2021 109
5.2. BCCMC Levies (US $/lb.) 111

Acronyms

APCQ	Association of Cranberry Producers of Québec
ARS	Agricultural Research Service (a branch of the USDA)
BCCMC	British Columbia Cranberry Marketing Commission
CETAQ	Club Environnemental et Technique Atocas Québec
CI	Cranberry Institute
CMC	Cranberry Marketing Committee
ERS	Economic Research Service (part of USDA)
FAO	Food and Agriculture Organization (of the UN)
IAF	Investment Agricultural Foundation (BC)
MAPAQ	Government of Québec, Ministry of Agriculture, Fisheries, and Food
NACREW	North American Cranberry Research and Extension Workers
NASS	National Agricultural Statistics Service (part of USDA)
OECD	Organization for Economic Cooperation and Development
R&D	research and development
SDC	sweetened dried cranberries
USDA	US Department of Agriculture

All opinions expressed in this report are those of the authors and do not reflect the perspectives of our funders or employers. The reader should keep in mind that, while a survey was carried out, the opinions expressed in this report are not purported to represent majority views. They are generally expressed here as reflecting multiple interviewees' opinions and/or as offering an interesting perspective on the industry. We believe that reporting differences of opinion is important for an independent report, even at the risk of making some in industry uncomfortable, and that such reporting has the potential benefits of voicing concerns that might not otherwise be heard in a form that might feed into developing industry consensus around strategy. Participants have shared their individual perceptions of the situation as they see it, and these perceptions inform the behavior of key stakeholders and influence the ability to resolve fundamental governance issues.

Acknowledgments and Methods of Study

This work was supported by the US Department of Agriculture, National Institute of Food and Agriculture, under Grant No. 2017-67023-26906, received by the principal investigator, Dr. Paul Gottlieb of Rutgers University. This case study is part of a larger study of agricultural clusters in the United States, including their precise mapping and examination, as well as parallel case studies on hops and racehorses. We would like to thank the funders. We would also like to thank my research assistants, partly funded through USDA and partly through Simon Fraser University's work-study program: Raphael Ochil, Leighton Kerr, Ester di Maio, Ronaldo Au-Yeung, and Amélie Lauzon of the University of Ottawa. Leighton deserves special acknowledgment for his significant work on the Canadian statistics and for helping to prepare the survey. We would also like to thank Patty and Sarita Hira for additional research and editing assistance. Patty also helped gather and organize the statistics for BC and Québec cranberry production. Special thanks are owed to Dr. Alois Sieben, of SFU's Department of English, for his assiduous work in editing the final manuscript.

Research was conducted through historical and statistical analysis, interviews with stakeholders in each of the seven main producing clusters, and surveys carried out through intermediaries in the same seven areas, during the period 2018–2022. Cranberry industry stakeholders were generally open and supportive once we could reach them. We made an early pitch about the research to Ocean Spray at the Cape Cod Cranberry Growers' Association in 2018; they have been generally supportive of the effort to provide a strategic overview of the industry, while still respecting our need for independence as researchers. The stakeholder interviews were approximately one hour in length and consisted of both predetermined and open-ended questions, with the promise of not ascribing statements to any individual. Cranberry growers and handlers were generally very friendly and open to the study, and we were able to attend the North American Cranberry Research and Extension Workers (NACREW) meeting. We would like to particularly thank the cranberry growers' associations in each of the clusters; all were very helpful. We were fortunate to be invited to the Washington/Oregon and Wisconsin growers' associations annual meetings, which gave us additional insights into concerns and allowed us to introduce the study to their membership. Unfortunately, the COVID-19 pandemic put a stop to the research for about two years. As a result, we had to shift some of the BC research to online Zoom interviews once Simon Fraser University (SFU) allowed the research to resume in spring 2022. Happily, we were able to conduct more than a dozen in-person interviews in Wisconsin in March 2022 to complete the study. The Québec Cranberry Growers Association (APCQ) and the Government of Québec were particularly helpful in piecing together the important story of the cluster formation there.

Particular thanks are owed to officials in the US Department of Agriculture (USDA) and the Cranberry Marketing Committee (CMC). At the USDA, Patty Bennett's Marketing Order and Agreement Division helped considerably in clarifying issues around the marketing order. Greg Lemmons, of the National Agricultural Statistics Service, and Agnes Perez, of the Economic Research Service, went out of their way to help with guidance on how to find cranberry statistics. At the CMC, Michelle Hogan's support for the survey was vital to this study; CMC also kindly permitted us to virtually attend their 2022 winter meeting, even though we had to get up at 5 a.m. on consecutive days for it. The CMC, the BC Cranberry Marketing Commission (BCCMC), and the APCQ all were kind enough to disseminate our survey to their growers' lists in winter 2021–2022.

We wish to thank the following list of interviewees. In accordance with SFU's ethics policy, all interviews were conducted confidentially, almost exclusively through one-hour in-person interviews, with some preset and some open-ended questions. A handful (fewer than ten) were conducted via Zoom, either because of COVID-19 concerns or because scheduling could not be worked out during field research trips. Expert interviewees were assured that their names would be listed in the report (with their consent), but no information or perspectives would be specifically ascribed to them. We do not list any names of the government officials or individual growers we interviewed for the study, to protect them. Cranberry growers' names are also not listed, to protect them, and while other stakeholders' names are listed in the interviewees list, no attribution connects information to names. Over the course of three years, more than eighty interviews, mostly in person, were conducted with stakeholders in Massachusetts, New Jersey, Washington, Oregon, Wisconsin, Québec, and British Columbia, and with USDA officials in Washington, DC. We found names of growers and handlers through web searches. We then sent e-mails and made phone calls to set up interviews; this usually required multiple efforts. We are thankful to the organizers of the 2019 NACREW and the 2019 Washington-Oregon growers' associations for allowing us to pitch the research to their members.

List of Interviewees
(Government Employees and Growers Not Listed)

Dawn Gates Allen and Brian Wick,
  Cape Cod Cranberry Growers' Association
Charles Armstrong, University of Maine Extension
Amaya Atucha, University of Wisconsin Madison,
  Department of Horticulture
Steve Berlyn, Mariani Premium Dried Fruits
Coreen Rodger Berrisford, BC Cranberry Marketing Commission,
  general manager
Marc Bieler, CEO, Bielers Canneberges, and founder of Atoka Products
Cassie Bouska, extension officer, Oregon State University
Shawn Cutts, American Cranberry Growers' Association (NJ)
Vincent DeMacedo, Massachusetts State Senate
Bob Donaldson, director, Oregon Growers' Association
Rosa Gallardo, Elizabeth Canales, and Xueying Ma,
  VacCAP consumer preferences researchers
Michel Gardner, agronomist consultant, Québec cranberry industry
François Gervais, CETAQ, Québec
Vincent Godin, président of APCQ and Emblème, Québec
Christelle Guédot, University of Wisconsin Madison, entomology
Nicole Hansen and Bill Hatch, Cranberry Creek Cranberries (WI)
Rebecca Harbut, Kwantlen Polytechnic University
Michelle Hogan, Cranberry Marketing Committee
Kim Houdlette, Makepeace Cranberries
Terry Humfeld and John Wilson, the Cranberry Institute
Massimo Iorizzo, horticultural science, NC State,
  head of VacCAP Research Project
Allison Jonjak, University of Wisconsin–Madison,
  cranberry outreach specialist, Division of Extension
Didier LaBarre, research, APCQ, Québec
Jordan Lamb, DeWitt LLP (WI)
John Lebeaux, Massachusetts agricultural commissioner

Tom Lochner, director, Wisconsin Cranberry Growers Association
Jim Luby, University of Minnesota
Heidi Lundstrum, E.S. Cropconsult (BC)
Chip Matthews, Pappas Lassonde, Inc.
Ocean Spray employees: Rod Serres (MA), Jeff LaFleur (MA), Samantha Tochen (WA), Don Kloft (OR), Jean Pierre Deland (Québec), Miranda Elsby (BC), Leroy Kummer (WI)
Jean Olsthoorn, agronomist consultant, Québec cranberry industry
Jacques Painchaud, retired, former official of MAPAQ (Government of Québec)
Dr. Kim Patten, Professor Emeritus, Washington State University, former director of the Long Beach extension station
Mat Patterson, director, marketing development, Government of British Columbia
Martin Plante, CEO, Citadelle, Québec
Susan Playfair, author, *America's Founding Fruit: The Cranberry in a New Environment*
Renée Prasad, associate professor, Agriculture Technology Department, University of Fraser Valley, British Columbia
Rutgers Research Station: Nick Vorsa, Amy Howell, and Jennifer Johnson-Cicalese
Hilary Sandler, Massachusetts Agricultural Experiment Station
David Brock Smith, Oregon state representative
Kalpna Solanki, chair, BC Cranberry Marketing Commission
Carolyn Teasdale, Government of British Columbia
Monique Thomas, APCQ director, Québec
Alan Thompson, Badger State Fruit Processing Company
Université Laval: Richard Bélanger, Jean Caron, and Silvio José Gumiere
USDA, Economic Research Service
USDA, Marketing Order and Agreement Division
USDA, National Agricultural Statistics Service (NASS)
Mike Wallis, executive director, BC Cranberry Growers Association
Bob Wilson, the Cranberry Network LLC (WI)
Nodji Van Wychen, Wetherby Cranberries

Chapter 1
Cluster Theory and the Challenge of Agricultural Cooperation

WHAT IS A CLUSTER?

Clusters are a central issue in economic development theories. They are geographically concentrated areas of activity focused on a certain industry and are a key concept for regional and industrial development strategy around the world, as the cluster concept suggests a certain "stickiness" of businesses and employment in a local area, often tied to specialized skills and knowledge. Alfred Marshall, one of the founding fathers of modern economics, provides a logical explanation: whereas previously self-sufficiency was the rule, professional peddlers and traders helped spread surplus goods in demand or goods that were hard/impossible to produce locally (such as exotic fruits and spices), leading to an increasing localization of industries or the making of complex products. As Marshall pointed out in the 1890s, the first reason for the emergence of clusters was the tacit and apprenticeship knowledge that came from specialization in a craft, such as cobbling or tailoring, creating an ability for a trained person to produce goods better and faster than an untrained person. Another intuitive reason was the simple concentration of natural resources in a certain area, such as a source of coal or iron ore lending itself to the concentration of metallic industries, or rivers providing sources of power for mills. Factories were often set up on the edge of town, creating a natural concentration of related activities, including those involved in textile production around the time Marshall was writing (Glass 1992).

Once an industry was established in a location, customers tended to patronize the products there, and more competitors were drawn to the area. This competition furthered the labor specialization and in turn improved technical skills in the area. There was also an "automatic" aspect of cooperation, as subcontractors and suppliers interacted with producers of goods. Beyond simply charting the emergence of industry clusters, Marshall anticipated many of the issues currently under discussion about them. He warned about the overreliance on one industry, which can be subject to a sudden falling off of demand. Since Marshall's writing, at the end of the nineteenth century, the costs for long-distance trade have declined, including reductions in global shipping costs, allowing competition across (virtual) space and thus threatening the core principles of cluster advantage. Ironically, such forces also enable new and larger geographic clusters to sell to diverse clients across the entire global market.

APPLYING CLUSTER THEORY TO AGRICULTURE

Marshall wrote about "industrial districts" (now known as "clusters," or geographic concentrations of related industries) in the UK—places, he noticed, often on the periphery of towns, where small industries and craftsmen would tend to colocate. Marshall suggested that colocation was based in part on the advantages to customers (think about a fashion district in any city) and in part on the advantages to the businesses, since they could share knowledge and skilled labor while differentiating themselves with their particular craftsmanship (1890, 154–158). Such ideas still hold traction. Every city has clusters: an entertainment district, a jeweler's row, an ethnic restaurant enclave, an auto mall, and so on. From a retail perspective, it seems at first blush counterintuitive for competitors to colocate where they directly compete. However, from the customer's point of view, it makes perfect sense to have one place to go to comparison shop more easily. We tend to associate clusters mostly with concentrations of suppliers, but really the concept depicts a complex interweaving of contractors and subcontractors in supply chains and convenience and proximity for buyers, including wholesalers and distributors as well as retail customers. Besides the farmers' and seafood markets found in many cities, we find famous cases of industrial concentration and specialization around a particular sector, such as the Milan fashion district, the financial centers of New York and London, autos in Detroit, and entertainment in Hollywood. While the existence of clusters is well-recognized, the causes that give rise to inter-firm concentration and cooperation are still poorly understood. More important, very limited efforts have so far been made in applying cluster theory to agriculture. The reason is obvious: agriculture is generally thought of as based purely on growing products where they grow best. Thus, the main idea has been that terroir—the combination of climate, soil, and water conditions—is the driving force behind agricultural location.

Despite ambiguities around what decides cluster location, the alluring prospect of maintaining specialized, high-paying jobs in a given location has grown increasingly attractive in this age of globalization. As a result, cluster development and maintenance strategies are proliferating at the national, regional, and local levels across the world. Most member countries of the Organisation for Economic Co-operation and Development (OECD) and many of their regions and towns have explicit cluster policies (OECD 2009). The rest of the world is starting to follow suit, particularly in East and Southeast Asia (Kuchiki and Tsuji 2011). The race is on to develop clusters that will create and maintain local industries and the jobs, incomes, and revenues they provide.

Yet, globalization raises doubts about whether clusters in agriculture or any other sector can be persistent; market forces should dictate production in the most efficient location. Any cluster policy efforts thus face a countercurrent recognized by analysts who suggest "the world is flat," with globalization eviscerating local competitive advantage (Friedman 2005), alongside the long-standing aspect of commodification. Commodification—the standardization of things that are produced—goes hand in hand with "Fordism," or the development of mass production techniques from the start of the twentieth century. By breaking down the production process into smaller segments, companies ensure that each worker can focus on the same rote task, thus leading to much greater output and quality control over time. The introduction of statistical techniques after World War II, popularized by Arthur Deming, revolutionized quality control of mass production, isolating potential sources of defects along the assembly line. Eventually, companies started to shift labor-intensive aspects of production to the lowest-cost locations, keeping in mind that there are many other inputs beyond labor, such as infrastructure availability and distribution costs. Thus, cheaper labor and transport costs, and not climate or a concentration in skills, are thought to be the primary factors for locational decisions in a global market.

Standardization of production and the revolution in communications and transport, such as developing standard containers for shipping and virtually instantaneous internet communication, accelerate the ability to break the production process down into standardized versus tailored or designed segments, allowing companies to move the standardized parts overseas, where labor costs are much cheaper. As overseas competitors learn more through production experience and flows of knowledge, including former students and expats returning home, they develop the ability to intervene into more complex phases of the production process, with the prizes being design and branding. This effective race for capturing value chains, in turn, further spurs globalization of production and the ability to create competitive clusters. These forces have accelerated with the introduction of machinery and artificial intelligence, revolutionizing manufacturing and reducing the need for individual craftsmanship. In short, it is hard to see how clusters can persist in the wake of such forces pushing toward standardization and globalization.

Agriculture, beset by weather patterns and *commodity cycles*, presents particular challenges around creating local advantage, especially insofar as production tends to be undifferentiated, thus undermining the main thrust of cluster theory—that specialized knowledge is tied to "niche" or differentiated products. The roller-coaster ride of earnings has perverse incentives, with good times marked by high prices leading to a delayed (because it takes time to mount) increase in supply that then floods markets, and bad times marked by low prices shaking out producers over time. Some of those producers may have borrowed to expand supply or entered the market during the upswing. For agricultural products, demand elasticities are low when you consider the entire market for human nutrition. Cross-price elasticities, between individual food items, are higher. The demand elasticity facing any single farmer is higher still, because of the large number of competitors and the uniformity of their output. It follows that farmers engage in a kind of zero-sum competition with each other, while being powerless over price and profits. The resulting condition of inescapable passivity/fatality, with farmers facing global agricultural market forces, is known as the commodity curse.

Though seldom discussed, clusters are found in some agricultural sectors, where producers seek to differentiate and market their products as being distinct. These attempts follow one of the few known strategies for escaping the commodity curse: only with product differentiation do prices tend to rise in any sustained manner. One can see this to a certain extent with gourmet cheeses such as Swiss blue cheese or French brie, whose characteristics and quality are associated with certain places. High-priced wines are the best example, with the appellation of Bordeaux or Napa reflecting both a certain style and quality across individual producers that is associated with a region. In previous work, Hira (2013 a,b) traces the long-term success of such clusters to institutional support mechanisms that are both inter-firm and supported by public policy, beginning with the granting of an exclusive appellation label. In other sectors of agriculture, attempts have been made to differentiate products in order to escape the curse. Such is the case with gourmet coffee or farm-to-table food, though, in most cases, it is doubtful that the farmer captures this extra price premium. The retailer, such as a coffee chain, or a restaurateur, or a microbrewery, is more likely to capture most of the markup, rather than the farmer.

This brings us to the project of Gottlieb et al., of which this book is one part, to examine whether and how clusters could be created in agriculture. Developing agricultural clusters would suggest the possibility of capturing more local added value and jobs where the farms grow the crops, as a form of rural development and in recognition that farmers rarely get more than a small percentage of the final price for their products. Thus, it would be a means of trying to smooth out the commodity cycle roller coaster of prices and farmer incomes and of helping farmers move toward product differentiation through higher quality as well as improved productivity. The primary question posed by the Gottlieb project is whether product differentiation can occur and, if so, in which products.

Cranberries fit exactly within the agricultural conundrum—an undifferentiated commodity that, on face value, has limited market potential, mostly during Thanksgiving and Christmas in North America. A tart fruit that has traditional value but is unlikely to compete with fruit heavyweights such as McIntosh apples or Valencia oranges, cranberries would appear to be a classic case for the commodity curse described herein.

Indeed, for our case study—cranberries—there exists a wide belt of suitable climatic conditions across the globe where they could be grown and processed. Yet, the production of cranberries remains largely concentrated in North America and, within it, in a few readily identifiable clusters. How could such geographic clusters persist in such a commodified, largely undifferentiable product? The relatively unusual story of cranberries involves the creation of a cluster from an undifferentiated product to differentiation through downstream supply chains—that is, in the processing and retailing side.

How, in turn, did the industry organize itself toward differentiation? As we discuss throughout the book, the answer lies in the creation of a cooperative mechanism, with policy support, to manage the supply chain. Nonetheless, these efforts at industrial organization of a sector are fraught and subject to continual challenges. There simply is no way to enforce discipline across hundreds of individual growers over vast spaces who respond to the same commodity price signals we describe above, tending to overproduce when prices are high and being subject to shakeouts when they drop. The solution has been to create an agricultural cooperative, one that we explore across several other products in a later chapter. In fact, the admirable success of the cranberry industry to achieve growth amid severe commodity price cycles rests in both parts on cooperation and innovation, with most growers working together as a unit but also innovating to grow demand in response to the challenges from a minority of independent operators. Ironically, we argue, the lack of discipline in the industry to completely control supply promotes its long-term growth by keeping the cooperative, Ocean Spray, on its toes in terms of market expansion, farmer ("grower") service, and innovation. However, as cranberry growing starts to creep outside the US clusters, the challenges for both cooperation and innovation—and the stakes for the multigeneration cranberry-growing families—are intensifying.

CLUSTER ORIGIN THEORIES DO NOT APPLY TO AGRICULTURE

The central question for modern cluster theory from the perspective of industry dynamics is why firms in the same market space colocate. The truth is that we have only partial answers. Scitovsky (1954) was one of the first to start examining clusters systematically. He posits the existence of "technological" and "pecuniary" externalities that help to explain concentration. Technological spillovers involve the sharing of knowledge, including a pool of skilled workers, that attracts other firms to locate near market leaders—popularly called "spin-offs" nowadays—reflecting the founding of new companies from personnel who leave leading firms. Pecuniary externalities are the decisions of key suppliers or contracting companies about where to source the different parts of the supply chain. These leading companies are sometimes referred to in the current literature as "anchor firms," which, often by historical accident, set up shop in a certain location, thus creating local agglomeration around their activities that becomes path-dependent over time. A current example is Walmart, which attracts business to its headquarters in Bentonville, Arkansas, the home of its founders. In agriculture, it is hard to find such anchor firms except where there are limited growing areas, such as Blue Diamond almonds, a co-op based in California. Rather, in agriculture, growing areas seem to feed into national and global markets regardless of where the crop is sourced. Thus, the wholesale and retail chain, such as Starbucks in coffee, is more important than from where specifically a given batch of coffee beans is sourced from.

Endogenous growth theory from economics focuses on the timing for industry specialization, so that natural factors such as resource availability provide the baseline conditions that allow for the initial rise of an industry. However, where a product is first developed matters, because being first leads to "positive externalities" in the sense of being further along in a learning curve than those who enter the industry later. For example, returns from initial sales can be plowed into R&D and keep the company ahead in product development. Historical accident and path dependency are commensurate with endogenous growth theory in describing knowledge accumulation and spillovers, such as an auto industry's inception giving rise to a local tire industry, which over time locks in certain advantages to industries that have had a head start.

This theory contrasts with the neoclassical theory of economic growth, which links it to natural factor endowments and specialization based on comparative advantage. From the latter perspective, clusters such as Saudi Arabia's petrochemical complex come from the geographic fortune of having a natural abundance of reserves. In response, one can argue that it depends on the industry. If knowledge is the key differentiating factor here, and knowledge can be created, attained, and used to improve products, then knowledge is not geographically confined, unlike abundant petrol reserves. Here again, at first glance, this cluster concept would be problematic for agriculture, in that innovation around basic commodities such as cranberries or wheat would appear to be far less dynamic and easy to spread. Thus, proximity to knowledge-creators such as R&D labs or universities should be far less important in agriculture than for sectors such as IT or craft agricultural goods like microbrew hops or varietal-based wine.

Another theory for why a cluster arises relates to increasing returns to scale. For example, the importance of "economies of scale," or the tendency for unit prices of goods, particularly industrial manufactures, to decline above a certain level of production, became a clear explanation for the need for large-scale factories that could serve as an anchor for a cluster. Paul Krugman's (1991) Nobel-prize-winning work on economic geography further noted that proximity to large demand centers such as large cities and to transportation infrastructure would promote concentration by reducing the costs of sales to markets. This builds on Alfred Weber's least cost theory of industrial location, which pointed out that manufacturing is likely to occur close to bulky/heavy raw materials, to reduce transport costs; the theory understands that the finished products will be lighter (Weber 1909). The proximity of steel mills to coal mines, such as in Western Pennsylvania, for example, is explained by the costs of shipping coal. The term agglomeration therefore began to be used to explain clusters, as potentially the result of a dual action of supply and demand optimization that created a virtuous circle—virtuous in the sense that, once several suppliers locate in one area, other suppliers and customers will come. Moreover, once educated and well-paid workers begin to live in an area, those providing additional products, services, and infrastructure will come to cater to them.

In the case of agriculture, this notion would seem to have some traction in terms of advantages bestowed to producers who are closer to big urban markets. Proximity to San Francisco factors in the theories behind the rise of Napa as a premier wine-making district (Hira 2015). The opportunity for customers to comparison shop can exert pressure on producers to maintain certain quality standards, and for shops to find new innovations. Discussing the geographic concentration of craft breweries in the River North neighborhood of Denver, Colorado, for example, Gorski notes that, "the emergence of

Denver's craft brewing district means drinkers can sample several tap rooms, including on foot or by bike. That is a great advantage for breweries hoping to lure new customers, but it also means there is no room to hide if the beer doesn't measure up. Breweries need to be on their game because customers have options" (2015).

On the other side, costs of land, labor, and congestion increase as concentration takes place, as we now see in Silicon Valley now, with some prominent companies such as Tesla looking for lower-cost alternatives, reflected in the move of some operations to Texas. Yet, such factors would also appear to be quite secondary to growing conditions in commodity agriculture, which takes place in rural, not congested areas. Thus, wheat grown in North Dakota remains competitive.

In the 1990s, supply chains became a clear focus of cluster research once Harvard professor Michael Porter popularized the policy discourse around clusters through his work on the sources of competitive and comparative advantage of nations, regions, and firms. Porter suggests that the vertical integration of supply chains may be one source of clusters, but equally important are horizontal chains of firms with complementary products (1990, 1998). Porter defines clusters as "Geographical concentrations of interconnected companies, specialized suppliers, service providers, firms in related industries, and associated institutions (for example universities, standards agencies and trade associations) that compete but also cooperate" (1998, 197).

Porter (1990) developed the now iconic diamond framework for firm competitive advantage that lends itself to explaining how regions can provide the enabling conditions for clusters. The diamond includes interaction among the local context (one that encourages investment); factor/input conditions (including human capital, information, R&D, and venture capital); related and supporting industries; and demand conditions. In this sense, a cluster can exist only if these conditions naturally converge; the implication is that they cannot be created. In later work, authors Delgado, Porter, and Stern in this vein state,

> Clusters facilitate new business formation and the growth of successful start-ups by lowering the costs of entry (e.g. by providing ready access to suppliers or low-cost access to specialized inputs, offering an environment in which the costs of failure may be lower), enhancing opportunities for innovation-based entry (as a stronger cluster environment will allow local entrepreneurs to develop and commercialize new technologies more rapidly) and allowing start-up firms to leverage local resources to expand new businesses more rapidly. Finally, strong

clusters are often associated with the presence of innovation-oriented local consumers, thus providing increased opportunities for entry into differentiated market segments. (2010, 500)

Given the large number of difficult-to-measure factors, it has been hard to test Porter's framework with any rigor despite the fact that it has become a rule of thumb for planners. More importantly, it is not at all suitable for the many other factors related to agricultural production, such as global market forces, weather events, access to storage, and so on.

GROWING CONDITIONS VERSUS SPECIALIZED KNOWLEDGE IN AGRICULTURAL CLUSTERS

In the more recent literature, the increasing fragmentation of global supply chains offers a counterexample to cluster theory and brings into question whether concentration in an internet age with the free flow of ideas is a thing of the past. Thus, one would expect that crop cultivation would shift to the cheapest places where conditions are favorable; this would suggest major shifts of agriculture production globally. If markets operate as most economists expect, there should be a general movement of agriculture away from high-cost areas in the EU and, to a lesser extent, North America, toward the temperate zones in the Global South.

However, even in manufacturing, global shifts have happened only in partial and haphazard fashion. Gereffi's (1994, 1999) concept of "global value chains" (GVCs) as applied to manufacturing suggests that the fragmentation of supply chains across the globe, which often includes many subcontractors, is driven by optimization in terms of costs for each *stage* of production, as well as the nature of who has power within the chain. For example, a large clothing retailer spurs a "demand-driven" chain, as opposed to petroleum production, in which the power lies more with the supplier. While the value chain literature better reflects power games within supply chains, the global production network (GPN) literature incorporates more realistic flexibility in the chains, in which, for example, one subcontractor could serve a number of different suppliers (Cooke 2013). In short, it is supply chain logic, rather than geographic proximity, that explains cluster location (Bathelt 2005, 205). The two can be seen as different sides of globalization, rather than competing theories as the authors suggest. In agricultural terms, most GVCs appear to be buyer-driven: it is Starbucks, not the farmer, who has the power in the relationship. This would appear to undermine the idea that agriculture is generally "sticky" to certain locations, particularly as it becomes more an industry and less a family, subsistence-driven, set of businesses. Agriculture *should* shift to the cheapest production location. However, we know that there are abundant distortions in agricultural markets, including abundant subsidies for farmers in the (global) West.

Another challenge for cluster theory is how to deal with the increasing fluidity of information in the internet age, a challenge that applies to agriculture as well. Delgado, Porter, and Stern (2010) find evidence that agglomeration leads to a greater number of start-ups and perseverance of start-ups in the United States. The fact that the various firms in emerging industries sometimes colocate is at the heart of the cluster phenomenon and why it is often associated with emerging, dynamic, craft, and innovative industries. Knowledge specialization comes in the form of "buzz," wherein tacit, craft-type knowledge is important, leading to agglomeration, and "pipelines," whereby knowledge is more easily formally transferred and thus spreads easily around the globe, through intra-firm networks (Bathelt, Malmberg, and Maskell 2004).

Boschma (2005, 71) goes even further in suggesting that geographic is only one type of "proximity" explaining cooperation; other types would be cognitive, organizational, social, and institutional. Geographic concentration, therefore, would be explained by the advantage of having regular face-to-face meetings, communities, or practices feeding into these other proximities. Cluster theory is thereby transformed from the concept of concentration, based on economic factors inherent to natural resource endowment or scale economies in supply and/or demand, into concepts that are more sociological in nature, involving the creation of tacit knowledge networks that allow for niche-quality differentiation and continual innovation as suggested by Piore and Sabel (inspired by Northern Italy), who claimed that clusters were constituted by small, flexible firms, giving rise to the term "flexible specialization" (1984, 17).

By contrast, some claim knowledge is sticky if tied to local institutions. The national innovation system (Nelson 1993) approach focuses more on generating and applying knowledge flows through creating synergies among the basic research (academic), commercialization (private sector), and subsidization/regulatory sectors (government), and less on the necessity for their geographic concentration. The basic model is one that suggests that coordination of these three functional sectors is necessary to pass through the "valley of death" from basic research on to commercialization. The triple helix framework (Etzkowitz and Leydesdorff 2000; Etzkowitz 2003) demonstrates this framework can work on a variety of geographic levels, thus lending itself to cluster studies.

The framework also gave rise to suggestions regarding innovation in specific industries, particularly the relatively recent "sectoral systems of innovation"

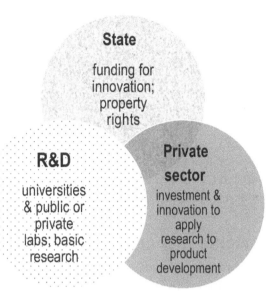

Figure 1.1: Triple helix
Source: authors, derived from Etzkowitz and Leydesdorff 2000

literature (Malerba 2002). Steinle and Schiele (2002), furthermore, usefully suggest that there have to be certain sectoral characteristics that advantage clustering, particularly, a value chain requiring modularity, and multiple innovating and dynamic competencies (i.e., complementary innovative products/services); advantages of a networked "club" approach to production and innovation, which allows for the ability to test out emerging new techniques and technologies; and markets that require time-sensitive and customized solutions.

An offshoot of the cluster concept related to knowledge is the regional innovation systems (RIS) literature (Cooke, Heidenreich, and Braczyk 2004). This literature emphasizes the importance of tacit knowledge and face-to-face meetings. A RIS would include training institutes and business associations designed to foster knowledge diffusion. This could be useful, for example, for coming to an agreement on product standards to ensure compatibility as suggested by Sturgeon (2000) in the case of Silicon Valley. A major university or laboratory could thus serve as an anchor for related knowledge-based businesses. Graduates could create spinoffs that then become anchor firms.

Suggestions around knowledge and innovation concentration appear to apply well to agriculture. Hira (2013 a,b) combines the concepts above and maps out such systems in order to gauge the elements that give rise to improved competitiveness in the wine industry. At the base of wine clusters are the unique characteristics of soil and climate in a specific location—captured by the wine industry term terroir—that relate to the particular flavor of a wine, though Hira argues that this has as much to do with specialized knowledge and regional branding, reflecting industrial organization, as with growing conditions. Where specific local growing conditions vary, and that variation matters for qualities of agricultural production, one can see the cluster concept as being compatible with globalization, with knowledge flows about basic technologies being shared fairly easily, but more innovative, nuanced, and tailored knowledge more likely to be "sticky" to certain regions and/or firms. However, it is a stretch to apply this concept to commodity agriculture—but even here, the key role of R&D in horticulture and extension services to push out new techniques would be quite apt.

AGRICULTURAL CLUSTERS AND PRODUCT LIFE CYCLES

Schumpeter's monumental 1939 work on business cycles introduces fundamental ideas that continue to shape the discourse surrounding learning, technological change, and industrial dynamics in regard to innovation. In the absence of his insights, basic models of economics would remain rooted in "statics," and would therefore fail to capture important realities related to change. Schumpeter's ideas are the origin of the modern notion of a life cycle, for products, industries, and firms.

For Schumpeter, competition incentivizes innovation. Over time, however, it is likely that successful firms in an industry will begin to calcify their processes as shakeouts lead to the evolution from perfect competition to a more oligopolistic market structure. Such firms (e.g., in the pharmaceutical industry) find advantages in moving from initial product to continual process and resource optimization, in the process enjoying built-up learning and economy of scale advantages. As they optimize their routines and shift toward the incremental improvement of existing platforms, they are likely to miss opportunities for more radical innovation. Thus, smaller firms and individual entrepreneurs find an opportunity to "disrupt" whole industries by deviating from patterns that have become set and ossified within an industry.

Hassink (2010) introduces the idea of "lock-in" to explain both geographic clustering and its decline. Functional lock-in describes vertical and horizontal supply chains, in which localized firms come to rely on each other in longer-term relationships to produce specialized products and services. Cognitive lock-in refers to the tendency to move toward a common perspective, which would naturally arise from communicating more often with your neighbors than with industry participants far away. The third lock-in is political, wherein policies and institutions come to be oriented toward cluster support. One can readily see how these phenomena could lead to a geographic cluster being locked into a way of doing business that becomes outdated over time. For example, political capture reduces the willingness of policymakers to discipline the local sector when needed, and it discourages the movement of public resources to emerging sectors/clusters. Generally speaking, lock-in opens the door to disruptors.[1] The only question left is whether the benefits of founding a truly disruptive firm in the industry's traditional home region will outweigh the costs. These issues loom large in agriculture, with extant competition among growing areas around the world. For example, Hira (2013 a,b) points to the rise of the new wine industries in Australia, which developed new techniques and forms of marketing to compete quite successfully with European and US incumbents.

Schumpeter's theories hold up well over time. If we think of the disruption of wired telephony in the face of wireless telephony, Bell Labs, the incumbent monopoly, provided much of the early research on cell phones but failed to enter the new market because it threatened its status on the older technology platform. Similarly, the internet has unseated retail stalwarts who failed to adapt, like Sears Roebuck and Co. Thus, even incumbents with serious early mover advantages and built-up knowledge may fail to participate in disruptive change.

But life cycles could occur in terms of how different agricultural areas produce the same crops. In other industries, disrupters such as Tesla and Biogen (a genome-based biotech firm) are often launched at some distance from the place occupied by older incumbents (this is a type of centrifugal shift—see discussion below). We can learn more about the life cycles of places by examining three phases in the life cycle of individual firms: (1) firm entry into an industry, (2) firm growth, and (3) firm exit—due, for example, to failure and liquidation. Frenken, Cefis, and Stam (2015) use this firm-level classification to consider how industry clusters evolve over time. From the firm perspective, entry is unlikely to occur in a vacuum. A new firm, started by an entrepreneur, is likely to occur in a region where relevant training, social networks, and markets already exist. In terms of firm growth, the ability to find new employees, capital, and linked upstream and downstream supply chain participants is optimized within a preexisting cluster. In terms of firm exit, they point out that there are plausible reasons to think that locational clustering could be detrimental to firms in some cases. The geographic cluster may lead to groupthink, consolidation of firms, and protectionist policies designed to insulate

---

1 Halberstam's journalistic account of the decline of Detroit in the face of new competition from Japanese auto makers is essentially a story of failure due to lock-in (Halberstam 1986).

firms from wider competition, eventually tempting Schumpeterian disruptors to enter the industry.

These notions fit very well with our observations about dynamics in the cranberry industry. As we detail in chapters 4 and 5, later entrants into cranberry production—Wisconsin and, more recently, Québec—are significantly more productive and likely to adopt new techniques than are incumbents in the cranberry business. Moreover, there is some evidence that the newest entrants, the companies in Québec, are more innovative in developing new products and overseas markets than the incumbent giant, Ocean Spray.

Vernon's work on production location decisions (1966) outlined the fundamental geography of the *product life cycle*, implying that there will be a centrifugal pattern of geographic change over time. Figure 1.2 shows how Vernon's model operates at the global scale (we have updated and revised the original conception to better reflect contemporary forces of globalization and supply chain modularization). Note that Vernon's model works within countries too, where it predicts a shift of production from urban to rural areas, often based on lower labor costs or differences in unionization (Norton and Rees 1979; Barkley 1988).

At the early stages of product development, according to Vernon, knowledge agglomeration lends itself to cluster advantages, such as those in Silicon Valley (e.g., development and manufacture of the first iPhone). Once a product

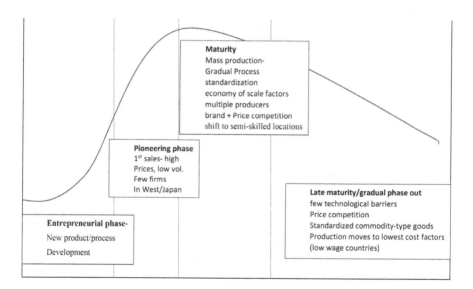

Figure 1.2: Vernon's product cycle—a revised version. *Source*: authors, inspired by Vernon 1966, and derived from Hira, Wixted, and Arechavala 2012

becomes standardized, however, the more labor-intensive activities will move to cheaper mass production sites overseas where there is semi-skilled labor, such as Mexico. Finally, when innovation is no longer a significant factor, production will move to the cheapest labor sources worldwide, as in the production of t-shirts in Bangladesh or Honduras. Even with seemingly high-tech functions like computer programming, standardization has allowed for a shift overseas, as in the IT cluster around Bangalore, India, effectively born out of American outsourcing. There, workers have a high education level, but they work cheaply by Western standards and do not require face-to-face supervision (Hira and Hira 2008).

In agriculture, globalization of some production has happened, such as the rise of new competition in lower-cost areas: wheat producers in Argentina or coffee producers in Vietnam. Yet, there are clearly limitations to applying the product cycle to agriculture. Coffee or wheat do not become obsolete as do fixed line phones. But techniques of production can become obsolete. In the case of cranberries, we link the higher productivity of Québec with breakthroughs in water management and efforts to improve organic growing techniques. While we have spent a lot of time covering cluster theories, we have not yet explained why there is so much ambiguity and controversy around them. The fact is that clusters are almost impossible to study in a scientifically rigorous way.

EMPIRICAL AMBIGUITIES LIMIT "RIGOROUS" STUDIES OF CLUSTERS

Along with ambiguity on the theoretical level is the more practical challenge of identifying and mapping out clusters that would allow for the development of a dynamic theory. These problems need to be sorted out before we can move toward a more scientific (testable) theory of cluster dynamics.

Types of Clusters

Markusen's (1996) classic article lays out three primary types of clusters that are often referred to in the literature. The first is the Marshallian industrial or Italianate district, wherein there is a rough equivalence among producers; it is called Italianate to reflect the small, highly skilled craft industries of Northern Italy. The second is the hub-and-spoke model, in which one to a few large firms dominate the space, with smaller subcontractors feeding off them; this configuration is common to large manufacturing plants. The third is the satellite platform district, wherein there are limited interconnections among firms in the same line of business, such as a retail district. In this case, the businesses may share the same location, but their business ties are with suppliers or purchasers who are located outside the cluster. More realistically, we can see an almost infinite set of changing configurations for clusters, depending on firm ties and relationships.

Cluster Boundaries

Further to this point, while the common image of a cluster is one of equal firms cooperating for mutual gain in a concentrated location, there is no reason whatsoever in real life for a cluster to map out that way. There are more likely to be asymmetries among firms, leading to an ever-changing map of relationships and flows among the firms. For example, Morrison and Rabelloti (2009) find, in an Italian wine cluster in the Piedmont region, that a handful of firms dominate knowledge-creation and make little effort to disseminate it. Examining innovation in shipbuilding, Greve (2008) finds that inter-firm networks play a greater role in technological innovation than geography.

What demarcates the boundaries of a cluster at any given time? Discovering the answer to this question may be more complicated from both a spatial and supply chain perspective than meets the eye. To begin with, how do we define concentration? Is it a region where a product is grown based on climatic conditions and historical path dependency, such as cattle ranching in northern Texas, or does it refer only to the Marshallian districts in cities and towns? There is certainly no boundary line on knowledge spreading into and out of the cluster, either. In a survey of Northern UK "knowledge-based" firms, Huggins and Johnston (2010) find it useful to distinguish between interaction based on network alliances, which they characterize as the strategic acquisition and spread of knowledge from firm to firm, and social capital, which is the sharing of knowledge through trusting relationships. They find larger firms more likely to engage in the former, and smaller firms in the latter.

Ambiguity about hard boundaries thus makes the survey approach toward network mapping most appealing, since boundaries are often based on levels of interactions among actors, rather than on functional or geographic space. For example, one could imagine a number of small fresh food producers working together on a farmer's market that would compete in harvest months alongside a year-round supermarket chain. How to measure concentration, therefore, is not an easy question, as it may be very specific to the type of product or service in question.

Cluster Measurement

Ellison and Glaeser (1997) created one of the classic studies of cluster measurement. Using US census data, they examined concentration at the state and county levels. They examined firm colocation for the same industry;

upstream-downstream colocation; and within-firm location of production facilities. Overall, they find that some concentration is present in all industries, but significant concentration varies widely across them. For example, fur, wine, hosiery, oil and gas, and carpets are the most concentrated, whereas rubber and plastics, footwear, canned specialties, malt beverages, and vacuum cleaners are not (912). Overall, they conclude that natural supply and knowledge factors play a role in the concentrated industries, and that proximity to large-demand markets does not. Still, they conclude that, "there remains in each case a great deal of heterogeneity to be explored" (921).

Feser and Bergmann (2000) provide one of the better-known empirical studies seeking to define and identify clusters. They develop an index that ranks areas based on the proximity of related firms using input-output tables for the United States. Not surprisingly, they find large factory industries such as metalworking and vehicle production to be concentrated, while agricultural goods such as meat and dairy are among the least concentrated. They note that the complexity of the supply chain varies considerably from one industry to the next, indirectly suggesting that more transaction costs might lead to greater agglomeration.

Delgado, Porter, and Stern (2016) use a combination of input-output and labor concentration (percent of workers in related industries in one area) indices to measure the degree of concentration of different US industries. They find greater concentration for some industries, such as aerospace and petrol refining, than others, such as lighting and electrical equipment. However, they note that, even within an industry, there are different segments of concentration. So, for example, airplane manufacturing is more concentrated than airplane engine parts and manufacturing. Spencer et al. (2010) conduct a similar exercise for Canada, identifying clusters of activities across the country using measures of labor employment concentration and colocation of related industries. They find that clusters are associated with higher incomes and employment, and greater patenting activity. Carroll, Reid, and Smith (2008) used location quotients and spatial autocorrelation measures to identify the geographic footprint of the transportation equipment cluster in the states of Indiana, Illinois, Ohio, and Michigan. Yang and Stough (2005) used location quotients to identify basic industries and their suppliers in the Baltimore, Maryland, metropolitan region. They then grouped the basic industries and their suppliers into functional clusters using Ward's clustering algorithm. Various efforts to study cluster dynamics are ongoing. One of the most well-known efforts is at Porter's Institute for Strategy and Competitiveness, which has created a Cluster Mapping Project for the United States. These interesting exercises of measurement hardly get to the questions of causality.

More recent efforts in the empirical literature attempt to better tease out potential for cluster policy. Slaper, Harmon, and Rubin (2018) find that the diversity of US clusters (reducing vulnerability to downturns for a particular product or service) as well as the extent to which they trade (i.e., are oriented toward export) both contribute positively to local GDP growth and employee compensation. However, they also note that the fastest growth occurred in natural resource sectors, which they attribute to the development of hydraulic fracturing in the oil and gas industry. Alarmingly, they conclude that productivity increases may not be accompanied by wage increases.

Delgado, Porter, and Stern (2016) provide an overview of the ways that clusters have been empirically studied, as well as some sample measures based on US statistics; in doing so, they elucidate some of the issues with the empirical studies. The ambiguous definitions noted above create measurement confusion as well. For example, concentration indices may examine the input-output tables (reflecting the transformation from raw materials to finished products) of a production process, exploring the concentration of subcontractors feeding off a few large firms; or the proximity of a number of competing firms in the same industry; and/or the existence of support institutions, such as business associations, university labs, and pools of specialized labor. Problems of measurement extend into the independent or causal variables, which are even more contested, reflecting the wide range of theories about why clusters exist. For example, historical accident may explain why a cluster starts in a particular place, such as the space industry in Houston, or autos in Detroit. These important historical events are not yet properly explained by cluster theory. Moreover, the measurement of tacit knowledge flows, as postulated by cluster theories, goes well beyond the simple measurement of employees in a certain industry; it should include, for example, the existence of training institutes such as local universities. Innovative ways to move beyond merely identifying clusters toward finding potential clusters is part of the next wave of research (Goetz, Deller, and Harris 2009).

Martin and Sunley (2003, 19–21) point to some of the other problems associated with the empirical measurement of clusters literature, beyond the fuzzy definition itself. First, analysts are not able to measure more informal and tacit types of knowledge exchange. Second, the literature relies on existing economic census data, which is defined, in turn, on given administrative and political units, ones that might not reflect actual economic geography (e.g., an industry spilling over borders). Third, there is no agreement within the literature about what constitutes geographic concentration. If the units are too large, they may include more than one actual cluster of activities; if too small, they are simple concentrations of business, which may or may not constitute a cluster. As they conclude,

> The extensive methodologies of top-down mapping exercises can at best only suggest the existence and location of possible clusters: they provide a shallow, indirect view of clusters. They cannot provide much if any insight into the nature and strength of local inter-firm linkages (traded and untraded), knowledge spillovers, social networks and institutional support structures argued to be the defining and distinctive features of clusters. (Martin and Sunley 2003, 21)

The vast literature using the case study approach to clusters helps provide such nuance but faces other issues. This literature illustrates the often-idiosyncratic nature of cluster origins. For example, Bassett et al. (2002) describe the rise of a documentary film industry around Bristol in the UK due to a BBC location decision there. Saxenian's (1983) and Sturgeon's (2000) classic studies of Silicon Valley from a historical perspective also make drawing lessons out for other potential clusters problematic, to say the least. In short, we see, on the one hand, that conceptual and measurement ambiguity prevent a pure statistical approach to cluster analysis. On the other hand, we see from our literature review that case studies establish a great deal of complexity, but have not been set up in a comparative way to understand whether and how cluster theories apply to undifferentiated commodity-based agriculture.

OUR APPROACH TO STUDYING AGRICULTURAL CLUSTERS

As we have discussed, cluster theory has been applied sparingly to agriculture. Agriculture is viewed as something that is naturally derived based on growing conditions, which goes against the core notions of a concentration of human, financial, and knowledge capital at the core of cluster theory. Most of agriculture is seen as a bulk commodity, subject to the whim of weather and unpredictable technology breakthroughs, and the roller-coaster ride of market prices. This is why agriculture is one of the most intervened-in sectors, in order to try to smooth out farmers' incomes, at least in countries that can afford to do so.

In general, we tend to think that growing conditions (soil, climate) and proximity to local demand markets are the obvious factors. We think of agriculture as undifferentiated commodities, thus the shared pools of knowledge that Marshall referred to were far less important. In short, *agriculture seems to best fit our natural default assumption for competitive advantage based on natural geographic advantages and tends to approximate the perfect competition assumptions for efficient markets.*

Our cluster approach posits a counterintuitive framework to the way we usually think about agricultural products. Agriculture production is usually thought of as "commodity" production—undifferentiated mass-production food or feedstock that is subject to the whims of weather and roller-coaster prices. If prices go up, farmers benefit for a time, but then they overproduce, leading to an inevitable decline. If prices go down, it may take some time for markets to respond; it's not easy for farmers to cut production when they have so much capital tied up in land, agricultural equipment, and inventories. Agriculture is not an easy business to enter or leave. Juxtaposed with the roller-coaster ride of commodity price swings is the generally heavy and continuing debt for land, buildings, and equipment. Yet, the individual farmer captures just a small percentage of the overall price, owing to his or her lack of leverage in the supply chain.

From this perspective, it is not surprising that agricultural production is becoming more concentrated, moving from family to industrial/corporate farming. The declining number of farmers has worked hand in hand with general consolidation in ownership by corporations or larger farmers, enabled by technological advances such as GPS-activated tractors and precision automated irrigation that reduces overall labor needs. The shifts apply equally to the cranberry industry. One large non-cranberry corporation, for example, has cranberry bogs in Wisconsin and in Québec; some suggest that the large pension fund TIAA (representing US higher education) has invested there. Several formerly family-owned operations such as Fruit d'Or and Atoka are now owned by large corporations. In Wisconsin, Butch Gardner, a trucking magnate, has been aggressively expanding into a vertical-integration operation of owning and managing cranberry fields and processing juice and SDCs (sweet dried cranberries) for domestic and overseas private labels. Their Badger State Processing website states that they now own 1,400 acres and can produce seven million gallons of juice and fifteen million tons of SDCs annually (Badger State Fruit nd; Leonhardt 2017). The American Berry Corporation also has a processing facility in Warrens, Wisconsin. According to informants (interviewees), the company represents California-based investors who took over the failed operations of a local cooperative, which continues to provide the fruit for the operation. It could be that these trends will continue, but the lasting image of the family farm as a symbol of a way of life still endures in much agricultural production. Some interviewees suggest that corporate investment in cranberries will be limited, because of the long-term wait for payoff and volatile prices, when other investment paths are available. The more important challenge for family farmers wanting to stay in the industry for the long run is to raise the capital to renovate their bogs to reach economies of scale. However, their access and willingness to take on debt is understandably circumscribed.

Consolidation also reflects an attempt to build up enough capital and diversification to ride out the roller-coaster ride of commodity price cycles. Commodity cycles wreak havoc in support institutions, macroeconomic stability, and long-term growth prospects for countries that depend too much on agriculture or mineral commodities (Sachs and Warner 1999). Considering the stability of some large agricultural producers noted as exceptions, such as New Zealand, some authors argue that resiliency to shocks from the commodity cycle or "natural resource curse" depends on the quality of governance (Collier and Goderis 2012). More pessimistically, the famous Prebisch-Singer hypothesis (Prebisch 1950) posited that even amid long-term commodity cycles, the overall purchasing power of commodities versus other goods (manufactures, advanced services) declines over time. This suggestion is contested within the econometric literature (Erten and Antonio Ocampo 2013). Beyond the limitations of long-term historical datasets and the dynamic aspects of changing economies and markets, there are the often confounding issues around endogeneity among commodities and other markets, such as the close link between oil prices and agriculture. Petroleum is an important input into current methods of agriculture, from seeds and fertilizer to tractors to food transport and plastics (Baffes 2007). Previous efforts such as the New International Economic Order from the 1970s, inspired by the temporary success of OPEC in running up oil prices and in creating commodity cartels or storage facilities to smooth out supply during price fluctuations, have all failed miserably.

Despite spectacular failures to manage commodity cycles on a global level, Western economies, including Japan, intervene heavily to manage them in their own agricultural sectors. Out of the scope of this work emerges the range of historical policies across time and space, from subsidies to farmers during price downturns to experiments to pay farmers not to grow crops to more controversial efforts to market surplus product abroad as food aid. Legitimate concerns for domestic food security, combined with intense lobbying by farmers for mechanisms designed to insulate them from commodity price cycles, have justified continual support, with varying levels of distortion and success.

As we argue throughout this book, specialized knowledge clearly plays a role in the ability to escape the commodity trap. For example, New Zealand's organization of key agricultural sectors, such as dairy and wine, around a common strategy has led to higher prices for its exports. Cluster organization allows it to improve and create a national "brand" around quality. In this context, it is the dream of every farmer, wholesaler, retailer, and policymaker to find a way to increase and stabilize incomes. Seen thus, the cluster literature offers an attractive possibility and has inspired policies across a variety of locations for keeping or developing jobs within a certain region. In a sense, it suggests farmers can cooperate to manage and innovate on the supply side.

A limited literature suggests that many cluster notions apply to agriculture. For example, Ng et al. (2017) examine rice "clusters" in Malaysia, finding that social capital and geographical proximity bolster localized learning. They find that both formal links through institutions and supply chain agents (e.g., fertilizer salespeople) and informal social capital help to transmit knowledge across farmers. Farmers also share small-scale innovation efforts informally. Events such as cultural festivals help solidify the social capital base.

The most developed literature around agricultural clusters centers on the wine industry. Some parts of the wine-production chain escape commodification through differentiation. Differentiation is often formally demarcated through the concept of terroir, which posits that the particular location of production imparts unique taste characteristics. Using network analysis, Giuliani and Bell (2005) and Turner (2010) further argue that proximity allows for tacit learning opportunities for craft wine production, albeit in uneven ways and through interaction between the global and the local. Beyond the work of Hira (2013a,b), very few of the works on agricultural clusters emphasize the role of public goods or institutions, thus undervaluing the potential for proactive policies. Zhang and Hu (2014), in discussing potato clusters in China, argue that the state played a crucial role in the success of the cluster they studied, by helping with growing techniques, land titling, capital access, transportation, and other aspects of the supply chain as part of what they call an "industrial policy" toward the sector. In this sense, when we speak of agriculture, like other clusters, we are referring to a tightrope of competition and cooperation—"coopetition"—whereby farmers who compete with each other nonetheless see the benefits of cooperation around collective goods. In fact, cooperation should be more common in agriculture than in other industries. Trade secrets copied by a handful of competitors will have virtually no impact on the innovator because the market shares are universally small. For similar reasons, horizontal cooperation in production agriculture is generally permitted in Western legal systems in a way that is not true for industrial sectors that are more concentrated.

We have seen that the agricultural clusters literature is largely limited to a few differentiated products, particularly wine, that thereby escape some of the aspects of commodification. By and large, there has not been much effort to adapt cluster theory to an agricultural context. For example, while those involved in agriculture recognize the crucial role of universities in basic R&D and local agricultural extension, in general, there is no explicit recognition of agricultural production as occurring in clusters. Indeed, when we think of most products such as wheat or corn, we observe that many agricultural products are grown on a massive scale, across wide swaths of the map. As long as the needed growing conditions are present, anyone should be able to produce that crop. Thus, natural growing conditions suggest that only crops that can be grown in certain geographically limited areas should cluster. Perhaps quinoa in the central Andes is one such example, but history tells us that native crops tend to spread globally, and perhaps in time, multiple quinoa growing regions will develop.

Even when producers have geographic conditions in common, we argue that there are important locational differences among different regions growing the same commodity. For example, we point to the vital role of local extension stations. At an Oregon cranberry growers meeting in 2020 attended by the lead author, for example, a grower pointed out to the presenter from the East Coast that the pathogen profile was distinct there; indeed the profile was also different in nearby Washington. West Coast growers, for example, have less fruit rot issues, given the milder summers there. Researchers who work in extension point out that the pest profile for each growing region is quite distinct. Additionally, Hira and colleague's (2013a,b; Hira and Swartz 2014) work on clusters in the global wine industry points to the importance of tacit knowledge as a source of locational advantage in the making of high-priced wine segments and provides case studies, such as Napa, illustrating how such clusters form and operate. Hira points out that the wine industry creates price stability and premia through differentiation by types of wine being linked to certain locations, such as Oregon Pinot Noir. This practice encourages cooperation within the regional cluster to ensure conformity with a common style or varietal, a joint marketing approach, and knowledge-sharing to improve quality and reduce costs over time.

Indeed, every cranberry grower interviewed for this report highlighted the importance of tacit knowledge for growing successful crops. Knowledge came from a variety of sources, from family members who passed down the farming tradition to sharing information with neighbors about techniques. The knowledge transfers in limited fashion, such as new pesticide treatments, because of differences in local growing conditions, or terroir, the unique combination of temperature, air, water, and soil in a given location. Thus, growers develop differentiated knowledge that optimizes conditions for each area. It is not too much of a leap to think that the same *could* hold for many other agricultural products. What has not been done thus far is to examine clusters of undifferentiated agricultural products, which is why cranberries are such an interesting case.

WHY CRANBERRIES ARE A GOOD TEST OF CLUSTER THEORY

Why study cranberries? This study is part of a larger investigation into agricultural clusters across the United States led by Dr. Paul Gottlieb of Rutgers University. Gottlieb's team developed a specialized dataset mapping out the geographic concentration of different agricultural products across the US in 2017–2018. From this new dataset, we found, surprisingly, that cranberries are one of the most concentrated crops. Since they are not limited to certain geographic spots (such as guava in Hawai'i), they are of particular interest from the perspective of cluster theory. Because they are one of the more concentrated crops in North America, we are able to use cranberries to examine the factors behind agricultural colocation, and thus to test out theories behind the geographic concentration of industry. In the rest of this book, we examine a number of both natural and human-based factors that might explain the concentration of cranberries in certain locations, and thereby provide a test of the validity of such variables, which we revisit in the conclusion.

A 2014 report by Alston et al., reflects the importance of the cranberry industry in North America. They provide the following estimates of its economic impact from 2009 to 2012:

- In the United States, $3.55 billion in value-added output and 11,610 jobs annually.
- In Wisconsin, $936 million in total value added and 3,977 jobs.
- In Massachusetts, over $250 million in value added and 1,682 jobs.
- In New Jersey, over $561 million in value added and 1,569 jobs.
- In Oregon, over $78 million in value added and 458 jobs.
- In Washington, over $122 million in value added and 488 jobs.
- In Canada, $411 million in value added and 2,708 jobs annually.
- In Québec, $365 million in value added and 2,269 jobs. (Alston 2014, 30)

According to the latest Food and Agriculture Organization (FAO) production statistics (see table 4.2), the US is responsible for 60% of global production, Canada 25%, and Chile for another 13%. Cranberries are, in other words, dominated by US and Canadian producers, allowing for this study to reach a fairly comprehensive sample of stakeholders.

In short, cranberries were selected because they are one of the most geographically concentrated products *and* because they are an undifferentiated product, just the opposite of what we would expect to see on the basis of economic and cluster theory. While there are constraints on growing conditions, as we describe below, there is unmistakable concentration into certain geographic clusters within the much wider range of possible cultivation areas. Most cranberries are grown in just five states and two Canadian provinces, and within the states and provinces, bogs are concentrated in certain closely linked regions. From a theoretical perspective, therefore, this study seeks initially to better understand why cranberries cluster, what the implications of the clustering are for the industry, and what role policy has played and can play to aid cluster and industry health.

CLUSTERS AS A POSSIBLE WAY TO OVERCOME COMMODITY PRICE CYCLES

The general observations about the commodity nature of agriculture make cluster theory even more important. If agriculture can start to differentiate its production, then there is a chance to reduce the vagaries of the commodity cycle. The commodity cycle refers to the rollercoaster ride of prices based on swings of demand and supply as reflected in the volatility of commodity markets, including agriculture and minerals. Bad weather or a pest can wreck supply, sending prices skyrocketing. This spurs new competitors to start producing agricultural goods, but it usually takes a few years to get up and running; in the meantime, growing conditions have normalized or been adapted to by the incumbent farmers. The result is a sudden downswing reflecting oversupply. This perennial problem is one of the main foci of agricultural policymakers; the sector as a result is rife with interventions, from subsidies to import controls. Because food is so central to survival, and farmland part of the founding and enduring mythology of national and regional identity, such interventions are often justified among mostly market economies as necessary to preserve "food security" and a way of life for family farmers. The heavy costs of such interventions reflect the essential problem of market distortions. In fact, no policy has eliminated commodity price cycles or the volatility that accompanies them. Could the development of clusters reduce the need for such haphazard and intermittently effective policy interventions?

This brings us back to some of the essential ideas behind cluster theory. If products can be differentiated by quality as well as by price, then farmers can start to create "branding" around the unique attributes of their produce, thus allowing for higher and more inelastic pricing and, in turn, more stable incomes, as we see with advanced name-brand products, such as Apple's phones. We see this in some categories of food already (the "farm-to-table" movement, the organic movement, and gourmet niches such as prized high-quality coffee), but by and large most agriculture is still produced as a bulk commodity. In previous studies, Hira showed how some New World wine regions moved from low-cost generic wine production to differentiated higher-priced production through cluster theory and policy support for innovation (Hira 2013a,b, 2015; Hira and Swartz 2014). However, not many agriculture products are easy to differentiate, and economies of scale in production, processing, or distribution may make it uneconomical to do so (most coffee is still bulk and price-sensitive). Studying how clusters function might either help to support product differentiation or provide farmers greater support from the commodity cycle, which seems to require collective action, if it is at all possible.

The main question we address in this study is this:

What are the strategies that an agricultural industry can employ to start to break the vicissitudes of commodity cycles? This question leads to several sub-questions:

1. Is it appropriate to think of agricultural products as being a legitimate category for the extension of economic cluster theory, or do they stand apart, based on the vital importance of natural input factors, such as climate and soil?
2. Is there a stable basis for cooperation among agricultural producers to help them effectively reduce supply volatility, differentiate and improve their product, and grow demand?
3. Given that most of the literature around clusters in agriculture has focused on highly differentiable products such as wine, can the human factors identified by cluster theory as key to success, including human and financial capital, proximity to supply chain and outlet markets, R&D and knowledge dissemination, and policy interventions, make a difference for a largely undifferentiated commodity-type product such as cranberries?

Answers to such questions would be extremely valuable in helping a wide array of farmers escape the commodity curse and governments in reducing their heavy protection and subsidy programs designed to help stabilize farmers' incomes. However, the lack of clarity about how to define a cluster bedevils its measurement in any readily accessible format amenable to statistical analysis. Moreover, we lack the data on the intra-industry and input-output level to map clusters in any kind of detail. (The fact that establishment-level data on agriculture are collected by a US federal department different from that used for all other industries contributes to the lack of good input-output data.) This same lack of data creates a barrier to the level of detail we can access in our analysis of cranberries. We faced similar limitations of incommensurate data over time and space, an inability to identify certain producers over time, and barriers to proprietary information in regard to supply chain relationships. Even in terms of basic support policies on the federal and state levels, as markets are subject to such diffuse forces, it would be impossible to assign a clear line of causality or effectiveness from statistics alone.

On the other side, we have seen the limitations of the case study literature, which provides extremely interesting insights into the workings of a particular cluster, such as Silicon Valley, generally through a historical or network analysis. However, such analysis is inherently limited in terms of generalizability. Lacking a clear sense of variables that can be generalizable or tested across cases, it is hard to reach conclusions from the study of a unique cluster about how they function more generally. The empirical cluster literature, whether of the statistical or case study variety, lacks dynamism in the analysis. Without dynamic models, it is impossible to establish causality for clusters.

As a result, this study takes a mixed methods approach. We employ quantitative techniques such as statistical analysis of supply and demand trends over time and space and a large survey to capture growers' perceptions. We employ qualitative techniques to map out supply chains and stakeholder interrelationships. The lead author spent time in each of the seven North American clusters conducting interviews and filling in perceptions and tacit information alongside analysis of academic literature reviews, historical archives, organizational websites, and diverse primary document such as legislative, policy, and regulatory notes. To the extent that the data and time budget allowed, we are thus able to both examine the cranberry industry over time and compare the different clusters against each other, as well as evaluate joint and separate responses and their effectiveness to market shifts.

Indeed, cranberries offer a unique opportunity for a comparative study of agricultural clusters and the questions around commodities, as they are primarily grown in five clusters in the United States (Massachusetts, New Jersey, Wisconsin, Washington state, Oregon) and two Canadian provinces (British Columbia and Québec). By comparing the seven clusters faced with generally similar industry conditions, we can examine the different roles of natural and human-built comparative advantage to industry success. Over the course of

2018–2022, Hira conducted research on the industry, including field research in each of the clusters.

Finally, the initial research revealed that comparing cranberry clusters affords us the opportunity to address another set of questions of great potential interest to those interested in agriculture and cluster theory:

> 4a. What potential role does industry organization, a largely neglected factor in cluster theory, play in the ability of agricultural producers to insulate themselves against the market and weather cycles of agricultural markets? Can supply chains be organized to reduce the commodity curse?
>
> b. Where there are multiple clusters in different locations producing the same product, what types of coordination are possible? How easily do knowledge and personnel flow across the clusters?

From the business strategy perspective, cranberries are a remarkable case of industry organization through cooperation, to share processing, joint marketing, and product innovation costs through cluster growers' associations and, primarily, through the Ocean Spray cooperative. In subsequent chapters, we examine how Ocean Spray seeks to organize the industry and the challenges of organizing the industry for common aims across seven different clusters. Ocean Spray's ability to provide discipline to the industry and to innovate in ways that improve both supply and demand are clearly under duress now, such that we find that the cranberry industry is at a crossroads, facing a possible chronic oversupply situation for the foreseeable future. Many in the industry say that it is in need of a "reset." What exactly that reset looks like depends on your perspective. In this book, we synthesize all of the available information on the industry, gather new data on the perceptions of stakeholders, and propose some policy paths that might help the industry move forward. We also examine cooperatives in other agricultural industries to seek out further lessons on cooperation. This brings us to the last set of questions we address, with the benefits to industry and policymaker readers in mind:

> c. How have commodity cycles been managed by the cranberry industry in the past? Why do previous efforts to manage them through the main cooperative organization, Ocean Spray, appear to be breaking down? What role can policy play in arresting further deterioration in conditions for cranberry growers? What are the best pathways for creating a long-term path of stable growth in the industry?

The first half of the book, comprising the first three chapters, starts with an introduction to the growing conditions behind cranberry production, including the importance of research support, to explain why we have a clusters for a commodity product. We then turn to an historical review of the industry. Two main themes emerge from this review that distinguish cranberries from some other agricultural commodities, such as wheat, responding to questions 1 and 2 above. The first is that cranberries, despite their commodity characteristics and wide potential growing range, clearly cluster around collective goods, in regard to the location of key supply chain activities. The second, more important, theme is that human factors, including policy, play an arguably equal role to natural ones in the cranberry industry's evolution, beginning with the strategic leadership of certain individuals such as Arthur Chaney and Marcus Urann. In regard to questions 3 and 4, we examine how cooperation in the cranberry industry was consolidated over the course of the twentieth century through one large co-op, Ocean Spray, helping to distinguish this industry from other commodity products, such as corn and soy. Unlike other agricultural commodities, the cranberry industry has been able to diversify its sales over time through product development and marketing, thus keeping growing supply forces in check until about 2000, from when the current disequilibrium started. This differentiation strategy to effectively grow demand offers an important set of lessons for other agricultural producers.

The current, potentially long-term disequilibrium is the central point of discussion in the second half of the book. Chapter 4 is a comprehensive review of supply and demand conditions, globally, and by state and province, based on all publicly available statistics, demonstrating how this uneasy management has fallen apart over time, with improvements in production, new entrants (Québec) from outside the United States moving into production in response to temporary price rises and policy intervention, and the accompanying declining ability of Ocean Spray to steer the industry.

Chapter 4 also presents a summary of confidential interviews with key stakeholders in the industry, revealing their growing concerns about the industry, and their nature. Informants are concerned about the future of the industry, and there are no easy solutions. The discussion offers a snapshot of cranberry growers' perspectives on the crisis and potential solutions through a survey conducted in summer 2021. Chapter 5 compares cranberry cluster governance by exploring two in-depth case studies of British Columbia, an Ocean Spray-dominated cluster, and Québec, an emerging independent giant in the industry.

Chapter 6 compares Ocean Spray's situation with that of other large US agricultural cooperatives. The purpose of this discussion is both to compare how

Ocean Spray has attempted to manage both cluster development and commodity cycles with that of the handful of other well-known and prominent US agricultural cooperatives, such as Sunkist and Land O'Lakes, and to draw out some preliminary lessons for the cranberry industry and, more generally, the possibilities and challenges of creating dominant industry cooperatives in agricultural products.

The final chapter, chapter 7, offers a conclusion in the way of offering the authors' perspectives on potential policy recommendations and industry reorganization. We close by revisiting its implications for cluster theory.

Chapter 2
Why Do Cranberries Cluster?

WHY CRANBERRIES CLUSTER: NATURAL, POLICY, AND SUPPLY CHAIN ADVANTAGES

Growing Requirements

Cranberries (*Vaccinium macrocarpon*) are vines in the Ericaceae family native to northeastern North America. Other forms of cranberry (*Vaccinium oxycoccus*) are native to other areas of North America, including the Pacific Coast. Cranberries were used and traded by Native Americans as a food source, as a poultice for wounds, and in dyes for cedar baskets. The name, originally "craneberry," comes from local settlers to Massachusetts for crane birds that were seen near the farms, related to its upright stem. Cranberries are associated with Thanksgiving and Christmas, but they were also crucial in early colonial days for long sea voyages as a source of vitamin C to fight scurvy, since they spoil at a slower rate than other fruits. For example, the Hudson's Bay Company shipped cranberries from British Columbia to San Francisco as far back as the mid-1800s.

The need for certain growing conditions induces a certain degree of clustering and limits cultivation, thus we can say that there is clear evidence for natural sources of comparative advantage. Cranberries require a temperate climate with sufficient days between 32°F–45°F and acid soils of peat or vegetable mold and a layer of sand (hence the natural origins near large bodies of water). Cranberries grow in bogs, where soil is interlaid with organic matter (e.g., dead leaves). The plants are flooded in the midwestern and eastern clusters in winter to prevent damage, and at harvest time, to help separate the berries from the vines.[1] Harvests generally occur from September to late October, depending on local conditions. Different varietals yield different qualities in terms of productivity, fruit firmness and color, and susceptibility to pests. Some interviewees suggest that different varietals have different optimality in terms of whether they are used for juice or for sweetened dried cranberries (SDCs).

---

1 Flooding is not done on the West Coast, where winter temperatures are more moderate.

It generally requires three to five years for a commercial cranberry farm to reach full operation (*Encyclopedia Britannica* and University of Massachusetts, http://ag.umass.edu/cranberry/about/cranberry). Girard and Sinha state that "on average, every acre of cranberry farm is supported by 4–10 acres of wetlands, uplands, and woodlands" (2012, 401). Cranberry growers find that such additional area is important for the health of the farm and see it as ecosystem preservation. Because cranberries are not sweet, they are less subject to pests, but there are concerns about rot, fungus, and pests in the industry, and pesticides and herbicides are commonly used. Colder temperatures help reduce such dangers, but if the temperatures grow too cold, the fruit vines can die. In general, though, cold winters are viewed as beneficial, and so climate change could have a long-term effect on industry location.

Interviewees suggest that it takes at least ten years to recoup initial cranberry investments in building a healthy farm. The higher costs of land in some clusters, and limitations on whether or how agricultural land can be converted to other uses play a big role. Thus, there are clear barriers to entry and exit from the industry. They also note how the introduction of new, higher-yielding varietals developed by both Rutgers University and University of Wisconsin, in addition to new farm growing techniques, such as more level and uniform beds, have vastly increased productivity post World War II, as we discuss in the next section. Having a farm of more consistent shape and level allows for more efficient fertilization and pesticide spraying, as well as harvesting. Because these advances were developed over time, they tend to be more concentrated in newer growing areas, and ones with cheaper land, and thus help explain the differences in productivity by region. Thus, one important observation at the outset is that there is a clear tension between the advantages of path dependency and endogenous growth, reflecting the positive contributions of first-to-market, historical learning, and multiplier effects of early clusters, versus the advantages of late entry and the ability to take the latest knowledge and improve on it. What we see is that the tension between these two elements inherent to cluster theory is easily resolved by understanding that both can be simultaneously true.

The Role of Environmental Regulations

Interviewees underscore the fact that cranberries are usually grown in wetland areas. Most states consider these as areas requiring environmental protection, to protect biodiversity as well as watersheds. Awareness of the crucial role of wetlands in water storage, cleaning, and biodiversity has increased over time, thus there are regulatory obstacles to expansion of new acres, providing some advantage to legacy areas. Some are pushing into "uplands" (in Wisconsin particularly), natural growing areas that are converted into suitable wetland-like conditions for cranberry growing, but growers interviewed universally agree that such conditions are disadvantageous.

Not surprisingly, most cranberry growers insist that cranberries are quite compatible with wetland services and, in fact, may enhance such services because of the needs for pollination and preservation of water sources for their own long-term success. The degree of environmental regulation can have a large effect on the operating environment for cranberry growers. In New Jersey, growers in the protected Pine Barrens region note how the lack of state promotion and, in fact, discouragement of expansion or renovation of farms, is related to the state government's concern around environmental issues related to wetlands. Existing farms are grandfathered in, but there is little evidence of active support for them. In Massachusetts, the state has a program for the purchase of cranberry land that owners want to sell, to reconvert it to conservation wetlands, but the funds are limited, restrictions designate acceptable parameters, and there are many bureaucratic hurdles, all of which effectively limits use of this option. Wisconsin growers and those in BC (Canada) also suggest that environmental regulations place brakes on further expansion. These limits may have played a role in the expansion of the industry to Québec. State environmental regulations, in fact, vary quite widely and have a major effect on location decisions. Wisconsin growers suggest that the state's cranberry-friendly water regulations going back to the nineteenth century contrast sharply with the situation in Minnesota and Michigan, where the industry has never really taken off because of greater restrictions. However, experts in both states also note that concerns about rural water use and quality are growing, since most growers depend on surface water.

Interviewees in both Canada and the United States are also very concerned about federal and provincial regulations on pesticides, on which most rely, and whether their options will be curtailed in the future. They express concerns about the costs of meeting regulations, the undervaluing of cranberry growing for environmental benefits, and whether such regulations will dampen possibilities for future growth. These concerns will only multiply as the industry seeks to expand in overseas markets, particularly the EU. So far, ready substitutes, natural or chemical, are not yet available for many of the most widely used pesticides. Québec is not spared from such concerns. Even while it is the leading producer of organic cranberries, increasing concerns about environmental regulations are putting limits on growth and potentially moving production to less advantageous locations, as we discuss further in chapter 3.

Why Aren't Cranberries Grown Everywhere They Could Be? A Refutation of the Natural-Conditions Explanation of Cranberry Clusters

The question of location goes far beyond amenable regulations. Throughout this study, the lead author's introduction of the research as one informed by cluster theory elicited the natural reaction from the industry that cranberries are grown solely based on where ideal conditions for growing them exist, akin to the terroir argument of winemakers. Certainly, the right growing conditions are a prerequisite, but we argue, they are only part of the story. While it is understandable that industry observers who have focused on improving growing conditions and outcomes in particular locations for generations would focus on these, the facts seen from a broader perspective don't jibe with this intuition. "Exhibit A" is the spread of the industry to Québec, where growing conditions were known to be suitable for generations, but industry only came around in the 1980s; we explore the origins and growth of the industry in Québec later in this book. This is not to say that natural conditions are unimportant. The higher yields in Wisconsin and Québec are undoubtedly a reflection of highly favorable growing conditions including temperature and proximity to water, as well as the abundance of local sand which works better than peat as a growing medium and is easier to maintain and renovate. As we discuss later, the higher returns are also a reflection of cheaper land and improved farm design, including economies of scale that help reduce the challenges associated with agricultural debt such as for paying off land and equipment.

On top of growing conditions and economic factors, social ties are abundantly important to the cranberry industry. Gareau et al.'s (2020) study of Massachusetts cranberry growers is based on a survey and content analysis of the Cape Cod Growers' Association and the University of Massachusetts Cranberry Station. A full 97% of the respondents to the survey saw social ties to other growers, the association, or the extension station as important.

The more subtle and interesting question is why other areas that enjoy similar growing conditions do not cultivate cranberries. A Massachusetts grower noted in an interview for this study the serious advantages of growing in more than one region, which reduce the chances of weather-related downturns (as well as potentially diversifying market outlets). According to some interviewees, large areas of Maine, Michigan, and Minnesota could grow cranberries; in fact, there could be a substantial expansion globally based purely on growing conditions. Janzen suggests that the "natural cranberry range extends from Maine in the North to North Carolina and Tennessee in the Eastern and Midwestern US, and includes the upper midwestern states of Ohio, Indiana, Illinois, Michigan, and Minnesota" (2010, 9), though others suggest the overall spread is more limited. Interviewees seem less clear on why cranberry growing has not spread, with some stating that the need for sandy soil and closeness to large bodies of water might be a limiting factor, but such reasoning is purely anecdotal.

In Maine, for example, early cranberry farms at the turn of the century went out of business in the 1920s due to a downturn in markets. In 1997, when prices were high, Governor Angus King launched the 2000+8 campaign, promoting 2,000 acres of cranberries by 2008. However, state support was short-lived; environmental regulations of wetlands and water usage restricted expansion. Financing from local banks was challenging, given the long payoff periods, and contracts with Ocean Spray were not honored by some growers, creating some intra-industry political issues. Once the governor left office, the price had dropped, along with state initiatives. There are currently twenty growers in Maine, and they produce almost exclusively for the local fresh fruit market (Harker 1997; State of Maine 1988, 1996).

The story in Minnesota is similar. Minnesota has less of the optimal acidic soil, and summers tend to be warmer than in Wisconsin. Environmental regulations around wetlands are also much tighter. In the 1990s, there were some experiments with cranberry growing, including by Makepeace, a Massachusetts firm, some wild rice growers, and some local indigenous tribes as a sideline. However, there was little state support outside of a few university studies, and the experiment died. Minnesota presently has one cranberry farm, a member of Ocean Spray.

There are just seven cranberry farms in all of Michigan. These figures are striking given that blueberries, which require similar growing conditions, are grown widely in both Maine and Michigan. One interviewee in Wisconsin suggested that this was due to differences in access to water, with Wisconsin growers having regulatory access to water historically, which was not granted in Minnesota and Michigan, but this explanation seems too facile. Other Wisconsin interviewees cited the factors noted in this book—the importance of economies of scale in processing and infrastructure as well as local R&D and extension services—as explaining the lack of spread to Michigan.

Another interviewee pointed to the failed cranberry-growing experiment in New Zealand and the long-term efforts and substantial funding required to establish even a limited industry in Chile as examples of the level of *tacit knowledge required in the industry*. In line with the previously discussed literature on agricultural clusters, most growers emphasize the importance of traditional, tacit knowledge, passed from one generation to the next. One Wisconsin grower said, we talk over poker or over golf and (continually) share ideas about how to improve yields. Tacit knowledge covers a wide range of activities, from strategies for farm creation and maintenance to pest management and timing of harvesting. The nuances of cranberry cultivation have largely been passed down by family members in tight producer communities, thus partly explaining both clustering and the inability of other areas to produce significant amounts. One handler, when asked how he developed innovative cleaning techniques to meet the higher demands of his SDC manufacturing customers, stated that his wife was a food scientist, had worked in a Frito-Lay factory, and thus was able to help his group design the entire plant, with standards well above industry norms. However, as we shall see below, the development of scientific knowledge in the industry has changed the possibilities for growing in new places and at higher yields. Nonetheless, *the mismatch between potential and actual growing areas reinforces the importance of examining cluster theory to explain the location of cranberry growing.* Clearly, there is something far beyond just growing conditions that explains agricultural location, at least for the case of cranberries. In the course of the research, we found another crucial factor, largely neglected by the clusters literature: namely, "lumpy" and less mobile parts of the supply chain. In the next section, we show that a certain level of *lumpiness* (referring to the need to obtain large production to reduce costs), through economies of scale or market power in parts of the supply chain, help explain clustering.

The Cranberry Supply Chain: A Crucial Factor behind Clustering and Stickiness

On the consumer side, the cranberry industry creates generally homogenized products, as so far it has proven impossible to create differences in the taste of cranberries; they are simply too acidic to be accepted for raw eating, unlike other types of fruit, like blueberries, which prevents a large farm-to-table movement or regional differentiation and marketing in the industry. Cranberries have distinct submarkets: the first is the smaller, fresh cranberry market, which sells its fruit primarily around Thanksgiving and Christmas. The fruit receives a premium for freshness and longevity, and it has to meet certain standards for fresh fruit sales (relating to size) set by USDA. A smaller section of this market is organic. Interviewees suggest that the upside of the fresh market is that the income stream from it is stable. However, the fresh fruit market is so small, and raises concerns about fruit rotting, that it has not attracted much industry attention. This could change if consumers begin to better understand the health benefits of cranberries. The second market is juice, which is made in large processing centers combining berries from the same region, as we describe below. This is the most commodified market and, until the recent post-COVID-19 spike, was flooded by concentrates that are by-products of the third market. The third market is the sweetened dried cranberries market (SDCs), which requires fruit to be of a large size and color and which, as the fruit dries, creates juice. Both the juice and SDC markets require Krugman-style economies of scale involving millions of dollars of investment in processing and plants, and transportation advantages from proximity to large markets. Other, much smaller, markets include pet foods and supplements. In these ways, cranberries are no different than other agricultural commodities. The supply chain for cranberries is also similar in general terms to that of other agricultural products, as can be seen graphically in table 2.1.

One of the principal findings of this study is that key nodes of supply chains are co-determinant with cluster location, development, and longevity. In terms of inputs, cranberries need specialized versions of general fertilizer; according to interviewees, this market is dominated by GROWMARK. In terms of harvesting and pesticide equipment, there appear to be a variety of manufacturers, as well as interviewees noting a lot of DIY efforts that are shared within clusters. In regard to cleaning equipment, interviewees note the dominant presence of Key Industries (https://www.key.net/en/applications/cranberry-processing/). A few in Wisconsin suggested that they also used some EU-based suppliers for equipment, channeled through local representatives, but this appears to be a unique feature in Wisconsin, reflecting its higher production volumes. Nonetheless, all interviewees state that local adaptation, either in house or by local craftsmen, is necessary, suggesting that local subcontracting reinforces geographic advantage. Interviewees also note concentration in the freezer truck segment. While fertilizers and equipment can be brought to any

Table 2.1: Basic Supply Chain Inputs for Cranberries

Growing Inputs	Processing Inputs	Sales Inputs
Land purchase	Land	Transport to Markets
Farm Development	Building	Advertising/Marketing
Seeds	Specialized Equipment	Labor
Fertilizer	Labor	Taxes, regulatory compliance
Labor	Packaging	Export costs- shipping customs duties, etc.
Harvesting equipment incl. fuel & maintenance	Storage	Further packaging for retail markets
Pesticides (Chemicals)	Freezers	
Taxes, regulatory compliance	Trucks	
Water equipment- irrigation, pumps, etc.	Taxes, regulatory compliance	
Royalties (if applicable) for new varietals		

Source: Authors

location, in short, because the cranberry industry is relatively small for agriculture, *local concentrations of knowledge are needed to adapt inputs* to local growing conditions, including equipment redesign and, sometimes, manufacture. A Farm Credit Bureau report for 2015 breaks down costs for cranberry growers into categories (reflected in column 1 of table 2.1) (Farm Credit East 2016, 10, 12). By far the largest category is labor, at 28% of the cost/barrel (a barrel contains 100 lb. of cranberries). We have not focused on labor in this report because labor policy is made nationally and thus could not explain clustering, but weeding and harvest season undoubtedly depend heavily on migrant labor, as in other sectors. "Custom hire" is the second largest category, at 12%, referring to independent contractors being used "for specific labor-type tasks such as harvesting, mowing or weeding." The third category is chemicals, at 9%.

There are two harvesting methods: dry and wet. Dry harvesting is used primarily for the small fresh cranberry market. It is very labor-intensive and thus tends to be done on smaller farms. Everything else uses the more cost-efficient wet harvesting method, whereby flooding water is used to float cranberries that are then scooped up using specialized equipment (a pump). Water is also used during the wintertime to prevent plant damage. In spring, the water is vacated, and growers use bees to pollinate the flowers, which then become fruit. Cranberries, once harvested in fall (September–November), need to be cleaned and processed using specialized equipment as soon as possible to preserve freshness. While it is much cheaper to wet-harvest cranberries, it also increases the chances of fruit rot. The cranberries are thus sent immediately to a cleaning station, where water is applied again, and they are put into specialized equipment to shake out debris and remove stems. They then are binned and sent to freezers for preservation. Once frozen, they are shipped to manufacturing facilities to be processed into juice or sweetened dried cranberries; 100 lb. of frozen cranberries yield approximately 1.7 gallons of juice concentrate. Juice and SDCs (sweetened dried cranberries) tend to be produced in different types of facilities, according to interviewees. Transportation further requires the use of specialized freezer trucks. For all these reasons, *cleaning stations tend to be set up near cranberry farms*, thus providing a key reason for clustering. The significant costs of transportation, furthermore, mean that proximity to large retail markets is a factor in location decisions (Alston, Medellín-Azuara, and Saitone 2014, 1, 8). In fact, interviewees noted that the lack of nearby processing facilities put a damper on efforts to grow cranberries in Maine, Minnesota, and Michigan.

Conditions such as economies of scale in the supply chain and to reduce commodity price cycles, combined with upward limitations on conversion of new land because of wetlands protection, are pushing the industry toward consolidation. Some of the farms in Wisconsin and Québec are huge corporate-owned operations, which enjoy the ability to take on debt, ride through commodity cycles, and add technology and updates in a way that family owners who have not paid off substantial debt or land struggle with. Some of these farms reflect the ability of the most successful families to increase their size into larger corporations; on the flip side, smaller family farms are being bought out and/or the older generation is leaving the business. According to multiple interviewees, moving toward a larger scale of production not only requires skills in, for example, financial and labor management, marketing, and inventory that are beyond their knowledge and experience, but also would take what they enjoy out of a self-owned, family-run business. While expanding could make sense in the long run, it entails considerably higher risks, given the commodity cycle, a risk profile that runs against the natural instincts of a family farmer.

Nonetheless, consolidation seems inevitable, given the higher productivity of larger operations and the limitations on expansion based on land-use restrictions in areas where the cluster supply chain exists. As mentioned in the following discussion on R&D and innovation, larger clusters will be able to provide more extension services, thus creating a virtuous circle of higher productivity and innovation, which means Wisconsin and Québec, with the most extensive research systems, will have such advantages over other clusters. Moreover, both of the largest clusters are part of a larger agribusiness scene, one that affords additional benefits, such as easier access to agri-finance and equipment suppliers, as well as political presence in state and provincial governments. One corporate manager in Wisconsin noted that recent technological advances allowed for automatic adjustment in watering and flooding based on continuous monitoring of temperatures and precipitation. Ironically, the same regulatory differences that pushed some production into New Brunswick, like the tariff conditions that pushed production into Canada, might someday lead to significant production outside of North America. So far, there are not any signs of success, despite experiments in Chile, New Zealand, Eastern Europe, and China. Clustering in the supply chain and the need for formal and tacit knowledge help to explain why.

Interviewees emphasize the importance of transportation costs and the necessary *proximity of processing facilities* to support the clustering of the cranberry industry. Research from the US West Coast supports this contention. Washington state interviewees, for example, suggest that their proximity to West Coast markets, primarily in California, allows them to remain competitive with cheaper Wisconsin-based growers.

In Oregon, growers and handlers cited the transportation cost advantage in another arena: greater proximity and forged personal relationships with export markets, principally in Asia. Asian consumers prize the health traits of red fruit, an attribute that is associated with West Coast fruit. One Oregon grower noted his involvement with an experimental farm in China as well as the personal ties that allowed him to develop steady contracts in a market the rest of the industry has been struggling to develop. Oregon growers and handlers noted that their proximity to the I-5 corridor, and the ports in Tacoma and Portland (especially for exporting), was a huge advantage. The development of processing facilities in Oregon allowed for the development of a strong independent market alongside Ocean Spray. Demonstrating the many shapes markets can take, a few Oregon growers acquired small-scale processing facilities in their own areas, and thus were able to fill some larger retail orders. Reinforcing the idiosyncratic and dynamic nature of supply chains over time and space, these markets are smaller in scale than the large, generally multiproduct, juice and SDC companies on the East Coast, and different even from the smaller companies such as (the formerly independent) Massachusetts-based Decas, in that the Oregon handlers do not generally enter into retail markets.

The two large growing regions in Wisconsin—northern and central Wisconsin—encompass 21,000 acres spread across twenty counties run by 250 growers (WSCGA nd). A 2022 news article suggests that seven thousand people are working in the industry, assigning an economic value of at least $330 million/year (Lorey 2022). The heart of the industry, including the location of the main industry associations, is in central Wisconsin, around the Wisconsin Rapids area, which forms "the Cranberry Highway," which tourists are encouraged to visit, starting with the Wisconsin Cranberry Discovery Center, a small museum, in Warrens. While interviewees in central Wisconsin wax eloquent about the formerly glacial soils, not found elsewhere in the region, the location has more pragmatic benefits. Wisconsin growers point to the convergence of three major highways in the central triangle, as well as railway lines, as a major advantage of their location, which permits them to ship easily to either coast. Geography clearly matters, both in terms of growing conditions and for developing a sense of cluster identity as well as cluster services. For example, northern Wisconsin has a distinct sense of community and significantly different growing conditions, such as peat beds and early harvesting varietals, amid colder temperatures, than central Wisconsin. Overall, there appears to be a strong culture of cooperation and compromise among Wisconsin growers; interviewees state that strong multigenerational relationships are at the heart of this. As one interviewee there stated, when industry meets, they "leave their [individual] hats at the door."

In Québec, industry organization is similar to that of Oregon, with a mix of Ocean Spray and independent local companies processing the fruit. Ocean

Spray bought the independent Québec processer Atoka, and it competes with local giants Fruit d'Or, Emblème, and Citadelle. So far, Atoka does not appear to have provided a strong new brand for Ocean Spray. Québec companies have been active in the United States as well, with purchases of juice maker Pappas Lassonde and, more recently, Decas Cranberry Products. One Québec interviewee stated that, to use their processing capacity efficiently, they need a certain amount of fruit. There can be a significant mismatch between fruit supply and demand at the processing level, just one example of the discontinuities and lag times that are common to agricultural markets, where growing times and weather wreak havoc on the ability to respond to market signals. In a high-demand situation, competition is created among processors for independently grown fruit. In a low-demand situation, the price might not decline enough in the short run to reflect true market demand, because the processors ("handlers") want to keep their operations running at peak capacity. In theory, the market should sort out the optimal amount of processing capacity, but "lumpiness" in terms of economies of scale and/or market power by the processors demonstrates that markets may likely never reach such optimal efficiencies, particularly when supply and demand take on long-term wavelike patterns.

While we have explained why cranberries cluster based on key nodes in the supply chain and proximity to large markets, the industrial organization landscape varies considerably from one cluster to another, reflecting local supply conditions and path dependencies. There is further variation in general patterns between Ocean Spray dominance and Ocean Spray rivalry with independent processors. These organizational patterns, along with historical evolution, reflect quite distinct cultures and governance systems in each location. Regardless, the location of processing remains important, well beyond the prerequisite of suitable growing conditions. For example, the area north of the St. Lawrence in Québec or New Brunswick (regions that have grown in recent years due to cheaper land) has much cheaper land, a colder climate (albeit a shorter growing season) with less pests, and more lax environmental regulations. However, several interviewees stated that further increases in cranberry cultivation in other areas such as Joliette are limited because all of the processing is located in the center of Québec, around the Plessisville, Victoriaville, and Drummondville regions, as well as expertise in agronomy, equipment, and the proximity of major transportation corridors. Microconditions in terms of growing might also play a role. One interviewee also said that the soil was not as good in Joliette or New Brunswick and that the occasional very heavy snowfalls negatively affect its potential.

We can now sum up the previous discussions to understand why cranberries and, potentially, other commodity crops cluster. All of these supply chain factors—particularly the heavy long-term sunk costs and specialized knowledge and equipment in both growing and processing around key transportation hubs (the downstream supply chain)—and not growing conditions, help explain the "stickiness" of the cranberry industry around certain clusters and in higher-cost areas such as Massachusetts and New Jersey. While economies of scale and natural growing conditions push the industry toward Wisconsin and Québec, proximity to large markets reduces transport costs, giving a different advantage to East and West Coast producers, though it is unlikely to be enough to close the production cost gap. Along with climate change, there is thus evolutionary pressure on coastal producers.

Creating a precise map of cranberry processing facilities is not possible, as their location is proprietary information. However, taking information from Google searches, the largest companies' websites, USDA, Statistics Canada, and through field research, we have prepared maps that identify the large-scale processing stations, as well as cranberry growing operations, to reinforce our argument. The maps delineate places that have five or more operations (please find details on the maps and the methodology behind them in appendix C; notice that the dots represent individual growing operations, *not volumes*, which the reader will find in the statistical analysis section in chapter 4).

The map in figure 2.1 clearly shows the colocation of processing stations and cranberry growers. The dots just over the border on the East Coast are the Québec cluster. Note that, while cranberries are growing in other states and provinces, they are limited in volume and density. The dots in Pennsylvania, Texas, and Nevada are Ocean Spray processing stations, designed to reach regional markets.

It is important to note that there are a number of smaller processing facilities across the regions, run by medium-sized independent handlers who produce their own juice and, sometimes, SDCs. These facilities tend to be clustered in the same areas as the processing stations noted above. However, we see that the density of agricultural operations co-varies with processing; it is impossible to say which comes first. What we can say, reinforced by our interviews with growers and other stakeholders, is that the processing stations create an ecosystem around cranberry processing. Again, this helps explain why growing has never really taken off in other areas, such as Maine or Minnesota or Michigan, and highlights the decisive role of government in helping form the cluster in Québec.

Zooming in on New England, in figure 2.2, we can see the sticking power of Massachusetts growers, with proximity to large urban markets and Ocean Spray's headquarters. In Québec, in figure 2.2, we can also see the centralization of most cranberry growers. There is also an Ocean Spray processing station in

WHY DO CRANBERRIES CLUSTER? 43

☆ Processing or Receiving Station
• 1 Dot = 1 Cranberry Farm

Figure 2.1 (*above*): Cranberry processing stations are placed in the key growing clusters. *Source*: authors, from USDA and StatsCan (see Appendix C)

Figure 2.2 (*right*): Processing stations in New England and Québec

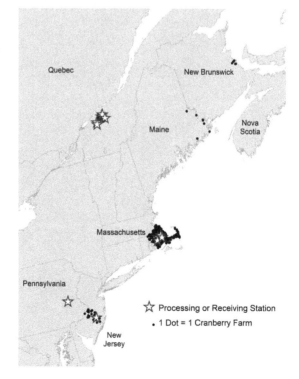

☆ Processing or Receiving Station
• 1 Dot = 1 Cranberry Farm

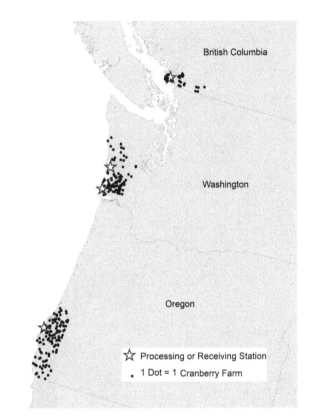

Figure 2.3 (*right*): Processing stations on the West Coast

Figure 2.4 (*below*): Processing stations in the Great Lakes

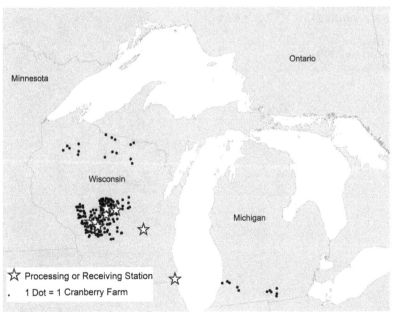

New Jersey, near the growers, and a juice-bottling plant in Pennsylvania. Our emphasis here is on cranberry growers and processors. If we wanted looked further downstream along the supply chain, we would need a different investigation and maps for juice processors, whose location does not co-vary with cranberry growers.

On the West Coast (figure 2.3), we see that the main processing takes place in Washington state, for Ocean Spray growers in BC, Oregon, and Washington state, and also that there are smaller-sized processors along the Oregon coast. In Oregon, some of the growers have their own processing facilities, though of a smaller scale, built out of necessity because of their independence from Ocean Spray.

In figure 2.4, we see the centralization of processing in Central Wisconsin. The dot at the southeastern corner is a long-standing transshipment point for the Chicago market, which was the original catalyst for the Wisconsin growers. Ocean Spray has a juice and sauce processing plant there.

What creates these clusters of vertical supply chain activity? The fact is that, even outside of Ocean Spray, growers make only limited attempts to handle their own fruit due to economies of scale, which create effective oligopolies among the handlers who process the fruit. These economies of scale help define the industry, which, over the last three decades, has consisted of a very slow and, at times, varying decline in Ocean Spray's dominance. This decline is challenging the ability of Ocean Spray to provide collective leadership for the industry, though it largely continues to do so, even amid its own internal challenges, including financial ones. The challenges come largely from the rise of new independent handlers in Québec and existing ones in Wisconsin, the two highest producers. Because of periodic surplus situations, the industry has implemented little vertical integration, with few handlers buying their own land. However, signs indicate land-buying becoming a possible future trend, with some companies in Québec, for example, now buying acres of cranberry land. Krugman's arguments about proximity to large markets are secondary to having processing stations in proximity to growers to preserve fruit freshness—though still valuable for explaining the stations in Texas—and interviewees noted the advantages of transport costs with proximity to West Coast and East Coast markets, or easy shipment to the EU via the port of Montréal.

Other perceptual and cultural factors, beyond the operational and business ones described throughout this book, reflect the interviewee refrain throughout the interviews that growing cranberries *"is a way of life,"* and thus *most interviewees are reluctant to leave no matter how thin the margins.* They enjoy being their own boss and making their own hours, and they are consummate problem-solvers. With land and equipment paid off, they are able to hang on for the indefinite future, even as their children move on to other industries. Stickiness works both ways: while it is a positive along the lines of cluster theory, as we discuss throughout the book, it also reflects *barriers to exit, including shifting to potentially better locations or product diversification.* One interviewee in Wisconsin put it this way: if you have spent family generations on a plot of land, invested years in time and effort to develop your farm, have sunk investments that took years to pay off, and do not find other businesses provide a similar way of life, it would be very hard to leave the business. The pressures on smaller producers, however, are real. While many have succession plans and prospective business heirs, others are looking for an exit strategy.

For example, Oregon growers around the southwest corner, Bandon area, find costs of land increasing and the local labor pool for harvesting drying up. The growers who want to leave the business struggle to exit, as the land is zoned for only agriculture, and according to a local expert, "other areas are more competitive in other crops and livestock." Recent state legislation allowed owners to build housing for themselves or their workers on growing areas of fewer than 140 acres, but they are still prohibited from economic diversification, such as running a bed and breakfast or retail outlet. Similarly, in Massachusetts and New Jersey, many of the farms are designated wetlands, preventing sales of the land for other uses. It is a central challenge only for some, but the industry is too small to afford to import seasonal workers, and there is no coordination with other agricultural industries to organize this. Additionally, the Oregon growers are too far from the busy touristy area a couple of hours to the north of them that would offer diversification and direct sales opportunities. One Oregon handler stated that he had looked into moving up to Florence (approximately two hours north), where there is much more tourist traffic (and it is closer to ports), but realized that he would be too far from the main processing and transportation (freezing) centers that have been built up around the Bandon industry. By contrast, Wisconsin and Québec producers are optimistic about their ability to continue production levels.

What became clear in our field research is just how unique each cranberry cluster was in its industrial organization, even while still meeting the same constraints of national and global market forces. This uniqueness suggests that multiple potential forms of industrial organization can meet the same market conditions. For example, it is notable that 90% of growers in Washington state belong to Ocean Spray, whereas just 50%–64% of those in Oregon do (Graves 2014).[2] In Québec, Ocean Spray may control some 25% of the market, while Wisconsin has a mix of both independent and Ocean Spray. Yet Ocean Spray

---

2 Interviewees suggest the actual number is closer to 50%.

is dominant in BC, New Jersey, and, to a lesser extent, in Massachusetts. Interviewees in Washington suggested that they had a stronger sense of community, and thus stuck with Ocean Spray, even when independent handlers were paying three to four times as much in the 1990s—but their options were far more limited than those in Oregon, as Washington has no close processing facilities besides Ocean Spray. By contrast, a number of other independent facilities are available in Wisconsin and in Oregon, giving ready options to those wanting to bail on Ocean Spray. All of this reinforces the point that the cranberry industry, by processing requirements more than growing conditions, lends itself to natural clustering and locational path dependency.

Additional Reasons for Clustering: Location of Research and Innovation Support

In one of the rare studies of agricultural clusters from the perspective of commodities (in this case, focused on agricultural production in Saskatoon), Phillips et al. suggest a three-pronged approach (2013, 7). The first focuses on natural locational advantages, which, in the case of agriculture, means growing conditions and/or proximity to markets. This approach applies to the cranberry clusters we study, set up where cranberries can be grown. The second applies to processes, such as local universities or policies designed to attract and keep businesses in any area. As we discuss below, each of our cranberry clusters is situated within a clear set of support institutions, centering around R&D and extension, including local Ocean Spray agents. The third is people, which our study links to "tacit knowledge," or the sharing of knowledge among farmers. It also encompasses entrepreneurs, such as Marc Bieler, as we suggest in our mini case study on Québec. In addition, as discussed in the previous section, we posit that supply chain exigencies and choices also affect locational decisions. These decisions are occasionally linked to proximity to markets, as in the case of Ocean Spray's processing plants in Texas and Nevada, but mostly we see a symbiotic relationship between clusters where cranberries are grown and where processing facilities are located.

Innovation has been vital to the cranberry industry's fortunes. Long-time interviewees of the industry describe dramatic labor-saving improvements over long periods of time. They describe the many hours of even more backbreaking work in the past, in which at least a dozen laborers were needed during harvest time to cull the cranberries; it is more typical now to see three to four additional workers. The original method was to use hand rakes to separate the berries. In the early 1950s, a mechanical raking machine was invented in Warrens, Wisconsin. Raking is still used by some to preserve the quality of the fresh fruit. Raking was replaced by the beater in the 1960s, as berries intended for juice products do not require the same care. A harrow, which is gentler on the vines and works faster and wider is now used. A large "cranboom" or flotation device is used to corral the floating berries. Whereas it previously required at least two people to bring in the net, growers now use an automated reel or tie it to a truck to bring in the net. Vacuum pumps suck in the berries, separating out water and residue. Whereas growers used to have to lay out aluminum pipe every year to drain the water, PVC pipe can now remain in place underground. The berries used to be placed on a large assembly line where multiple workers would sort out and dry the berries for quality for the fresh markets. A cranberry mill was introduced to sort soft from firm fruit by its bounce, but workers remained integral until the last few decades, when machine sorting and optical scanners came to be used, though visual inspection of random samples continues. Automatic driers create an assembly-line system for processing the berries and putting them into freezers for storage. In short, labor-saving has helped preserve the family-centered focus of the industry. In the future, precision drones and continual monitoring are expected to improve the efficient use of water and pesticides.

Ocean Spray has been the leader in providing such collective goods in innovation. In 1929, the USDA, working with the New Jersey and Massachusetts agricultural experiment stations, began a cranberry hybridization program to produce cultivars that would be resistant to false blossom disease. However, it produced only one generation of improvements (Eck 1990, 57). The first juice products, introduced during the 1930s, were the Cranberry Juice Cocktail (1931) and Ocean Spray Cran (1937); both were not sweetened. In the 1950s, the NCA introduced the first TV commercials and, in 1957, frozen cranberry-orange relish and frozen cranberries. Researchers helped develop the water reel or "beater" in the early 1960s, designed to beat the berries from the pedicel (stalk), thus reducing labor costs in harvesting. The 1960s were a time of great innovation, with the introduction of sweetened juices, including the Cranberry Juice Cocktail, Cran-Apple, and Grapeberry (later CranGrape) emerging between 1963 and 1968 (subsequent developments, which largely fall under the leadership of Ocean Spray, are described in the next section) (Long, Jacques, and Kepos 2017, 315–316; Stang 1993, 290).

In 1939, the Wisconsin Agricultural Experiment Station, with the assistance of the USDA, the state government, and Wisconsin Cranberry Sales Co., began a new cranberry breeding program. Researchers there developed six new varietals (Vorsa and Johnson-Cicalese 2012, 195–196). Interviewees note several innovations that have changed the industry over the last few decades: the development of integrated pest management (IPM), including precision agriculture (e.g., selecting the specific areas for pesticide and water application); the replacement of the beater with the harrow, which is easier on vines; and improvement in various equipment, such as vacuum tubes.

Several attributes are most prized by the industry, with a conditional bifurcation based on the end use (fresh, juice, or sweetened and dried). These attributes include color, with redness being favored, though the degree of redness desired is limited for use in sweetened dried cranberries. Size, naturally, affects the amount of fruit that can lead to juice, but again, for SDC, it has to be within a certain range. Firmness is prized. And of course, similarly prized is resistance to pestilence, including a wide range of insects, rot caused by fungi, viruses, and other diseases. A 2017 survey of the industry in New Jersey, Wisconsin, and British Columbia was conducted by Gallardo et al. (2018); 92% of respondents were growers. The survey asked growers to prioritize what breeding traits they wanted to see in their crops. The top priority for Wisconsin and BC was fruit quality, while disease resistance was the highest priority in New Jersey, due to higher rates of fruit rot, according to the authors of the survey. In terms of fruit quality traits, firmness was the most important trait; in Wisconsin and BC, this was followed by fruit size; for Wisconsin and New Jersey, anthocyanin content ranked third. After fruit quality, improved plant yield was the second most important trait. Vorsa and Johnson-Cicalese (2012, 197–198) state that identifying breeding characteristics is complicated by the fact that there is no certified nursery system for cranberries and that cranberries reproduce asexually through stolons. It can thus be challenging to trace the varietal origins of fruit on a particular farm.

As suggested by cluster theory, local knowledge-creators and brokers play a big role in the competitiveness of different cranberry growing locations. The triple helix theory covers the extensive industry-researcher-policy cooperation in the cranberry industry, spurred on by the issues unique to its cultivation. Caruso, Bristow, and Oudemans (2019) state that diseases related to cranberries are "unique" and include fungal pathogens that affect both the fruit and the leaf, but there are few issues involving nematodes, bacteria, or viruses. False blossom disease, caused by a virus, is an exception; it wiped out 9,000 acres in New Jersey and Massachusetts in the 1920s and 1930s. Fruit rot, caused by a variety of fungi, is an ongoing concern. If left untreated, it could consume up to 50% of the crop on the East Coast. Interviewees across the board pointed to the important value of their local extension stations and Ocean Spray representatives, who help them troubleshoot problems as they arise and are generally available on a regular basis. They also noted that problems vary widely among growing areas, due to "microclimates" and unique conditions leading to different types of issues. In BC and Washington state, for example, there has been a recent emphasis on the tipworm issue. A new team of scientists, funded by the Canadian government through the National Science and Engineering Research Council (NSERC) with matching funding from Ocean Spray, is studying fruit rot via a new microarray technique that allows for more precise identification of the fungi that cause the rot. Ocean Spray was drawn into the project by Canadian scientists at Université Laval, in part because of the more generous matching funding option, according to interviewees.

Beyond breeding for new varietals, most research funding seems to be focused on short-term local pest problems, because of different pest profiles and because most funding comes from grower-managed state or provincial boards. There appear to be few collaborations across crops or between the United States and Canada, though researchers across different clusters, and particularly across Québec, Wisconsin, and New Jersey (Rutgers) appear to have regular contact with each other. Language barriers may play a role, according to one expert. Focused on local problems, clusters' state and provincial associations resist collaborating on larger research issues. Thus, by default, Ocean Spray funds most long-term collective goods type research.

One concerning aspect of the cranberry industry is that we could not find any formal (long-term) training program in any of the clusters, which brings us back to the vital importance of tacit knowledge and social capital associated with cluster theory. Most growers/managers appear to learn through the annual cranberry schools and the training offered by Ocean Spray, which includes financial management and analysis for growers. A 2012 initiative by the Wisconsin Cranberry Board created the Cranberry Leadership program to help create professional managers. The program offers participants access to a variety of skills, from agricultural research to social media, creating a cohort effect among the next generation of the state farming families and some professional managers. It requires a modest payment by participants, but much of the program is paid for by the board and the state cranberry foundation. However, the program trains only a small number, estimated by interviewees at fifteen for the first cohort.

Neither Québec nor BC have the equivalent of agricultural extension agents (scientists who act as bridges between growers and researchers and are generally located in stations nearer to farmers). Extension agents act as key "bridges" between growers and researchers in the United States, helping growers to see the value of contributing to industry research and providing researchers with a ready source of funds. Lacking extension agents, communication between growers and scientists depends instead on funding for specific research projects, or personal networks (often through former students) between researchers and growers or growers' associations. For example, the Québec

Cranberry Growers' Association (APCQ), including several activist growers, helped fund irrigation research at the Université Laval that reportedly helped contribute to significantly higher yields. When asked which researchers they would go to for cranberry issues that the growers and APCQ cannot solve, the interviewees stated that there is no concerted or consistent cranberry research program at any local university. The growers used to rely on the Government of Québec (MAPAQ) for help, but MAPAQ no longer has a dedicated person to research solutions. So, growers have to look for experts in a particular issue (e.g., entomology) across Québec's universities. On one hand, this situation creates challenges for regular R&D in the sector; on the other, there appears to be strong funding from the provincial and federal governments, which is matched by the growers, for applied research projects. Canadian cranberry agronomists and growers state that they have very good relations with US counterparts, and that there generally is a free flow of information, though a few expressed some reservations about the partial openness of Ocean Spray. In line with the "global pipelines" (alongside tacit local knowledge) concept of cluster theory, the flow of tacit knowledge from exchanges with Wisconsin growers was widely cited by Québec producers as being behind their rapid learning curve. In general, cranberry growers and extension workers attend the "field schools" in different provinces and states, along with NACREW, the annual researcher and extension workers' conference, which all help to disseminate knowledge.

Each cluster has its own idiosyncratic research community around cranberries. In Wisconsin, a station devoted to cranberry research was set up by the state legislature in 1903, including an experimental farm of five acres in the Cranmoor district, but closed in 1917. In 1918, Rutgers University helped establish the New Jersey Agricultural Experiment Station, which studies both blueberries and cranberries. The Washington Cranberry and Blueberry Station was opened in 1923 as part of the Washington State Agricultural Experiment Station in Long Beach; it changed its name to the Coastal Washington Experiment Station in 1960. The station helped create the Crowley cultivar. Early researchers prioritized diseases, including false blossom diseases (Eck 1990, 13–15). One of the challenges for cooperation in the cranberry industry is that growing conditions are remarkably different from one cluster to another. For example, the types of pests and diseases the plants suffer from differ markedly, complicating joint R&D (Playfair 2014, 157).

The Wisconsin Cranberry Board is clearly the most significant state-level supporter of research, with an annual budget of $400,000–$500,000. The mandatory state levy has helped fund significant research that benefits the industry, as we discuss below (State of Wisconsin nd). The ten cents/

barrel levy is based on a state marketing order that funds research through the Wisconsin Cranberry Board. Research priorities are decided by the Wisconsin Board (with seven board members elected to three-year terms and term limits), with inputs from the Growers Association and the Research Foundation, and generally reflect grower interests in horticulture and improving yields. The growers have had some success in getting federal lawmakers to fund US-government Agricultural Research Service (ARS) specialists who specialize in cranberries and have been instrumental in developing some of the new varietals. The Wisconsin Cranberry Board also funds annual research projects, as well as University of Wisconsin Madison researchers and graduate students specializing in cranberries. The university maintains a Fruit Program, including researchers and extension agents whose portfolio includes cranberries and who participate in the annual cranberry school to disseminate proceedings (UW Fruit Program nd). There appear to be at least five researchers working as extension agents for cranberries in the state, including one who is posted closer to the farms centered in Wisconsin Rapids. In addition, there is an affiliate USDA ARS Cranberry Genetics and Genomics Laboratory, including three full-time researchers who appear to have joint appointments and a team of graduate students working on plant breeding and on entomology. One local scientist also reinforced the recognition by Wisconsin's congressional delegation for the importance of the industry, citing a recent effort by Senator Tammy Baldwin to obtain federal funding for additional scientist positions at UW Madison and for the research station. As one Wisconsin researcher put it, "We work together closely with the Growers' Association and with our USDA counterparts, who also teach on campus. . . . There is no doubt that there is a symbiosis between our presence and that of the cranberry industry. The two work hand-in-hand to explain cluster location." Because the board is focused on scientific research, with relatively little attention to marketing, it works in a complementary fashion with Ocean Spray. Similarly, interviewees report a culture of cooperation across different-sized growers in the state, based in part on long-standing family and interpersonal ties.

Interviewees noted that a years' long effort to establish a research station with an experimental farm has finally come to fruition. The station is owned and operated by the Wisconsin Cranberry Research and Education Foundation (Wisconsin Cranberry Research Station, nd). The land was originally purchased in 2017, and funding has come from private sources as well as USDA. The station is currently researching the cold-hardiness of different varietals, as well as targeting pesticide and fertilizer use (Kirwan 2021).

The Cranberry Research Foundation, based in Massachusetts, conducts research on behalf of the local industry; according to interviewees it provides approximately $25,000/year in funding, mostly to the local extension station. Research is also sponsored by the Cranberry Marketing Committee (CMC) and the Cranberry Institute. The CMC provides a quarterly production report that is widely used in the industry. The CMC not only administers the marketing order (see section 4.10), but also promotes exports. It uses a Seattle-based consulting firm to help prepare an overseas marketing plan for the industry and works with USDA to help growers and handlers make contacts in overseas markets, with matching funding from USDA. The CMC has recently sponsored health research, set up by the industry's acceptance of the USDA marketing order (as we discuss below).

The Cranberry Institute (CI) was created to provide research with representation from the whole industry, though Ocean Spray still controls a majority of the seats. It is notable that the CI depends on voluntary contributions of industry handlers (not growers), with the lion's share coming from Ocean Spray. The CI combines funding for research projects, based on majority votes deciding an agenda, with a vetting of submitted proposals. It also helps to monitor regulatory conditions, such as restrictions and guideline differences between the US and overseas markets and helps coordinate lobbying efforts (which are not permitted by the CMC). According to interviewees, the fact that a majority of the board members of the institute are growers has both good and bad sides. On the good side, funded research is responsive to the needs of growers. On the bad side, handlers may lack the knowledge or motivation needed to consider long-term strategy regarding marketing or R&D. Many interviewees make the same point about Ocean Spray. A number of growers noted the potential importance of the CI in providing timely and breakthrough research. They also cited its value in synthesizing information, particularly about pesticide use, in easy-to-understand formats for growers.

The Washington State Cranberry Commission also funds research projects, funded by a ten cent/100 lb. levy on growers. Interviewees suggest that the levy provides research funding of approximately $13,000/year for research projects. A commission of elected grower representatives chooses the projects for funding. Washington growers organized through the Pacific Coast Cranberry Research Foundation also fund the operating costs for an extension station in Long Beach, run by Washington State University and manned by recently retired Dr. Kim Patten, as the state stopped funding the station some years ago. The search for Dr. Patten's replacement is currently under way (Washington State Legislature nd).[3]

---

3 Dr. Patten worked in pest management in aquaculture as well, so the replacement will have to cover both industries.

The story of the foundation is remarkable. It was led by former extension agents Malcolm and Ardel Macphail, who helped organize local growers to voluntarily fund the extension station and to push for the continuation of state funding for the salary of the researcher/extension agent. The story shows the power of personal leadership and community ties. By contrast, Oregon has no mandatory levy, and the industry seems relatively neglected by the state. The growers' association is voluntary and charges a modest $150/year in dues, which amounts to a few thousand dollars per year that had been going to Dr. Patten. While there used to be two agricultural extension agents in the Bandon area, the state has now reduced it to just one position, to cover livestock, dairies, and horticulture including cranberries.

In Québec, the main researchers are at the Université Laval. The ties with Wisconsin are important for both regions (as we discuss in chapter 5). Ocean Spray also provides its own system of extension agents in each of the clusters. The agents are considered agricultural research scientists, but according to interviewees, most of their time seems to be devoted to working with farmers as problems arise. They are an important supplement and work harmoniously with state extension agents. Interviewees note the important role Ocean Spray's agents play in knowledge translation, moving new innovation and research into useful information for growers. They seem open to helping non–Ocean Spray growers as well, correctly seeing cluster issues as shared problems. Their contribution is viewed in a very positive way by the growers interviewed.

The development of a large organic segment of the cranberry market reflects consumer preferences as well as concerns about the use of chemical pesticides. Cranberries are prone to fungi, rot, and pests. In turn, this vulnerability raises questions about the heavy use of water, and possible water and ecosystem effects (including on bees, who have an important role in pollination) from pesticides (Luhning 2014). New European Union (EU) regulations regarding the widely used rot pesticide Bravo have caused considerable concern in the industry. Several upset growers see this as a failure by the industry to lobby the US government adequately to pressure the EU on their behalf. Current research includes, therefore, both the urgency of finding new pesticide compounds and the challenges of organic growing.

By far the most important innovation in recent years has been the development of new, more productive varietals, whose development was led by Nick Vorsa of the Rutgers Experimental Station; Juan Zalapa of USDA, stationed in Wisconsin; and the Grygleski family in Wisconsin. Beginning in the early 2000s, these new hybrids have been widely introduced, in an ongoing process, and are revolutionizing the industry. They are the most important innovation since the Stevens hybrid was developed by the USDA in 1929 through a breeding program to create resistance to false blossom disease. Seedlings of the Stevens hybrid were released in the 1940s and had become widely disseminated by the 1970s, leading to major increases in yields (Silver Creek Nursery nd). Beyond yields, each varietal has different harvest times, qualities, and optimal growing requirements. The varietal mix varies considerably from one region to another (US Cranberries nd, a). Although scientific research in cranberry cultivation is limited, it is making a significant difference in the industry. For example, new varietals developed by Rutgers University vastly increased productivity (by perhaps one and a half to two times the yield), leading to major increases in supply, particularly in Wisconsin and Québec. Different types of the new varietals have different levels of royalties, which leads to wide variation in adoption. It is worth noting that some processors expressed concerns about whether all the new varietals have optimal characteristics for SDCs. Moreover, new farm design and harvesting techniques have contributed to dramatic increases in productivity. Several interviewees stated that advances in farm design; greater use of and improvements in equipment, such as booms for precision pesticide management; and large advances in understanding about water exposure leading to changes in irrigation and drainage techniques were as important as the new varietals in increasing yields. However, knowledge is still sticky, and some growers and support institutions in other regions state that they are not as confident to switch to the new varietals, because their knowledge and experience is with traditional varietals and because of concerns about lower quality and different attributes of the new ones, including firmness. Some interviewees stated that some of the new varietals ripen earlier, throwing off their ability to manage the labor and other harvesting tasks learned from traditional varietals. Several also stated that the new varietals had to be harvested quickly, as the fruit tends to take on water and rot faster. Others stated that spreading out harvests based on when different varietals ripen makes their lives easier, so that they can manage the load with less hired labor. Some suggested the newer varietals also appear to require additional fertilizer/nutrition and harvesting investments. Not surprisingly, there is some resentment among growers about the royalty payments, which they find particularly high for the Rutgers variety, which they state was funded in good part by Ocean Spray.

Experts in the industry caution that it will take years to really see how the new varietals play out. When asked about why the new varietals focused on yield, given the commodity price cycle, they reply that it takes thirty-some years to really develop new varietals, and these were started in the 1980s, when there was a supply shortage (around the time that SDCs were developed). Given that beds were often completely renovated as they were put in, it takes years to reach consistency in fruit production and acquire the tacit knowledge to manage each varietal. Overall, growers are cautiously optimistic, noting that each new varietal will have its own characteristics and requirements, and more time is needed to reach any clear conclusions. In addition, in some regions, such as Massachusetts and Washington state, the overall age of growers is increasing, and as they get closer to retirement, they are not able to undertake a long-term project; thus, new varietals will only increase the gaps between regions' productivity.

While the new varietals may eventually create cranberries superior across all attributes, clearly it is a good idea to preserve biodiversity of varietals. For example, diversity may reduce risk factors, such as susceptibility to certain fungi or pests. The "holy grail," as one scientist put it, would be to develop newer varietals that have sweeter taste (lower acid to sugar ratios) and could increase the amount of cranberries in juice blends, or even someday allow for widespread consumption of cranberries as fresh fruit. The Grygleski family and University of Wisconsin–Madison have produced a slightly sweeter varietal called the "sweetie," but it is not sweet enough to match consumer preferences. One Wisconsin researcher noted the theoretical possibility that cranberries could be crossed with blueberries, a close genetic cousin.

USDA-NIFA is the lead funder of a $12.8 million project called "VacCAP," which includes researchers across the US looking at traits of both cranberries and blueberries. According to participants, the research in both crops was based on a pilot grant that permitted a survey of growers of both crops on their breeding priorities. In cranberries, the priorities were color, firmness, and fruit size, related to improving the quality of SDCs. Researchers suggest a sizable portion of the present crop is not up to the standards of SDC production. The research, in part, seeks breeding techniques to reduce the acidity of cranberries, which would make their taste less astringent; to find cultivars that are less susceptible to fruit rot; and to gauge health-conscious consumers' willingness to accept added sugars in cranberry projects (VacCAP nd). The researchers found that consumers put a significant discount on cranberry juice labeled as having added sugar, even when compared with juice blends that might have more sugar or when countered with a label about health claims. VacCAP is an example of what could be done on the health research side—a multistate, multidisciplinary project with a sizable budget.

In sum, although growing conditions are important, they are wholly inadequate to explain cranberry clusters. We see through cranberries that a wide swath of concepts from cluster theory are applicable to agriculture, particularly,

- the factor of path dependency, or historical lock-in
- the importance of economies of scale

- the role of both formal knowledge through R&D and local extension stations and tacit knowledge through sharing growing and harvesting techniques
- the vital role of location next to supply chain factors—processing facilities in this case—as well as to large markets on the East and West Coasts
- the role of policy, both in engendering a new cluster, as is the case with Québec, and in its lack of effort in holding back the industry, as is the case in New Jersey

In the rest of this book, we explore further the human factors behind clustering, including both industry organization and policy decisions. One thing we shall see is how uneven and idiosyncratic each cluster is, and how each presents a dynamic moving target. But first we begin with a review of the history, and then a statistical analysis of trends in the industry, in order to understand the long-term evolutionary factors that led to the current formation and shape of the North American cranberry clusters.

Chapter 3
The History of Cranberries: Escaping the Commodity Trap via Cooperatives

The history of cranberry cultivation reflects, without design, an evolutionary shift toward industrial organization that can provide collective goods and a model for other agricultural producers to consider. The need for collective goods derives from ongoing efforts in pest management and improvement of yields, as described in chapter 2, but, more importantly, recognition over time of the benefits of supplier cooperation. As in all agriculture, this need relates most fundamentally to the problem of commodity cycles and the lag times between market signals and grower responses. Supplier cooperation can assist with supply management, to reduce the pain of "busts," and, more promisingly, to assist with common marketing and product innovation to grow demand. In this chapter, we examine how path dependency clearly affects industrial organization, including the location, cooperation, and competitiveness of producing clusters. Similarly, we trace out the vital role of contingency and personal leadership in shaping industry structure—in this case, the highly unusual development of the Ocean Spray cooperative.

PATH DEPENDENCY: EARLY CRANBERRY CLUSTERS ON THE EAST COAST

The initial locations of cranberry cultivation in Massachusetts and New Jersey help to explain these states' longevity in the industry, even as they lose competitiveness due to factors we have already discussed. Timing clearly matters in terms of cluster location and longevity. Cranberry cultivation, going back at least to the eighteenth century, was centered in Massachusetts at the outset. Playfair notes that wild cranberries were much prized by the early colonists, as they were viewed as being imbued with medicinal qualities and thus considered "the choicest product of the [Massachusetts] colony" (2014, 1) when presented to King Charles in 1677. The berries were used widely on whaling ships, for example, to prevent scurvy. They presented advantages over blueberries and grapes because of their longer shelf life and thick skin (2).

Mason states that cranberries were first cultivated in North Dennis, Massachusetts between 1810 and 1820. "Very soon thereafter, it was discovered that a thin layer of sand over the ground improved the quality of the berries," and sanding had become a common practice by 1850 (1926, 65). Eck notes that Henry Hall, a Revolutionary War veteran, first attempted to cultivate cranberries on Cape Cod in 1810 (1990, 4–5). A book by Eastwood from 1859 discusses the "many ponds" abounding in the leading growing area, Cape Cod, that lent themselves to cranberry cultivation. The author notes the use of cranberries by the native Pequod people going back centuries (Eastwood 13). He dates attempts at farming cranberries to 1844, along with many years of difficulties (21). It is fascinating to note that cultivation was spurred by views of the cranberry as a "must have" luxury item for the wealthy. The primary markets were Boston and New York, though attempts to sell cranberries in bottles in Europe were beginning (71–72). By 1875, the ability to grow cranberries on peat bogs was widely known, and cultivation spread to Western Massachusetts (Mason 1926, 65).

Eck suggests that the cranberry market began to form in the 1820s, when wild and cultivated fruit were intermingled (1990, 7–8). Boston was the major market, and a shipment point to Europe, where the fruit sold for $20/barrel, and to New Orleans, Mobile, Savannah, and Charleston, fetching as high as $35/barrel. The market started to expand rapidly in the 1860s in response to increased demand, including from whaling ships, as the fruit was slower to rot than others and had high vitamin C. In Western Massachusetts during this period, cranberries were called "red gold."

Cranberries were also native to New Jersey, and Benjamin Thomas of Pemberton began to cultivate them in 1835. Procopio and Bunnell state that cultivation in New Jersey began in Ocean and Burlington counties and remains concentrated in the Pinelands region there (2008, 772). Eck recounts the story of "Peg Leg John," John J. Webb, who dropped his berries down a staircase, thereby noticing that the sound berries bounced, while the rotten ones stayed stuck, a principle later used in separators. In 1828, Ebenezer Childs, a New Englander and pioneer storekeeper in Green Bay, Wisconsin, began trading cranberries, which also grew wild in Wisconsin. Cultivation there began in 1853 by George A. Peffer in the Fox River Valley, exceeding 1,000 acres in 1869. Anthony Chabot, a Frenchman, started a cranberry bog in Long Beach, Washington, in 1883, using cultivars from New Jersey and Cape Cod. Chabot was producing approximately 7,500 barrels/year until the bog dissipated in the 1890s under the management of Pacific Cranberry Company. This bog and other areas were revived in 1904 by J. M. Arthur of Portland, Oregon, who started the Breakers Hotel in Long Beach. He created the Pacific Cranberry Marsh company in 1904, at which time there were four producers in the area.

Outside investors expanded cranberry growing in the area in the 1910s, but issues with pests, weeds, and distance to markets led to major losses. These issues spurred local growers to develop the Cranberry Research Station under the leadership of D. J. Crowley of Washington State University in 1922. After a major shakeout, Crowley's new methods led to a revival in the 1940s, once farmers could raise the investment capital to implement them (Pacific Coast Cranberry Research Foundation 1997, 29–33). In 1885, Charles Dexter McFarlin planted the first vines in Empire City, Coos County, Oregon, giving up gold panning to plant the vines he had brought from Massachusetts (Chandler 1957, 1). Informants note that the industry grew fast because cranberries are high in vitamin C and slow to rot (when dry harvested), thus were widely used for sailing and whaling vessels during the nineteenth century.

Durand Jr. (1942) confirms 1853 as the first year that wild cranberries, also native to Wisconsin, were harvested there. Prices reached $11/barrel in 1872. Cultivation was primarily in central Wisconsin, which has marshland conditions and sand and peat land that are too damp for other types of agriculture. The roots of industry organization lie in the efforts of Judge J. A. Gaynor of Wisconsin Rapids to deal with drainage and water rights, for which he obtained a state grant of $250 in 1893. He was instrumental in creating an Agricultural Experiment Station at the University of Wisconsin in the region that included cranberry studies. The original founders tended to pass down their farms to family members. Stevens and Nash (1944, 277) suggest that cranberry cultivation began in 1860 in Berlin (much farther east than the current center). They trace the "Berlin Boom" to a Mr. Sacket, who came from the East Coast with knowledge of how to cultivate cranberries. By 1865, he had produced 938 barrels, which were sold in Chicago from $14 to $16/barrel; cranberry cultivation rapidly spread from the example.

Interviewees in Wisconsin discussed the rich tradition there, with stories passed down through generations. Many got their start through "investors" from Chicago who asked them to start cultivating the wild cranberries growing there for sale in the fresh food markets during the holiday season, where they were a hit. Along with the efforts of the research station, there was a great deal of private experimentation.

An 1892 book titled, simply, *The Cranberry*, was published by the Bradley Fertilizer Company as a how-to manual for cranberry farmers. It lists the 1891 crop as New England, 480,000 bushels; New Jersey 250,000; and the West, 30,000 (28). Playfair states that, in 1895, 3,255 acres of land in Cape Cod and 3,766 in Plymouth County (Massachusetts) were devoted to cranberry cultivation, and these figures tripled by 1905, fueled by rising demand (2014, 22). By 1945, cranberries were the chief export for Massachusetts.

COMMODITY CYCLES WRACK THE INDUSTRY

From the outset, commodity cycles marked the cranberry industry. Ups and downs based on oversupply have long roots in the cranberry market, including a crash in 1900 (Playfair 2014, 126). This cycle led to two responses: first, to cultivate overseas markets and, second, to try to increase demand. Regarding the first response, Playfair notes that, as of 2014, 30% of the harvest was exported, despite increasing competition from Canada, Chile, and other emerging supply countries (2014, 127).

Jesse and Rogers note that cranberry production increased from 300,000 to more than 750,000 barrels between 1910 and 1929, though grower prices occupied a wide range, between $4 and $14/barrel during the period (2006, 8). Part of this increase can be attributed to the development of flood harvesting, which, according to Stang (1993, 290) began in Wisconsin in the early 1900s and spread quickly, saving enormous amounts of labor. Before canning, informants suggest that cranberries were mostly consumed fresh, during harvest time, which coincided with their association with and use for Thanksgiving and Christmas.

Mason suggests canning had become a big industry in South Hanson, Massachusetts, by the early 1920s (1926, 68). Mason lauds the cranberry industry's impact in southeastern Massachusetts, where it was able to make land valuable that would "otherwise waste." According to her, at the time there was no significant cultivation of cranberries outside the United States; quantities had been dwindling in Nova Scotia and Prince Edward Island since 1917. While only 5,000 cans were sold in world markets before 1922, by 1924, more than 100,000 were packed by the United Cape Cod Cranberry Company for shipment around the world.

Eck reports that the cranberry industry in Washington state grew rapidly from 1883 until the start of World War I, after which growers were unable to "deal with the intricacies of cranberry culture," and the crop declined significantly (1990, 6). In 1912, Edward Benn began cultivating cranberries in the Grayland area, which became the source of new growth.

During the 1920s and 1930s, the cranberry industry was devastated in New Jersey and Massachusetts by false blossom disease. This, along with the Great Depression, helped to drop acreage in New Jersey from 11,000 to 2,800 acres from the beginning to the end of the 1930s (Jones 2003, 354). By the 1940s, Wisconsin had become the second-largest producer, after Massachusetts (Matusinec et al. 2022).

Hyson and Sanderson note that yields increased considerably, from 365,000 barrels in 1900–1904 to more than 650,000 in 1938–1942, due to improved techniques (1945, 332). Farm income increased from $2 million to $10.4 million over the same period. In their article, the authors explain that, despite concentration in the cranberry industry, they did not believe antitrust action was warranted. Their reasons include the long periods required for cranberry investments to pay off; the dynamic movements of both demand and supply over time, leading to limits to profit-taking; and the nonparticipation of some significant suppliers (368–369).

By the 1950s, a million barrels of cranberries were being produced annually, and issues were increasing around unsold fruit. More importantly, in 1959, the US Department of Health, Education, and Welfare stated that the herbicide aminotriazole, used in cranberries in Oregon and Washington state, caused cancer in mice, leading to a widespread consumer scare. Fresh cranberry sales plummeted to zero that year. The USDA indemnified growers at $8/barrel ($1 below the market price) under a special federal program, beginning a history of federal policies of supply regulation (Jesse and Rogers 2006, 4, 10).

Acreage grew steadily over this period, and yields increased by about 50% in the 1960s because of improved production techniques, including mechanical dry picking and varietals, to about 30 barrels/acre (Jesse and Rogers 2006, 10). The industry turned to the USDA in 1962 to ask for help in controlling supply through the Cranberry Marketing Order. The USDA set aside a certain amount of fruit from the market that could only be exported, given to charity, or used for nonhuman consumption. The annual set-aside amount was decided by a seven-person committee called the Cranberry Marketing Committee; in 1962, it was 12% of the crop (Eck 1990, 349).

Problems of oversupply were matched by limited demand. Cranberries were initially thought of as a product to be consumed during Thanksgiving and Christmas. An informant in Wisconsin relates the development of juice to the "cranberry scare" of the 1950s, which spurred Ocean Spray to develop alternative markets. The industry expanded demand by marketing it as a condiment to meat at any meal (once canning made that possible) and encouraging its other potential uses, such as in jams, barbeque sauce, and candies. The development of juice cocktails by the mid-1960s rapidly expanded the market and reduced pressure for set-asides (Eck 1990, 349, 352). Ocean Spray introduced the first juice blend, Cran-Apple, in 1963 (Lambert, Rogers and Lass 2004). Ocean Spray vastly expanded the market for cranberries in the early 1970s with its marketing. The trick was to create a more palatable juice that contained enough sugar to change the taste from tart to sweet (Playfair 2014, 144).

By the late 1970s, the takeoff of cranberry juice blends had reversed the surplus, and prices had risen to $40/barrel by the early 1980s. During this period new competitors to Ocean Spray entered the market, including Clermont,

Cliffstar, Decas, and Hiller, who were able to undercut Ocean Spray's prices. The boost in demand lasted into the 1990s and led to increasing acreage, new varietals, and a doubling of production between 1970 and 1990 (Jesse and Rogers 2006, 10). In 1995, Wisconsin overtook Massachusetts for cranberry production, thanks to its lower land costs and greater mechanization in newly cultivated areas (Jesse and Rogers 2006, 11).

Jesse and Rogers explain the ensuing crash in part as supply catching up with demand, which had a one-time boost in the 1990s related to medical claims (2006, 12). Furthermore, the 1986 departure of Northland Cranberries, Inc., from Ocean Spray—its largest member, producing 200,000 barrels a year—and the 1993 departure of another large grower, Donna Jeffords, producing about 100,000 barrels a year, vastly ramped up competition. By 1987, Northland was the largest cranberry grower in Wisconsin (Lambert, Rogers and Lass 2004). Informants in Wisconsin noted that Northland was the product of the singular vision of John Swendrowski, a former high school English teacher and football coach turned loan officer for Wood County Bank, who saw the potential for cranberry investments as prices started to climb in line with juice consumption. He used his financial savvy to buy up multiple marshes (up to twenty-five) and develop his own supply chain. He created a buzz and distribution around his then-innovative 100% juice product, which mixed cranberries with apple or pear juice to sweeten it. He later guaranteed at least 27% of the juice was from cranberries, touting the health benefits. He managed to develop strong retail distribution in the northern Midwest and then began expanding nationally, including the purchase of Seneca juice. This shifted cranberry prices up dramatically, leading to a major expansion in acreage, as Northland offered a premium for growers to switch from Ocean Spray and spurred on new entrants.

Northland began to build its own processing capacity in 1995 and eventually became the second largest US cranberry processor, selling some products under its Northland label. It introduced a 100% juice blend to distinguish itself as a healthy alternative to Ocean Spray, which added sugar and water to its juices. Ocean Spray responded with new grapefruit and juice blends and a deal with PepsiCo (discussed below). Both companies also bought up other smaller juice companies and expanded cranberry production. Since Northland had contracted with Cliffstar and Clement Pappas to provide fruit at above-market prices, then left the deal, Northland had to scramble to find new growers, further stimulating production. Some interviewees claimed Northland's aggressive expansion shifted prices up to the point of significant supply increase, thus creating a larger commodity wave. The bubble burst in 1998, when prices dropped from $64 to $38 a barrel. As a result, the industry invoked the Cranberry Marketing Order during 2000–2001, having the government purchase large inventories to reduce supplies (Jesse and Rogers 2006, 12; Lambert, Rogers and Lass 2004). Informants also suggested that Northland was at one time close to purchasing Pappas, which would have given it processing and distribution leverage. Northland also made a reported $800 million bid for Ocean Spray, which was overwhelmingly rejected in 2003. Ocean Spray's sales were reportedly ten times as large as the offer at the time. However, according to informants, as the price burst, Northland's debt became overwhelming, and the company was broken apart and sold off, including a processing center in Wisconsin Rapids bought by Ocean Spray for $28 million in 2004. A 2002 suit against Ocean Spray for monopolistic practices was settled out of court, and Northland was effectively broken up by 2004 (*Milwaukee Business Journal* 2004). Remaining juice assets were acquired by Apple and Eve in 2005, which itself was acquired by Lassonde in 2014, though one can still find Northland-brand juices.

The USDA established the Cranberry Marketing Committee to administer a total marketable quantity of 5,468 million barrels in 2000–2001, not including fresh and organic fruit, based on formulas derived from past grower production. In the following year, the 2001–2002 cranberry harvest was lowered further, to 4.6 million barrels, to try to help increase prices, as some growers were struggling. In the meantime, the industry suffered through conflict, with Northland undergoing financial restructuring and suing Ocean Spray in 2001, alleging price fixing. A.R. Demarco Enterprises, Inc., one of Ocean Spray's largest growers, also sued Ocean Spray, alleging a conspiracy to drive out smaller growers and shareholders, and lobbied the USDA, all in order to achieve more value upon selling the company (Lambert, Rogers and Lass 2004). The Northland implosion remains an important historical incident for some industry members, particularly in Wisconsin, which they saw as reflecting predatory behavior by Ocean Spray. They pointed to the purchase of Atoka as an example of that, though informants downplayed any rivalry. Some Wisconsin interviewees suggested that the Québec producers have learned from the Northland incident and thus have developed strong financial plans to compete with Ocean Spray.

What we see in the early decades of the industry is the dominant position of East Coast growers, the ups and downs of commodity cycles, and the steady improvement of technology and management leading to ever-increasing supply trends. As discussed in chapter 2's focus on innovation, these primordial industry forces continue today. We now turn to how the industry started to organize itself in response.

RESPONDING TO COMMODITY CYCLES: FORMALIZING COOPERATION

Cooperation has a long history in the cranberry industry, well preceding the formation of the Ocean Spray cooperative, and is deeply ingrained in the industry culture. Eck asserts that the cranberry industry was first organized in New Jersey when growers met in Vincentown in 1869 (1990, 11–12). In 1871, growers formed the American Cranberry Growers' Association, which had committees to investigate topics such as marketing, drainage, pests, and standards measures. In 1871, the Wisconsin growers formed the Berlin Cranberry Association, superseded by the Wisconsin State Cranberry Growers' Association in 1887. Around the same time, A. U. Chaney and Judge Gaynor formed the Wisconsin Cranberry Sales Growers' Cooperative, which worked on marketing issues such as fruit grading and price pooling.

Eck notes "the fact that the cranberry was a perishable crop produced in widely disbursed geographic areas, the sales of which were restricted to a relatively short period, led producers to experiment with cooperative marketing organizations relatively early in the industry's development" (1990, 345). Marple Jr. and Harding contribute some additional advantages that have stimulated the industry toward cooperatives. First, following the Capper-Volstead Act of 1922, cooperatives do not face antitrust lawsuits, as long as they do not engage in predatory pricing. Second, vertical integration cuts out fees to middlemen in the supply chain. Third, net proceeds from member operations are not subject to federal taxation if they are distributed to members (2002, 82–83).

According to Playfair, the Cape Cod Cranberry Growers' Association was formed in 1888 to standardize berry color and size, engage in joint marketing efforts, and support the exchange of farming ideas (2014, 118). Mason adds important details. In 1895, the larger growers of Massachusetts and New Jersey formed the Growers' Cranberry Company, and Massachusetts growers also formed the Cape Cod Cranberry Sales Company. Operations included sales offices in Philadelphia and Boston, designed to predict market movements and market products. Growers were paid individually, based on the price received for sales of their batches. In 1906, a heavy crop flooded markets, pushing them toward cooperation. The Cape Cod Cranberry Growers' Association pushed the state to fund research, leading to the establishment of the Cranberry Experiment Station at East Wareham in 1893 (1926, 66). According to Eck, the station became home to many of the most preeminent cranberry researchers in the country until the 1960s (1990, 12–13).

In 1905, Arthur Chaney helped set up a cooperative of midwestern growers called the Wisconsin Cranberry Sales Company, which included

90% of Wisconsin growers. Around 1907, the New England Cranberry Sales Company was created to establish a brand with quality standards, and joint marketing and distribution for its members, using the label "Eatmor." This company had a different model, choosing to pool berries and sell under standard labels. Pooling meant that the price received for a particular berry was pooled over the season, with returns distributed to individual growers, based on the price and the amount they contributed (Eck 1990, 345). In 1907, Chaney convinced the New England Cranberry Sales Company and its counterpart, the New Jersey Cranberry Sales Company, to create the American Cranberry Exchange, a marketing cooperative. The exchange had an elected board and took entire crops from local sales companies to markets, paying members partially upon delivery. It worked toward price stabilization through offering a portion of total sales to each farmer based on their portion of berries delivered by quantity and quality. The cooperatives made strong efforts to improve quality by dumping subpar berries. The exchange sold only fresh berries (Playfair 2014, 118).

The Growers' Cranberry Company merged with the American Cranberry Exchange in 1911, while the Cape Cod and New Jersey sales companies went out of existence. The exchange was marketing 75% of the crop in Wisconsin and around 65% in New Jersey and Massachusetts, with the residual crop marketed by individual growers or through local marketing organizations. On the West Coast, the Pacific Cranberry Exchange was established in 1917, mirroring the American Cranberry Exchange for local producers (Eck 1990, 346).

In 1919, the American Cranberry Exchange was reorganized into nonstock, nonprofit, and cooperative organizations in response to the Clayton Amendment of the Sherman Antitrust Law. However, the marketing operations and grading and pooling system remained the same. The state organizations continued to play an intermediary role between the growers and the exchange, keeping shipment records and furnishing boxes, barrels, and labels for growers, while distributing shipments and overseeing the pooling accounting system for the exchange. The state organizations received 2% of total sales, while the exchange received 5% of gross sales and was in charge of advertising; by 1920, 2% of gross returns were spent on ads. Growers were receiving 54% of each dollar of sales in 1920, far greater than the margin for other perishable food items at the time (Eck 1990, 347).

As of 1925, most small growers were members of the three state cranberry sales companies (Massachusetts, Wisconsin, and New Jersey), working through the American Cranberry Exchange, which acted as a selling agent for all sellers. The nonprofit exchange pooled berries and graded them by fixed standards. After members were paid for their berries according to amount and quality, the excess was divided among members according to their acreage (Playfair 2014, 118).

Marcus L. Urann, a Maine lawyer, was a founder and member of the board of directors of both the New England Cranberry Sales Company and the American Cranberry Exchange. In the early 1920s, he began a canning business under the Ocean Spray brand. In 1930, his company, now called Ocean Spray Preserving Company, invited the Makepeace Preserving Company and the Enoch F. Bills Company, of Massachusetts and New Jersey, respectively, to join together to form Cranberry Canners, Inc. (CCI), and thus reduce competition. Because they were not in the fresh fruit business, they did not compete with the American Cranberry Exchange (ACE). However, they began adding companies who served as large suppliers to Ocean Spray during the 1930s. In 1940, they expanded to include Wisconsin producers (called the Midwest Cranberry Cooperative) and, in 1941, to Washington state and Oregon. In 1946, the CCI renamed itself the National Cranberry Association (NCA) and began to sell fresh fruit, putting it in conflict with the ACE. In 1953, the ACE sought a merger, but NCA denied it, leading the following year to the dissolution of ACE and its major company, the New England Cranberry Sales Company, with most of the ACE growers now joining the NCA as individual members (Lambert, Rogers and Lass 2004).

Writing in 1954, Zane suggested that the cooperative movement made a huge difference in the growth of the cranberry industry in the United States, helping farmers gain access to loans, stabilize production, and standardize quality; giving growers more choice in distribution; increasing market demand through joint promotion and advertising; increasing grower returns from distribution; and reducing risk of damage and spoilage through pooling. However, Zane also warned about price undercutting by outside competitors and the tendencies for individual growers to clash within the organizations, astute observations that remain relevant (1954, 66–71). The culmination of all these efforts was the development of Ocean Spray as the de facto leader of the industry.

OCEAN SPRAY: A COOPERATIVE SOLUTION TO OVERSUPPLY THROUGH INNOVATION

Ocean Spray is a cooperative, in which growers purchase stock to become members (Playfair 2014, 122). Its headquarters is in Lakeville-Middleboro, Massachusetts, where it has a large cranberry-processing facility. The plant has been open since 1966 and produces more than 65 million pounds of dried cranberries and more than 2.2 million gallons of cranberry juice concentrate annually. Its activities cover the gamut of industry supply chains, including research and development, marketing, and agricultural supply chains. Other large competitors in Massachusetts include Decas Cranberry Products (now part of Fruit d'Or), who works with more than 125 independent growers; Cott Corporation; and Lassonde Pappas and Company (MDAR 2016, 6). Ocean Spray's headquarters near Cape Cod allows it to market itself to millions of tourists who pass through the area. In 1988, it was charged under the Clean Water Act with illegal dumping of effluent from its Middleboro, Massachusetts, plant. The company paid a $400,000 fine and donated another $100,000 in water treatment equipment to the town. Ocean Spray now prides itself on being an environmental leader in wastewater treatment (Long, Jacques, and Kepos 2017, 317).

Ocean Spray provides extension advice to growers on a regular basis, through regional representatives. It provides regular data alerts on weather and pests and helps growers with issues that they face. Through its extensive network, it creates a database on the appropriate conditions and yields of different varietals, including the new ones developed by Rutgers. In regard to long-term research in agriculture, Ocean Spray works with the Cranberry Institute to develop the targets for research that are then put out as a request for proposals. According to interviewees, it also has its own $150,000 budget that it uses to fund university-based research on topics of interest.

History of Ocean Spray

Ocean Spray has played a vital role in the history of cranberries in the United States; its roots and role in the evolution of the industry are deep. In 1912, Marcus Urann, a Maine lawyer, used the label "Ocean Spray" for his canned cranberry sauce that included both white and red berries. Jones (2003) points to Urann's leadership and personal qualities in establishing Ocean Spray. He made personal pitches to growers about pooling for processing, to ensure that markets would be assured, fewer low-quality berries would be disposed, and all "would share equally" in the profits. Moreover, by working together, growers could work to increase the size of the market and overall demand. He reportedly chose the name Ocean Spray because he believed that it would have a strong appeal to those living far from the coast (Jones 2003, 355). In addition to ensuring equal returns per barrel and giving growers an outlet for processing through canning, Ocean Spray offered extension help in the field. This helped create a culture of open sharing and mutual assistance, including to new growers (Jones 2003, 357).

Canning allowed Urann to profitably use lesser-quality cranberries (Playfair 2014, 119), and to sell them year-round. Canning had become a mass-production line by 1930, taking on 44% of the national crop by 1942. In 1946, Cranberry

Canners, Inc., was renamed the National Cranberry Association, and proceeded to market under the Ocean Spray label. By 1949, it was marketing 55% of the national crop, versus 28% for the American Cranberry Exchange (ACE). The two heavyweights (NCA and ACE) agreed to form the Cranberry Growers Council in 1950 to coordinate fresh fruit (ACE) and processing (NCA). The council was dissolved in 1953, however, as differences arose regarding distribution, and previous agreements were also dissolved. ACE folded when the New England Cranberry Sales Company and the A.D. Makepeace Company, two of the largest members of ACE, disbanded and sold their assets to NCA. In 1954, NCA sold 186,000 barrels of fresh fruit under the Ocean Spray label (one-third of the total market), expanded its frozen processing efforts (cranberry-orange relish and frozen cranberries), and began to promote cranberry cocktail mixes (Jesse and Rogers 2006, 31). Jesse and Rogers state that growing disparities in the size of different producers, particularly the fast growth of Wisconsin farmers, created tensions that led to conflict within the cooperative movements, which were still governed by one vote/grower (2006, 26).

In 1957, the National Cranberry Association changed its name to Ocean Spray Cranberries, Inc. (Eck 1990, 348). The previously mentioned cranberry scare of 1959 (regarding the herbicide aminotriazole), which occurred just before November, had brought the industry to its knees, according to Jones (2003, 358). It made growers realize that they could not rely solely on Thanksgiving dinner for their market. A number of farmers abandoned the industry, and the federal government ended up paying cranberry farmers $8.5 million in indemnities. After this period, Ocean Spray became actively involved in pesticide management, both in managing, testing, and recommending new products and in monitoring to avoid any negative effects or scares. Currently, Ocean Spray goes as far as paying its farmers to allow for testing of pesticides on portions of their bogs. Informants noted the tricky business of differing regulatory spheres among Canada, the United States, and the European Union, a task now entrusted to the Cranberry Institute to monitor, with Ocean Spray attempting to guide or influence them.

Jesse and Rogers suggest that five main goals were set by Ocean Spray in the mid-2000s, reflecting the overall mission (2006, 49–51). The first is the desire to surpass a break-even threshold so that some members can stay in business. The second is to continue to expand marketing opportunities, such as through new outlets for SDCs. The third is to further develop overseas markets. The fourth and fifth are to achieve grower alignment around strategy and to exercise leadership. R&D in horticulture has helped grow supply, but the main collective goods from Ocean Spray revolve around product innovation and marketing.

Ocean Spray's Leadership in Product Innovation

Ocean Spray's research was crucial to expanding markets in juice and SDCs (sweetened dried cranberries) in the postwar period. Jesse and Rogers (2006) provide a detailed case history of Ocean Spray in recent decades that will not be repeated here, save some highlights. In 1966, Ocean Spray began distributing Cran-Apple juice, and in 1967, cran-prune juice, the latter of which was subsequently dropped (Jesse and Rogers 2006, 27). Jesse and Rogers give much credit to Ocean Spray CEO Harold Thorkilsen for rapid growth in the 1970s (2006, 27–28). Among other accomplishments, he expanded into grapefruit juice, further developed overseas markets, invested in improved processing and packaging, and conceived of the plan to posit cranberry juice as a healthy and natural choice. In 1979, he successfully held off a potential antitrust lawsuit from the Federal Trade Commission (Long, Jacques, and Kepos 2017, 316). His success, ironically, led to increased external competition and internal turmoil, the latter related to the CEO's efforts to streamline decision-making in the board of directors, reducing it from twenty-five to thirteen members. This led to his resignation in 1987.

Ocean Spray also developed the new product category of SDCs. Dried cranberry "raisins" were developed as early as 1912, but only when Ocean Spray learned how to infuse them with sugar did the product really take off, in the mid-1980s (Stang 1993, 292). Equally important was the introduction of cranberry juice boxes in 1981, allowing Ocean Spray to temporarily become the leading US seller of canned and bottled juice drinks. During the 1980s, the company also introduced a host of new products, such as Mauna-La'i, a guava-lemon drink; Firehouse Jubilee, a tomato juice; Ocean Spray Liquid Concentrates; and Cranberry Fruit Sauces. In 1985, Ocean Spray purchased Milne Fruit Products, Inc., of Washington state, a large fruit provider to a variety of food companies. Milne had tripled in size by the early 1990s and provided valuable revenue for Ocean Spray (Long, Jacques, and Kepos 2017, 317). Milne was later sold by Ocean Spray (*Natural Products Insider* 2004).

New products continued to roll out in the 1990s, including

- Refreshers fruit juice drinks and Ruby Red grapefruit juice in 1991
- Cran-Cherry juice in 1992
- Ruby Red and Tangerine grapefruit juice drink in 1993
- Cran-Currant black currant cranberry juice drink in 1997
- Ruby Red and Tango Grapefruit juice drink in 1998
- and a 100% juice product in 1998 introduced in response to the challenge from Northland

Innovation occurred in product diversification as well:

- Cranberry Newtons with Nabisco in 1993
- Fruit Waves hard candy with Warner-Lambert in 1994
- Breakers with PepsiCo, a soft drink with 2% juice, and Cranberry English Muffins with Thomas' English Muffins, in 1994
- Cranberry Almond Crunch cereal with Post in 1996

In 1991, Ocean Spray entered an alliance with PepsiCo to distribute new single-serve juice options it had developed. Sales in this category doubled in the first few years. However, PepsiCo purchased the Tropicana juice company in 2000, right after PepsiCo had signed an extension with Ocean Spray, which sued and lost in 2000. Ocean Spray subsequently sought additional distributors for its single-serve products (Jesse and Rogers 2006, 39). As of 1998, the co-op included about 980 grower-owners, with a mix of small family-owned business and large businesses. The largest owned about 8.5% of the shares. Juice products had fundamentally changed the seasonal nature of the cranberry market and, by 1998, represented 70% of Ocean Spray's revenues. At that time, Ocean Spray cooperative members also reflected approximately 10% of the grapefruit harvest (Marple and Harding 2002, 79, 81).

The 1990s were also a period of acquisitions. In 1997, Ocean Spray bought a major stake in Nantucket Allserve, Inc., which produced Nantucket Nectars, a juice line. In 1998, Ocean Spray acquired Australia-based Processing Technologies International, a food technology company that had developed the technology to produce Craisins. Since Craisins (their brand name for SDCs) had become the number three brand in the dried fruit market, Ocean Spray wanted to apply the technology to other fruit products (Long, Jacques, and Kepos 2017, 319).

Amanor-Boadu, Boland, and Barton suggest that tensions were building in Ocean Spray in the early 2000s related to disaffection among some grower-members who were experiencing prices below $35/barrel (2003, 2). As production had increased in recent years, new entrants clashed with second- and third-generation members with smaller farms. A 2001 annual meeting led to a rejection of the possibility for the company to explore selling the company (21). The rejection left some hard feelings among some members, according to interviewees; Oregon growers, for example, had by and large supported the sale, and many left the co-op. They also noted that internal Ocean Spray board voting changed, with representation moving from one vote per grower to voting by acreage, which left smaller growers feeling marginalized.

In 2004, Ocean Spray engaged in two major moves. First, it sold Milne Fruits of Prosser, Washington, in a move it said was designed to allow it to focus on its core business of cranberries. Second, as part of an antitrust settlement case with Northland and Clermont, it purchased Wisconsin-based Northland's cranberry processing station (in Wisconsin Rapids, Wisconsin). It also agreed to a ten-year deal to convert Northland and its growers' cranberries into concentrate, though Northland retained the right to produce its own juice line (Just Drinks 2004a).

Under CEO Randy Papadellis, appointed in 2003, Ocean Spray continued to develop new products. In 2004, it introduced Juice & Tea, mixing juice with iced tea. Craisins were part of new trail mix lines. In 2006, it signed a new agreement with PepsiCo to market new single-serve cranberry drinks and develop new juice-based products. In 2008, Ocean Spray introduced Cran-Energy, a cranberry, vitamin, and green tea blend. In 2009, it expanded its lines to include pomegranate juice and, in 2010, blueberry juice. In 2013, it moved into "extracts," powders or gels that could be mixed with water, and the Pact brand, which sold the water and extract already mixed. In 2016, Ocean Spray purchased a receiving station in Chile, incorporating the owner as a co-op member and thereby expanding their reach even farther (Long, Jacques, and Kepos 2017, 320). Some interviewees blamed Papadellis for claiming that growing anti-sugar sentiments would ruin the business, on the one hand, but then doing nothing about it, on the other.

What Explains Ocean Spray's Longevity?

As one Wisconsin grower pointed out, the lack of vertical integration in cranberries also means that large handlers have to rely on a multitude of growers. Ocean Spray creates a layer of cooperation between the oligopolistic handling part of the supply chain and the farmers, thus improving the chance for farmers to capture value-added and, potentially, to coordinate on supply in response to commodity cycles.

Jones suggests that cultural components go beyond market forces to explain growers' loyalty to Ocean Spray, using them to explain why, at the height of the recent oversupply crisis in 2000, growers were unwilling to sell the company (2003). As she states, "Since the 1950s, Ocean Spray cranberry growers have typically seen themselves in terms of their membership in the Ocean Spray cooperative rather than as cranberry growers. This association with the cooperative is so powerful that both members and independents alike believe that without Ocean Spray, the cranberry industry would not exist as it does today" (345). Jones explains how some unusual aspects of the cranberry industry underlie the possibilities for cooperation: limited suitable growing areas; a general lack of need for government subsidies; the long-term nature of investments in the industry; the tendency to pass down growing to subsequent generations, including seventh-generation families, or more, tending to the crop; and the vertical integration of supply chains that Ocean Spray captures (349). Interviewees across North America stated that they stick with the industry because "it's a way of life," their families "have been doing this for generations," and they "really enjoy it." Many seem to have a deep sense of community with other growers. In the Grayland section of Washington state, every interviewee stated that they regularly hired out family and employees from other companies, pitched in to fix equipment or other tasks to help fellow growers, shared knowledge, and generally supported each other, regardless of whether they were large or small, Ocean Spray or independent. In Long Beach, Washington, one grower said that he readily loaned out his equipment, labor, and knowledge to fellow growers, at no charge. At the same time, a number of interviewees across the country stated that their children are generally uninterested in continuing in the business, and the average age of growers is likely to be over fifty (though no data are available). This suggests that, along with the market trends we discuss later, a shakeout in the industry, particularly among smaller farms, is *en marche*.

By contrast, interviewees who are independents are fiercely so. They tell a common narrative of resentment against Ocean Spray, based on its "market manipulation." The prime example they give is the flooding of the market with SDC-derived concentrate that Ocean Spray had stored up for years in the 2000s before finding a way to dispose of it legally through the recent marketing order. They suggest that Ocean Spray pushes competitors out, citing Northland, and that it enters into emerging markets such as fresh fruit, sometimes with lower prices designed to push out competitors. Some of these growers were at one point rejected for membership by Ocean Spray, and thus their resentment is personal. Most seem to be strongly independent-minded, by both personality and philosophy, suggesting that they prefer the risks and rewards of market competition to the security offered by Ocean Spray, and citing the previous deferred payment scheme of Ocean Spray (based on meeting firmness, color, and preservation incentives) as problematic (the payment system has now been changed to a continuous one). They express concern over the lack of autonomy of the Ocean Spray board, which they say is too closely tied to the emotions of the growers, who never want to lose money and are unwilling to invest in potentially risky and long-term market development, citing the abandonment of diversification in grapefruit products.

Regarding diversification, some Ocean Spray grower interviewees stated that Ocean Spray had no choice in regard to abandoning the bold experiment of expanding to grapefruits, as grapefruit growers had experienced a crop disease, making it impossible to provide most of the fruit from their own growers without jeopardizing their ability to resort to a USDA marketing order in situations of oversupply—recall that the terms of the marketing order stated that 50% of the production must come from fruit grown by members of a cooperative. Some growers pointed to the issues that arose from the grapefruit investment as a lesson to stick to what they know; undoubtedly, they inductively also prefer to run the cooperative smoothly by basing their strategy on the one product they know well.

The response from most Ocean Spray growers interviewed to the independents' charges demonstrates their strong sense of loyalty to the co-op. They believe that grower representation allows even the family farm to reap the benefits of the entire supply chain, and they compare their situation with those of other producers who are even more at the whim of market fluctuations. While acknowledging the potential for short-termism, they insist that most Ocean Spray board members spend time learning or come in with expertise beyond growing, and that many, if not most, growers' fierce loyalty leads to the ability to consider the long term. Thus, the glue is the corporate culture, belief in the cooperative, and the multigenerational makeup of the membership, who have made tacit pacts and exhibit a general spirit of compromise, reinforced by long-standing personal ties.

According to some within the organization, board members are chosen for popularity, not for competence or willingness to make hard decisions. They also cite the aforementioned issues surrounding the infrastructure needed to produce concentrates, as well as the lack of leadership on sugar-free and health supplement products as examples, though some Québec companies are in supplements. They suggest, furthermore, that Ocean Spray's overreaction to price increases in the 1990s led to oversupply and that its reluctance to ease growers out of business perpetuates it. Moreover, they note with alarm the large corporate debt, which they trace in part to overpaying growers in recent years. In 2020, Ocean Spray underwent a change its leadership, which might provide a fresh perspective, though the natural reaction seems to be to "circle the wagons" when criticisms are aired, and the general response from the cooperative to the authors was to dismiss criticism as being "hearsay" of a very small and unimportant minority. Indeed, Ocean Spray does not seem to have a long-term supply plan, which should be of concern. There seems to be faith in finding a new product and/or developing overseas markets, but these ideas are not tied to any clear industry strategy.

Jones notes the fact that Ocean Spray provides collective goods to the industry, helping to spread best-management practices such as testing for the use of pesticides; helping to control and manage supply; spreading new technology; and, of course, succeeding in growing the market overall (2003). Its guidance of the industry through the Great Depression and the 1959 scare has helped cement grower family loyalty. It is also synonymous with cranberry products and, so, a vital marketing vehicle (361). Moreover, it has negotiated on behalf of the industry with government.

Nonetheless, we argue that Ocean Spray is clearly at a crossroads, along with the industry as a whole. Many growers across the regions are fiercely loyal, with one saying that "the interests of the farm, the co-op, and the brand are clearly aligned." They point to the proven track record of the benefits of pooling investment to develop retail outlets. They see cautionary tales in other agricultural product markets that are less organized or sell out to other companies who then dismantle the co-op. However, as we intimated in chapter 2, a bifurcation is growing between the interests of more highly productive Wisconsin and Québec growers and the traditional mainstays of Ocean Spray along the two coasts.

Growers along the coasts, facing tighter margins, are predictably more loyal to Ocean Spray. For example, growers in Washington state relayed to me the benefits of loyalty. In comparison with approximately 50% of growers in Oregon, who became independent in the 1990s when prices were higher, most Washington state growers stuck with Ocean Spray. By the mid-2000s, they relayed, Ocean Spray was paying better prices and provided (and continues to provide) them a sense of security. As one grower related, "I don't have to worry about whether someone's going to buy my fruit, or try to find a buyer. ... They [extension help] are always there to help me if I need anything." Some Washington state growers noted that, even if prices from independents were equivalent, Ocean Spray's pricing system is better. They stated that independents pay according to a "pack out" system, whereby growers are paid only for good fruit. Ocean Spray takes a sample of the fruit and, as long as it meets standards, pays a base price plus incentives for the percentage of higher-quality berries and, for the fresh market, berries that last longer (a sample is taken and put in freezers). Overall, Ocean Spray seems to have a staying power along the two coasts, but it still cannot avoid tensions with the larger producing area in Wisconsin, which is central to its long-term fortunes.

For example, some interviewees stated that many of Ocean Spray's quality bonuses have now been rescinded, reflecting internal battles between the coast producers, who have better color attributes, and Wisconsin producers, who have better firmness and size. Firmness and not color is more important, now that the market has shifted to SDCs. Even with the steady support of Ocean Spray, almost all the Washington interviewees said that they had to keep full-time non-cranberry jobs, to make ends meet. This reflects the small size of their farms, with a lack of economies of scale that would probably not have lasted this long without Ocean Spray, which of course raises the question of whether Ocean Spray prevents or slows down the logic dictated by market forces, to start to wind down operations in higher-cost areas.

At the time of this publication, the long-term tensions between independent producers and Ocean Spray were dissipating somewhat by the end of our research, with a spike in prices after the acute phase of COVID-19, attributed to perceptions about cranberry health benefits. As a "market maker" facing eroding control, Ocean Spray is in a tough position, one reflected in recent changes to management and the board of directors. Some are concerned that the previous battles with takeover artists will be relived, and the magic of the cooperative formula will be lost. At the same time, every independent agent we spoke with said that they still saw Ocean Spray as the leader of the industry, the one actor everyone "needs to do well." Interviewees placed some of the blame on ineffective management at the company, and some were cautiously hopeful the new management team will find avenues for product innovation that would increase demand. Early opinion of the new CEO, Tom Hayes, the former CEO of Tyson Foods, is positive among those interviewed in early 2022. He has brought in a new team. Nonetheless, independent growers in Massachusetts and Washington relayed that they did not want to be part of a larger organization, revealing personality differences that matter as much as management in business decisions. As several growers in Washington remarked, "The tension is a good thing, as the independents keep Ocean Spray in check"; we authors agree that, even if it is at times contentious, some level of independence in the industry is good—but the question is, how much? If Ocean Spray loses its role, who will provide collective goods essential for industry market expansion and product innovation? Before we turn to answering that question, we first examine more closely the market forces pushing the industry toward a crossroads.

Chapter 4
Market Forces Threaten Cooperation

THE LONG-TERM OVERSUPPLY CHALLENGE

In this chapter we examine basic market trends in the cranberry industry to elucidate the underlying long-term forces behind the commodity cycle pressures in the cranberry industry. We point out why the current (2022) spike in prices is unlikely to last, and thus why the cycles of boom and bust will continue, promoting industry evolution once again. We begin by providing an overview of demand market segments. We then turn to supply trends on the global level and do a deep dive into how supply in North America has changed over time, highlighting the sources and trajectory of the current oversupply crisis. As we demonstrate, the main novel factor in supply comes from new Canadian producers; along with productivity increases from the new varietals discussed in chapter 2, this factor suggests long-term increases in supply that so far have not been met by increases in demand or expansion into new markets. This emerging fact ties into knots the main cooperative solutions discussed in chapter 3, namely Ocean Spray's efforts to manage supply and increase demand through product marketing and development and, as a last resort, the intervention of the USDA. to restrict supply, since Canadian producers are not included. A secondary factor is the lack of popular new products that have been developed to grow demand as in the past.

CONSUMPTION INCREASING, BUT NOT FAST ENOUGH

Amanor-Boadu et al. state that there are six basic markets for cranberries: fresh (unfrozen and frozen); juice (pure, blend, and concentrate); powdered; dried (sweetened and unsweetened); sliced; and sauces and jellies (2006, 45). Girard and Sinha note that categories of cranberry consumption for 2009 could be broken into 10% for fresh fruit; 15% for cranberry sauce products; 20% for dried fruit products; and 50% for juice products (2012, 401). The total US market was $2 billion, and 20% of consumption takes place during Thanksgiving. There are no historical statistics for cranberry consumption, but the

Cranberry Marketing Institute provides figures for the last decade (https://www.cranberryinstitute.org/about_cran/Cropstatistics_about.html).

In table 4.1, we see an unsteady rise in cranberry consumption, particularly in processed cranberries (dried and juice). Fresh fruit sales appear to have a low growth rate of 1.4% per year, with an average of 264,802 lb. per year, and represent just 3.9% of the total market. Processed sales are increasing at a reasonable 3.3% rate on average, but sales in this category, as well as in fresh, show great volatility from year to year, as reflected in the high standard deviation figures. The year 2017 shows considerable improvement but, in light of the longer-term volatility, cannot yet be taken as a sign of a long-term improvement. Still, per capita consumption in both categories is steadily increasing, reflecting a steady increase in demand.

The USDA also gives a longer per capita consumption timeline for the United States, presented in figure 4.1, which also shows downward trends.

What we see is that, while overall sales are increasing by about 2% per year (calculations by author, from cranberry marketing committee, found at https://www.cranberryinstitute.org/about_cran/Cropstatistics_about.html, accessed May 1, 2019), *per capita consumption has declined* from previous decades, even after the introduction and takeoff of sweet dried cranberries in the 1990s. Informants suggested that demand is declining because

Table 4.1: Global Cranberry Consumption

Crop Year	Processed Sales (lbs.)	Annual Growth Rate	Fresh Fruit Sales (lbs.)	Annual Growth Rate	Per Capita Consumption Fresh (lbs.)	Annual Growth Rate	Per Capita Consumption Processed (lbs.)	Annual Growth Rate
2008	5,328,003		252,694		0.08		1.75	
2009	5,535,668	3.9%	241,219	(-) 4.5%	0.08	0.0%	1.80	2.9%
2010	5,717,010	3.3%	257,012	6.5%	0.08	0.0%	1.83	1.7%
2011	5,315,314	(-) 7.0%	258,980	0.8%	0.08	0.0%	1.70	(-) 7.1%
2012	5,237,404	(-) 1.5%	265,364	2.5%	0.08	0.0%	1.67	(-) 1.8%
2013	5,555,709	6.1%	270,383	1.9%	0.09	12.5%	1.76	5.4%
2014	6,164,931	11.0%	258,767	(-) 4.3%	0.08	(-) 11.1%	1.92	9.1%
2015	6,203,247	0.6%	270,229	4.4%	0.08	0.0%	1.93	0.5%
2016	6,260,106	0.9%	288,697	6.8%	0.09	12.5%	1.94	0.5%
2017	7,053,075	12.7%	284,672	(-) 1.4%	0.09	0.0%	2.15	10.8%
Average		3.3%		1.4%		1.5%		2.4%
Standard Deviation		5.7		4.0		6.8		5.2

Source: Authors from Cranberry Marketing Committee, accessed June 2019

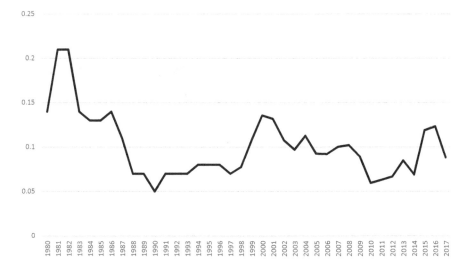

Figure 4.1: US per capita consumption of cranberries, 1980–2016 (lb./person). *Source*: author, from USDA

of generational change, as most still associate cranberries with holiday side dishes, and younger people are less apt to celebrate the holidays or consume cranberries with them. Fruit consumption varies over the period, but it is notable that blueberry and cherry consumption have increased at a steady rate.

Informants suggested that cranberry juice consumption in the United States has been flat or declining, while most growth is in sweet dried cranberries (surpassed, however, by growth in supply).

As shown in figure 4.2b, cranberry juice consumption rose from 0.1 gallons per capita in 1988 to 0.3 in 2010, settling down to 0.2 gallons per capita in 2020. This slight increase in the period is in contrast to total juice consumption, shown in figure 4.2a, which peaked at 9.2 gallons per capita in 1998, declining to 5.3 gallons per capita in 2020. Given this context, the slight increase is remarkable and may speak to the perceived health benefits of cranberry juice; however, it does not show any long-term growth trajectory, given the more recent decline from 2019. In fact, the range has stayed between 0.2 and 0.3 gallons per capita since 1993. The bucking of the overall decline trend for fruit juice is seen more plainly in fig. 4.2c, which shows a dramatic increase in cranberry consumption as a percentage of total fruit juice consumption.

While overall demand is increasing in the sweet-dried category, juice sales have been in a slow, years-long decline, though a post-COVID-19

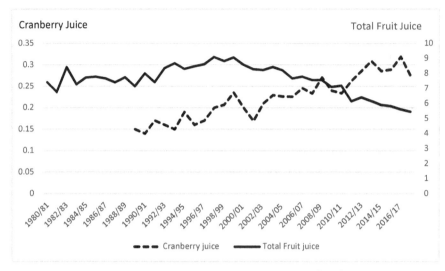

Figure 4.2a: US per capita juice consumption, 1980–2017. *Source*: author, from USDA ERS. *Note*: units = gallons, single strength equivalent

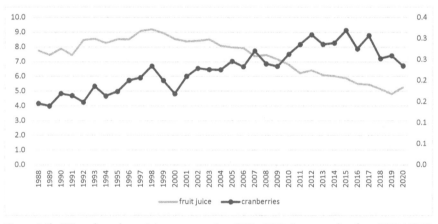

Figure 4.2b: US total cranberry juice consumption, 1988–2020. *Source*: author from USDA ERS. *Note*: units = processed weight, gallons, cranberry juice axis is on the right, total juice axis is on the left

spike occurred, related to perceived health benefits. Since no good statistics are publicly available for SDCs, it is hard to evaluate the size and growth of the market; however, growers and handlers interviewed for this report suggest that it is currently the main market driver, but that demand growth was flat. Still, they said prices were much more consistent for SDCs than for concentrate. Some of that surplus concentrate, according to interviewees, was donated through the US government to schools and charities and to overseas markets through the US Agency for International Development

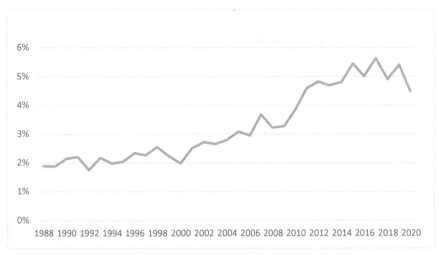

Figure 4.2c: US cranberry juice consumption as a percentage of total fruit juice consumption, 1988–2020. *Source*: author, from USDA ERS

(AID), but this is hardly a long-term solution. Even more concerning is that the growth is overmatched by the more spectacular increases in global supply over time.

CONCENTRATION OF PRODUCTION IN NORTH AMERICA

The FAO gives the statistics shown in table 4.2 for global production in 2019 of cranberries, demonstrating that cranberry production essentially takes place in three countries, the United States, Canada, and Chile.

It is interesting to note, from FAO stats, indications of the potential for production in the former USSR in 1990–1991. Note the data indicate that Chile started in 1991, but did not reach more than 1,000 hectares until 2005, so is a relatively recent entrant. Turkey's production also starts from 1991. Canada's production reaches above 1,000 hectares in the same year. These statistics help explain the ensuing glut we describe below. One small three-acre farm in New Zealand (https://cranberrieswestland.com/about/) appears to be quite recent, though no exact founding date is given. Deloitte's 2020 report for the Association of Cranberry Growers of Québec (APCQ) states that 63% of cranberry production in 2019 occurred in the United States; another 32% in Canada; and 5% in Chile. In subnational leaders, Wisconsin was responsible for 45% of production, Québec for 26%; Massachusetts for 20%; and BC for 6%; the remainder were 2% or less.

Table 4.2: Global Production of Cranberries by Country, 2019

	Acres harvested (hectares)	Tonnes	Yield hg/ha
U.S.	16,430	381,018	231,904
Canada	6,292	160,046	254,364
Chile	14,476	82,000	56,645
Turkey	n/a	10,982	n/a
Azerbaijan	600	2800	46,667
Romania	80	547	68,395
Ukraine	200	400	20,000
North Macedonia	48	281	59,158
Latvia	87	209	24,060
Tunisia	28	182	64,308
Belarus	90	178	19,778
Spain	n/a	100	n/a
Bulgaria	75	90	12,000

Source: Author from http://www.fao.org/faostat/en/#data/QC, accessed May 7, 2019

Chile has appropriate growing conditions for cranberries, and in recent years cultivation has taken root there. Cran Chile has 1,500 acres in cultivation in southern Chile. The berries are grown in mountain plateaus and irrigated by streams formed by melting snow. The company was formed in 1992 by Warren Simmons of the United States, who found ideal conditions in Chile's Lake District, including fewer issues with pests than in the US growing areas (Playfair 2014, 165–166). Informants suggested that one bog has recently gone out of business there, and that Ocean Spray owns the other, using it to export cranberries primarily to Asia and partly to the EU, taking advantage of Chile's free trade agreements, particularly one with China. Informants suggested that there are limits to Chile's growth. One of the two growers has pulled out from producing there, and there is supposedly a lack of good sand. If cluster theory is correct, the lack of cluster support likely looms large.

Rumors circulate within the industry about efforts to create new bogs in Eastern Europe, Russia, the Netherlands, France, and Germany, as well as New Zealand and China. Another study would be required to investigate such claims, but so far not much evidence exists of any significant new supply growth. If the analysis here is correct in pointing to the overall failure so far to establish new growing regions outside of North America, with the limited example of Chile, a great deal of policy and industry effort will be required to establish new clusters.

MARKET FORCES THREATEN COOPERATION 83

CMC Global Supply Statistics

The US Cranberry Marketing Committee (https://www.cranberryinstitute. org/about_cran/Cropstatistics_about.html) provides statistics in a different format, emphasizing just three countries. We should note first that these numbers don't align with the numbers provided by FAO in table 4.3. Putting that aside, if we focus on the supply figures provided in table 4.3 for the moment, we see the steady increase in supply that precipitated a volume control regulation in 2017–2018.

Considering the three main producers, the United States produced approximately 66% of the crop in 2018, Canada, 31%, and Chile 3.4%. While the United States therefore maintains a dominant supply position, this number is down considerably from the 77% production share it commanded in 2011, with Canada having only 19%, and Chile steady at 3.5% at that point. Clearly, the major increase in supply is coming mostly from growth in Canadian production. Indeed from 2011 to 2018, Canadian production grew 113%, compared to 11% in the United States and 24% in Chile!

LIMITED DEVELOPMENT OF EXPORT MARKETS
US Cranberry Imports and Exports

USDA's Foreign Agricultural Service keeps statistics on cranberry trade; however, the data appear to be limited to more recent years. Data from previous years are recorded as zero, which seems incredible; therefore, it must not have been tracked.

Table 4.3. Global Cranberry Production: Major Increases in the United States, Canada, and Chile, 2011-2018

Year	United States	Canada	Chile	Total
2011	775,500	191,080	35,400	1,001,980
2012	793,700	295,400	35,480	1,124,580
2013	881,860	276,600	46,500	1,204,960
2014	805,780	337,300	40,800	1,183,880
2015	805,340	327,200	43,200	1,175,740
2016	925,070	395,890	48,800	1,369,760
2017	808,520	265,270	48,000	1,121,790
2018	861,516*	406,393	44,000	1,311,909

Notes: *approx. 110,000,000 pounds restricted and will not enter the market; units are: pounds x 1,000)
Source: Author from U.S. Cranberry Marketing Committee

US Imports

In regard to imports, 1989 to 2018 saw a major and growing surge from Canada:
- Fresh imports grew from $7.4 to $61.4 million, an increase of 8.3 times
- Frozen imports grew from $125,000 to $18.7 million, an increase of 149 times
- Prepared/preserved imports (including jams/jellies and possibly sweet dried) grew from $22 million to $27 million from 2012 to 2018, an increase of 1.2 times[1]
- Juice imports increased from zero to $21.5 million from 2004 to 2018

US Exports

Figure 4.3 demonstrates the significant markets for fresh cranberry exports. As we can see, the number of markets is limited, and the export volumes are curiously volatile. On the basis of existing data, we cannot tell why; more investigation is needed.

Figure 4.4 demonstrates the top prepared/preserved cranberry export markets. We can see the significant decline of US exports to Canada and to the Netherlands, likely reflecting Canadian production increases. Chinese market growth demonstrates promise.

No figures are available for juice exports before 2012, but it is curious that the Netherlands is the major juice export market destination, commanding an average 61% share from 2012 to 2018. Probably it is a way station for exports to the EU—Canada (12%), Mexico (7%), and Australia (2.9%) are the other top destinations; it is notable that the exports to Australia have declined precipitously during the period. Here again, more investigation is needed to better understand the reasons behind these figures. Overall juice exports show an alarming overall decline, with world export totals declining from $76.7 million to $48.3 million during the same period. Prepared and preserved exports to the world increased during the same period, from $116.6 million to $296.8 million, presumably mostly through sweetened dried cranberries.

SUPPLY AND DEMAND: THE CHIMERA OF THE EMERGING CHINESE MARKET

The easiest solution for long-term oversupply, if there are no new product innovations, is to develop overseas markets. As in sectors across the board,

---

[1] Whether SDCs are included in this category is not clear, and we have received differing answers from USITC and USDA.

MARKET FORCES THREATEN COOPERATION

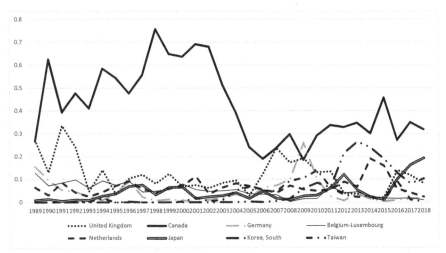

Figure 4.3: US fresh cranberry exports: significant markets, 1989–2018, percent of world total
Source: author, from USDA FAS

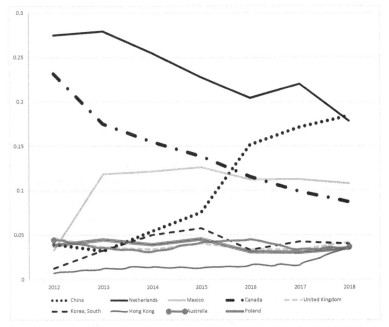

Figure 4.4: Top US export markets, prepared/preserved cranberries, 2012–2018
Source: author, from USDA

China is the most tantalizing market for cranberry growers, given its huge potential market and limited production. Chinese consumers reportedly perceive strong health benefits from cranberries and do not mind the tart taste of the fruit. As in so many other markets, the Chinese market is a double-edged sword, offering supply competition as well as a potential vast market of demand. Employing a research assistant who could read Mandarin, we were able to piece together the following basic facts.

Table 4.4 illustrates that China's increasing demand in cranberries, from 2014–2015 to 2016–2017, has been juxtaposed with an active increase in imports by double-digit percentages for three consecutive fiscal years. While 2017–2018 witnessed a slight decline in net import increase, China remains one of the largest importers of the berry, receiving more than 6% of total global exports. However, as the US-China trade war increased the Chinese tariffs on cranberries and other fruits by 15% in 2018, imports decreased by more than 55% in 2018–2019, from 184,094 (2017–2018) to 82,117 (2018–2019) barrels.

Recent data reveal that Beijing had become the second-largest importer of US cranberries in 2017, before the US-China trade war, receiving approximately 8,000 tons of US exports (Ye and Dai 2021). It is not clear how much imports decreased as a result of the Chinese tariffs imposed on cranberries, but producers interviewed for this book suggested that there were significant losses. Reflecting its general mercantilist approach to trade, China appears to be interested in import substitution policies for cranberries. China now has the largest and the only cranberry bog in Asia, the Honghai Manyuemei Production Base (Red Sea Cranberry Production Base), located in the city of Fuyuan in Heilongjiang Province in northeast China. Production appears to have started with the introduction of North American cranberries and research on the cultivability of cranberries in Fuyuan in 2010 and large-scale cultivation of cranberries and production of its products in 2015. Approximately 4,200 acres have been planted, about 500 acres of which would be harvestable by the end of the year, according to 2019 figures (Ye and Dai 2021). This statistic seems to reflect clear challenges to ramping up production; it is worth noting that several key North American experts interviewed for this report mentioned receiving consulting offers from China.

Table 4.4: Total Chinese Cranberry Imports, 2014–2019

	2014/15	2015/16	2016/17	2017/18	2018/19
Imports into China (Barrels)	82,843	128,319	194,848	184,094	82,117
Net Increase in Import	N/A	54.89%	51.85%	-5.52%	-55.39% (U.S. trade war)

Source: Author from "Overview of Export Data," Translated from Xiangrong Chen, et al. "Research on the Development of Cranberry Industry in China" ["Manyuemei chanye zai zhongguo de fazhan yanjiu"], *Rural Economy and Technology* 20, no. 19 (Dec 2020): 221.

The city of Fuyuan is continental seasonal in climate, located at a latitude similar to that of British Columbia and Québec. It has one of the only three remaining black soil belts in the world (the other two are in the Ukraine and the Mississippi River region) and the largest wetland in the country—the Sanjiang Plain Wetland. The pH value of the soil in Fuyuan averages between 5.2 and 6.8, and the pH value at the Honghai Production Base is around 5.5. In addition, the water-holding capacity of the land at the production base is strong, and the temperature and humidity of Fuyuan are very suitable for the growth of cranberries. The plantable cranberry land in Fuyuan is about 3,000hm^2–6,000hm^2 (7,413–14,826 acres) giving Honghai a great chance to expand its production base in future years, especially considering the growing demand for cranberries and cranberry products in the Chinese market (Ye and Dai 2021). In terms of transportation, Honghai Production Base is five kilometres from Fuyuan airport and eight kilometres from the nearest railway station. All these factors make Fuyuan a suitable base for the development of the cranberry in China.

At the municipal, provincial, and state levels, China seems to have few environmental regulations on the level of the United States or Canada. Peng Hai, a local production manager, revealed that the local (from our understanding both municipal and provincial) government(s) gave tremendous technical support to the production base, in an interview with the *People's Daily Online*: "The number of research institutes and experts on cranberries was historically limited; however, the Honghai was able to establish cooperation with the Heilongjiang Academy of Sciences, the Northeast Agricultural University, and the Heilongjiang Academy of Agricultural Sciences, among others to conduct research on breeding and other aspects of cranberry production (Xincainet 2021)." While Hai also mentioned preferential policies by the Fuyuan (municipal) government, the details of these policies are not available (Xincainet 2021).

Fuyuan was historically a "national-level poor county" (Fuyuan is a so-called county-level city). With the expansion of the scale of the cranberry industry in Fuyuan, however, farmers were able to lift themselves out of poverty in 2018, achieving an average annual income of "hundreds of thousands" of yuan, which significantly contributed to Xi Jingpin's victory in ending extreme poverty in early 2021. The municipal government has a strong interest in turning Fuyuan into an "Eastern Capital of Cranberries," while at the same time creating a "comprehensive cultural industry" of cranberries and building "China's first cranberry-themed cultural festival" in the city of Fuyuan through business and tourism (Xincainet 2021). Some scholars further suggest that the Chinese cranberry industry can create a cranberry economic development circle covering Europe and Asia, with Fuyuan as an industrial centre and a node for Sino-Russian border trade, with Shanghai as the marketing "bridgehead" (Chen et al. 2020).

Awareness of cranberries among Chinese people reached an historical high of 71% in 2021, compared to 66% in the previous year, in accordance with the latest statistics from Nielsen. Among consumers, 20% had purchased snacks made with cranberries, and 29% had reported consumption of cranberry drinks, such as fruit tea. More surprisingly, 29% of Chinese cranberry consumers had reportedly used cranberries as side dishes for their everyday meals for not only breakfast but also lunch and dinner. Data from the 2020 China Fruit and Vegetable Juice Industry Summit also demonstrate great potential for the Chinese cranberry market. The number of new products made with cranberry juice as a raw material has witnessed a growth of 48% over the past five years, and the use of cranberry puree has increased roughly between 30% and 40% annually over the same period (Andrew D 2021).

Perhaps owing to the fervent allegiance of Chinese consumers to diet regimens and therapy, the health benefits of consuming cranberries (such as claims about prevention of urinary infections and anti-*Helicobacter pylori* attributes) have also received wide positive coverage in Chinese independent media. Nonetheless, it is important to note the state media of China holds an opposite view; in fact, in 2015, the *People's Daily Online* published an article titled "Cranberry Contains Similar Nutrients as Other Fruits: Health Benefits of Cranberries Being Deified," stating that "the health benefits of cranberries have been falsely advertised by corporations. . . . Cranberry is similar to strawberry and blueberry; after all, it is just another type of fruit" (*People's Daily Online* 2015).

Chinese consumers nonetheless seem convinced about the benefits of cranberries and prefer fresh ones, which are deemed to have more health properties. The rise of e-commerce in recent years and fast logistic networks in China allow for preserving the freshness of cranberries when delivered to the hands of consumers. In fact, the Honghai Production Base has been cooperating with Chinese e-commerce giants, such as Jingdong Shengxian (Jingdong Fresh) (*People's Daily Online* 2015). The companies guarantee speedy delivery to preserve freshness, and thus local cranberries have ready logistical and freezer supply chains.

One Québec informant suggested that Chinese production should be viewed in a positive light, because the local industry will act to promote local consumption. This includes a cranberry festival held by the emerging Chinese cluster. This theory is plausible, along with the fact that current production in China is unlikely to meet potential demand.

To be clear, North American cranberries still appear to have a comparative advantage over those produced in Honghai, an area in northeast China, in the Manchuria region. Table 4.5 reflects the unit price of Chinese-produced frozen and dried cranberries, respectively, at 20,000 and 45,000 yuan/ton, roughly US$3/kg for frozen ones and $7/kg for dried ones (at the 2021 exchange rate of 6.4), five and eleven times more expensive than processed US cranberries, which average about $0.6/kg or $27.4/100 lb. in local US markets. This comparative price advantage is even larger when it comes to fresh cranberries. While Honghai-produced fresh cranberries sits at 180,000 yuan/ton or US$28/kg, US fresh cranberries average about US$1.5/kg or $66.80/100 lb. in 2019 in local US markets, according to the USDA (Agricultural Marketing Resource Center 2021).

The barriers to North American cranberry producers and exporters for utilizing their comparative advantage in price in the Chinese market are tariffs and transportation. While it is not yet known how many tariffs China will impose on the import of cranberries, as the Biden administration plans to review the phase one trade agreement that former president Trump forged with China two years ago, North American cranberry producers and exporters should explore the Chinese market for fresh cranberries in addition to the market for processed ones because of the huge price difference ($1.5/kg in the United States compared with US$28/kg in China), which may make up for the increased tariffs and additional transportation costs (think about fresh Malaysian durian).

More serious still are the serious challenges to understanding and facilitating export to the Chinese market, including finding suitable local partners. Existing efforts are haphazard at best. For example, one Oregon grower

Table 4.5: Chinese Market Prices for Different Types of Cranberries (2018)

Type	Unit Price (10,000 Yuan/ Tonne)	Amounts Sold (10,000 Tonne)	Percentage of Total Sales	Total Sales (100 million Yuan)
Frozen Cranberry	2	1.8	30%	3.6
Fresh Cranberry	18	1.2	20%	21.6
Dried Cranberry (Juice Concentrates)	4.5 (15)	1.8 (2.4)	40%	8.1 (27)
Anthocyanin Extract	50	0.12 (0.6)	10%	6
Seeding, Technology Transfer, Equipment rental				10
Derivatives				3.2
Total				79.5

Source: Author from Chen 2020

mentioned some support from the Oregon state government in meeting phytosanitary requirements in China, but most said there was no support from anywhere for learning how to export. State representatives headed by Representative Smith were able to get the US Obama administration to change USDA phytosanitary requirements for frozen cranberries and other berries, extending their expiration date from fourteen days, standard for other berries, to an indefinite period. An Oregon-China Business Council organizes annual trade missions, but, alongside CMC programs to provide basic market intelligence, these efforts serve rather to underscore the lack of a harmonized industry approach to developing overseas markets. As we review in the next section, production trends in North America suggest expansion of overseas markets will be as vital to the cranberry industry's fortunes as the introduction of juice and SDCs has been historically.

INCREASING SUPPLY LIKELY TO OUTPACE DEMAND GROWTH

From the USDA (NASS and ERS) and Eck (1990), we have been able to compile a fairly long time series on cranberry production in the United States, summarized in figures 4.5, 4.6, and 4.7. In figure 4.5, we see a gradual increase, with the exception of 1929, the onset of the Great Depression. Cranberry production plateaus until the late 1950s, when it decreases (related to the cranberry scare discussed above), then acreage really takes off in the 1970s. We can see a smoothing out of growth, with initial volatility in the early 2000s becoming steadily incremental increases in the 2010s, resulting in a potential long-term oversupply condition in the market. The closing gap between acres harvested and increasing production reflects higher yields over time, inevitably adding to the tendency for supply to increase and prices to flatten or decline.

This trend is reinforced in figure 4.11, reflecting the fact that productivity in the industry has clearly increased, with yields per acre really taking off in the postwar period.

The "market correction" of the last few decades reflecting our above analysis can be clearly seen in the value of the production ($1000s) in figure 4.7, with the 1997 and 2008 spikes very visible.

National price data also demonstrate the run-up to and the crash of 2000, followed by a period of volatility from 2010 to 2020. As we explain below, the run-up was based on the introduction of new cranberry products, primarily juice, to the market in the 1970s, increasing demand. Unfortunately, we have not been able to identify reliable sources of historical juice supply or consumption statistics over time.

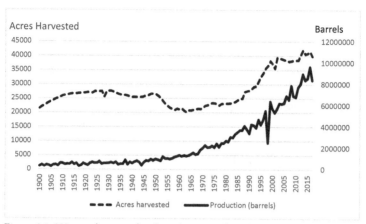

Figure 4.5: US acres harvested and production in barrels, 1900–2016. Source: author, from USDA

Figure 4.6: US yield per acre, 1900–2015. Source: author, from USDA

Figure 4.7: Value of US production ($1000s), 1934–2017. Source: author, from USDA. Note: Blanks indicate missing data

The important point revealed by figure 4.8 is that cranberries suffer from the same commodity price swings as do all agricultural products, creating serious challenges for the industry to deal with significant volatility and uncertainty; the principal response that largely distinguishes the cranberry industry from other agricultural industries is the movement toward cooperation as a response, as discussed in chapter 3.

It is impossible to find data on the break-even point for production, as that varies across time and space and depends on a wide spectrum of supply and demand and sales figures, which depend on the individual transaction. However, the slump to the low $30 price range in 2018–2019 is quite alarming, perhaps reflecting increasing supply from the new varietals and moves toward consolidation. Although up-to-date reports on current production costs are not available, a Farm Credit East report (Farm Credit East 2015) on Massachusetts cranberry growers reveals that the cost of producing cranberries per barrel for the period averaged $32.39/barrel, reflecting a gradually declining trend. Meanwhile the average price received in the state for 2014 was $37.08, up from $31.60 in 2013. Without precise data on costs, we cannot ascertain the profit margins for cranberries, but undoubtedly price declines will squeeze them, as reflected in our stakeholder interviews, which universally express concerns about long-term trends.

Figure 4.8 illustrates a substantial overall price premium from Ocean Spray. This makes one wonder how sustainable such prices are, though reports

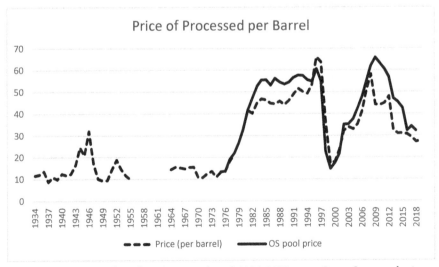

Figure 4.8: US processed cranberry price per barrel, 1934–2017 versus Ocean Spray pool price, 1975–2018. *Source*: author, from USDA and anonymous *source*; processed price. *Note*: Blanks indicate missing data

in 2021 were that prices were back up to approximately $37/barrel, which some growers attributed to health consumption shifts during the COVID-19 pandemic of 2020–2022. However, the same growers noted increasing costs for everything from petrol for transport to plastic for packaging. There is no way to tell whether the premiums make sense over the long run without a review of internal data from Ocean Spray, which are not available to us; however, the premia help cement the long-term attraction of growers to the co-op. Interviewees also reveal that, with the current post-COVID price spike, Ocean Spray prices are slightly lower than those of independents. Such information reveals the efforts of Ocean Spray to moderate price swings for its members.

INCREASING DIVERGENCES IN PRODUCTIVITY BY CLUSTER

While Massachusetts is most often thought of in regard to cranberries because of its pioneering status, Wisconsin is the largest producer. This is seen clearly in figures 4.9 and 4.10, which demonstrate the overall dominance of Wisconsin and Massachusetts in cranberry production. Note in particular the difference in the trajectory of Wisconsin production from that of Massachusetts, with the inflection point taking place in the early 1990s. The decline in production in New Jersey from the late 1950s is also notable. As discussed in chapter 2, the cheaper land and larger plots in Wisconsin have led to larger economies of scale.

Wisconsin's takeoff in production can be further reinforced by the graph shown in figure 4.10, showing its leadership in total production from the 1990s.

What is most notable is the growing gap in productivity between Wisconsin and other US states. While productivity has increased across the board except for Washington state, Wisconsin's achievement stands out.

Caron et al. (2017) provide a more updated binational picture of yield per acre, as reflected in figure 4.12, which Caron designed to demonstrate the importance of water management in Wisconsin and Québec.

In an interview with Caron, he ascribes the higher curves in Wisconsin and Québec to better irrigation and water management, noting that recent dips in both places are linked to "a compaction of beds" in both (see also Jabet et al. 2016).

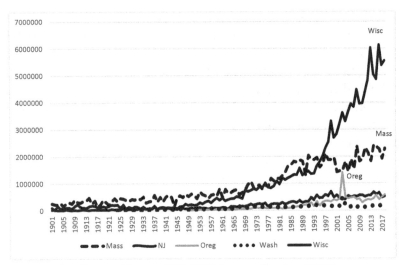

Figure 4.9: Acres harvested by state, 1900–2017. *Source*: author, from USDA

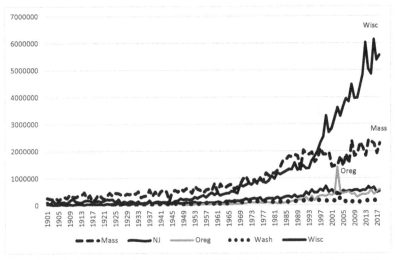

Figure 4.10: Total production (barrels) by state, 1900–2017. *Source*: author, from USDA

As the graph in figure 4.13 makes plain, there is a national market for cranberries, with not much differentiation by price and location, though the price spike in 2008 in Oregon deserves further investigation.[2]

Through the NASS county-level production statistics reflected in the agricultural census, we were also able to find the number of farms and acreage

---

2 My guess is that this may be a data entry error by USDA, but I have not been able to determine this with certainty.

MARKET FORCES THREATEN COOPERATION 95

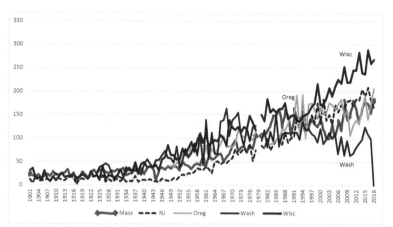

Figure 4.11: Yield per acre (barrels/acre) by state, 1900–2015. *Source*: author, from USDA

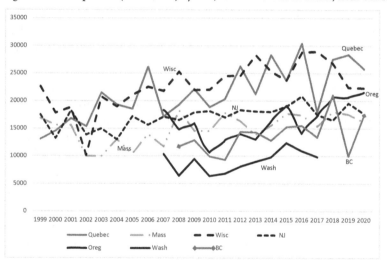

Figure 4.12: Yield per acre (lb./acre), 1990–2020, Québec and Wisconsin versus other US states and BC. *Source*: author, from Jean Caron, Université Laval

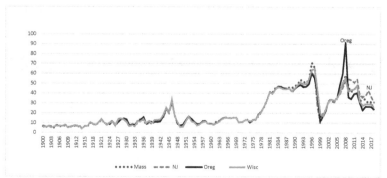

Figure 4.13: Price per barrel by state converges, 1900–2015. *Source*: author, from USDA. Note: Data for Washington and Oregon begin in 1924

by state for 1997–2017, for selected years. Clearly, there is a major decline in the number of farms in Massachusetts, which lost 347, or an astonishing 49%, during the period; in New Jersey, which lost twenty, or 43.5%; and in Washington state, which lost 26%. The cranberry industry in these states is in full-blown crisis. As one Massachusetts grower relayed to us, he needs to work a full-time job and then work in any free time on his bogs, just to keep up with bills: "But I'll tell you honestly, it's really tough. We don't go to coffee shops or hang out like we used to. We have to do everything ourselves. We can't afford to hire anyone anyway." We heard the same stories in Washington state and Oregon, with numerous informants telling us that they had other full-time jobs. Specifically, in Oregon, cranberry farming was combined with timber and livestock, so that cranberry growing was a second job, "by necessity."

This indicates that the USDA statistics (which do not provide the number of farmers) underestimate the extent of the problem. Indeed, based on internet searches of cranberry growers and discussions with informants, around ten out of thirty-two, or 31%, of listed Washington growers are no longer in business, while one in nine, or 11%, of listed Oregon cranberry growers/handlers are out of the business. Informants suggest, for example, that the number of farmers in Long Beach, Washington state, went from approximately thirty-five in 2000 to just around twenty now. Interviewees in Oregon suggested that at least 30% of growers had left the business, either selling or simply leaving their land fallow, and they believed that the numbers were worse in Washington. By USDA acreage statistics, Wisconsin lost approximately 6%, while Oregon had no change over the period. In terms of acres harvested, there is some considerable movement toward economies of scale in Massachusetts and New Jersey, with the total acres increasing by 12% and 12.5%, respectively. By contrast, the total number of acres declined elsewhere, by 2.4% in Washington, 33% in Oregon, and 25% in Wisconsin. We do not have access to acreage size, but if we divide the total acres by

Table 4.6: Total Acres/Farm by State, 1997-2017

	1997	2002	2007	2012	2017
Massachusetts	21.70	30.51	28.50	33.90	37.34
New Jersey	84.87	75.73	86.59	118.38	131.35
Oregon	17.39	18.37	20.19	20.97	23.13
Washington	13.29	15.27	14.61	16.21	18.45
Wisconsin	63.92	73.81	71.09	85.65	91.94

Source: Author from NASS, accessed Aug. 19, 2019

the number of farms, we see the breakdown by state, as shown in table 4.6, giving us the rough average size of each operation.

This calculated table reinforces the fact that cranberry production areas are consolidating, through both exiting and consolidating into larger bogs, an observation reiterated during the informant interviews.

DOCUMENTING QUÉBEC'S ENTRY AS A SUPPLY SHOCK

We turn now to a more in-depth analysis of Canadian production, relying on Canstats, the government agency. We note first that historical statistics are more limited in Canada than in the United States. Detailed statistics on domestic demand for cranberries is not available. Most supply has traditionally come from BC, with the Atlantic provinces playing a lesser role.

Figure 4.14 shows overall Canadian cranberry production, demonstrating the long-term increase in production, accelerating significantly with the entry of Québec into the market over the last two decades.

In Figure 4.15, we illustrate the dominance of the two major producing provinces. The rocket-like ascension of cranberry production in Québec from

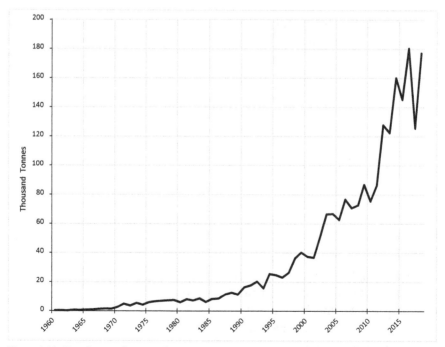

Figure 4.14: Canadian cranberry production, 1960–2018. *Source*: Leighton Kerr, from Stats Canada

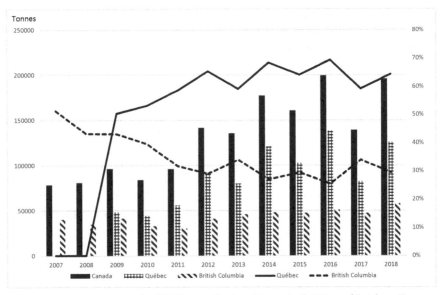

Figure 4.15: Impressive growth of Québec production. *Source*: Andy Hira and Leighton Kerr, from Stats Canada

2009 is impressive. The lines illustrate the relative percentages of Canadian production, while the bar charts provide total tons.

Figure 4.16 gives the "disposition" or final usage of Canadian cranberries for 1996–2018. We see that while absolute production is increasing, the proportion of exports is decreasing. The implication is that domestic demand in Canada for cranberries is increasing, but not enough to match the total increase in supply. Most of the new Canadian product is for export.

We were able to obtain a snapshot of export destinations by province for BC and Québec for 2018. The differences in export destinations are remarkable. We found 98% of BC exports go to the United States (as most BC growers belong to Ocean Spray, berries are sent across the border to Washington state and California for processing). For Québec, 51.2% of exports go to the United States, while 40% go to the EU, an impressive diversification compared to US producers. Figures 4.17 and 4.18 break down export destinations, separating US states, to show the geographic orientation of the different markets. The distinct EU profile for Québec is easily seen in figure 4.18.

According to informants, the entry of Québec as a major supplier, projected to be the second largest in coming years, after only Wisconsin, was unanticipated by much of the industry. Québec followed the Wisconsin model of large rectangular plots and high-yielding varietals, achieving a high level of productivity in a short time. Massachusetts and New Jersey growers reported being "wooed" to Québec by promises of subsidies and cheap land,

MARKET FORCES THREATEN COOPERATION 99

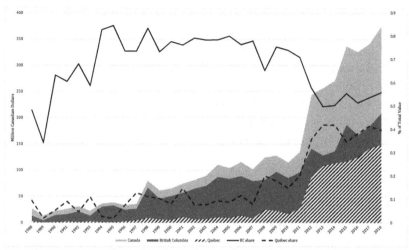

Figure 4.16: Exports as share of total Canadian production, 1996–2018. *Source*: Leighton Kerr and Andy Hira, from Stats Canada

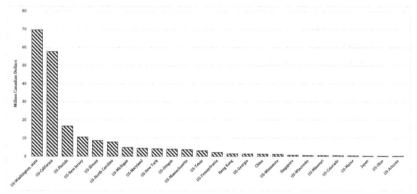

Figure 4.17: Top destinations for exports of BC cranberries, 2018. *Source*: Leighton Kerr, from Stats Canada

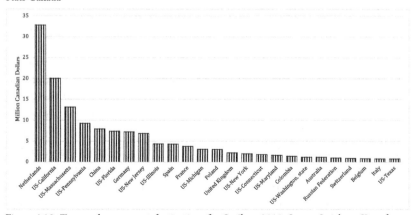

Figure 4.18: Top cranberry export destinations for Québec, 2018. *Source*: Leighton Kerr, from Stats Canada

thus helping to transfer the tacit knowledge necessary to establish the industry there, whereas inadequate policy support in Maine led to a failure to establish a viable "critical mass." Québec challenges the industry beyond its increase in supply. The vast majority of Québecois growers are independent of Ocean Spray, and many more are focused on the organic supply. Informants suggest a major climatic advantage for Québec and Wisconsin will grow over time, as they suffer from fewer pests due to having longer freezing periods. These trends are already happening, as we demonstrated in our statistical analysis of US production trends.

KEY TAKEAWAYS FROM THE STATISTICAL ANALYSIS

What we have seen from this statistical overview are two compelling facts: (1) a growing likelihood of a chronic oversupply situation in the cranberry industry, as productivity increases and cultivation in new regions outpaces growth in demand, and (2) growing disparities in productivity separate the financial viability of cranberry growing in different regions for the reasons discussed in chapter 2, leading to a shakeout of some producers exiting and others consolidating into larger plots. This is already reflected in the economies-of-scale advantages that add to natural growing and land price advantages in Wisconsin and Québec. As cluster theory predicts, both horizontal and vertical integration trends are occurring in the cranberry industry to smooth out lumpiness in the supply chain, reduce or better manage commodity cycle volatility, and create market power to improve margins. This clustering will further concentrate industry ownership and separate out large entities from smaller independent ones more likely to struggle. Significantly higher-cost producers in coastal clusters, such as Massachusetts and New Jersey, will likely exit if such trends continue. This suggests that a more proactive and innovative policy approach in the United States is direly needed. The policy would either improve smaller producers' productivity or help them exit the industry.

Our analysis so far reflects the remarkable historical collective cooperation of the cranberry industry, through Ocean Spray, to try to address agricultural oversupply through creating collective goods, including retail marketing and product innovation, is in peril. There is great hope that Ocean Spray will develop a popular new product, along the lines of previous breakthroughs such as blended juices and SDCs, to increase demand, but this magic-bullet approach is clearly insufficient to itself form an industry strategy for the future. In the meantime, the oversupply situation led to the temporary (2017–2023) invocation of volume regulations under USDA marketing orders, the subject of the next section.

FEDERAL MARKETING ORDERS WILL NOT SOLVE FUTURE SUPPLY PROBLEMS

The Cranberry Marketing Orders are governed by federal regulation Title 7.B.IX/Part 929 governing agriculture (National Archives 1992). The statute creates a Cranberry Marketing Committee (CMC) of thirteen growers, with nine alternates, along with one public member (and an alternate) and one at-large member who represents Ocean Spray, who, interviewees suggest, is generally a University of Massachusetts or University of Wisconsin expert. The current geographic allocations give the Massachusetts and Wisconsin regions four members each, and New Jersey and Washington/Oregon each have two members. There is also one member of the public and an alternate member of the public. Members are nominated by "major cooperatives" and "non-major cooperative" growers, with equal votes by district for each category (US Cranberries nd, b).The at-large member effectively gives Ocean Spray a majority. However, all actions require ten concurring votes (eleven if the public member votes), not a simple majority. No compensation is paid to members, but expenses incurred are reimbursed. Meetings are open to all growers and handlers. Funding comes from assessments of handlers based on their percentage of sales. Expenses can include the costs of holding the meeting as well as R&D and marketing, as determined by the committee. Informants noted that the CMC tracks inventories, even in non-volume-regulation years, so that it has a database of production by grower and handler. Where inventory needs to be destroyed for volume regulation, the CMC sends out a representative and otherwise audits reported numbers from handlers. Some informants are concerned about the accuracy and thoroughness of the CMC's numbers.

When a volume regulation is initiated, as was the case in 2000–2001, 2001–2002, 2017–2018, and again in 2018–2019, when it was set at 7.275 million barrels,[3] the total amount of cranberries that can be sold through normal outlets is restricted. Each grower is given a percent of the total volume based on their previous sales history; this is the amount each can sell. Excess cranberries can be sold overseas, given to charitable institutions, or used as feedstock for animals or for research and development. The most recent order exempts organically grown fruit and small handlers who resold less than 125,000 barrels during 2017–2018, and allows handlers to put up to 50% of "excess" cranberries into dried fruit or "other processed products." Informants note that in the latest marketing orders, exceptions were given to handlers who

---

3 A barrel is equivalent to 100 lbs., according to the act.

could demonstrate that they had previously sold 100% of their product; this was the case for the independent handlers.

The recovery of cranberry prices in the wake of the COVID-19 pandemic led to the 2017 order being rescinded in 2023. It is unlikely that volume regulations will be as effective if put forward in the future for at least two reasons. First, informants said that, because of exemptions, Ocean Spray alone had to dispose of much of its inventory, mostly in the form of juice concentrate left over from making sweetened dried cranberries. Independent handlers and growers, working off lower and more accurate market prices, stated in interviews that they are "in balance," as they do not accumulate inventories, and the problem lies with Ocean Spray's previous overpayment to its members (which some claim led to increasing corporate debt) and stockpiling of concentrate inventories. Thus, it is more likely that Ocean Spray would make its own adjustments. Second, Canada and Chile cannot be subject to volume regulation. Informants said that, while the CMC was able to develop agreements with Canadian producers on a recent volume regulation, the Department of Justice made it clear that any collusion with foreign producers was strictly prohibited. Some growers are experimenting with creating their own branded products, such as fresh and frozen cranberries of higher quality, jams, and honey, but even considering individual successes, such efforts will certainly not solve the larger problems of oversupply.

WHAT EXPLAINS THE PERSISTENCE OF LESS COMPETITIVE CLUSTERS AMID PRODUCTIVITY DIFFERENCES?

Our analysis brings us to two compelling questions that deserve attention. The first question is: *Why don't other states simply copy Wisconsin's approach and increase their productivity?* To answer that question, we can see that the transformation of regions from low to high productivity is no easy task, as illustrated by the efforts in Massachusetts. What we see is that path dependency in the cluster looms large in terms of the concentration of handling and processing facilities in the state, as well as the surplus of talent; however, historic advantage is eroding over time.

In our interviews, we found signs of alarm in both Massachusetts and New Jersey—long-standing families in the cranberry business had gone and were about to go out of business. In recognition, the Massachusetts state legislature created the Cranberry Revitalization Task Force in 2016 to examine methods for improving innovation in the industry; New Jersey offered no equivalent response. This action was in response to a severe economic collapse in 1999–2000, which led to seeking federal assistance through direct cash payments, USDA purchases of surplus cranberry products for federal food aid programs, and mandatory production restrictions by USDA. Informants said that a virtual cranberry innovation center was set up to help farmers adopt new practices around the 2006–2008 period. The task force sought to improve productivity of each farm and increase the use of technology in the state (MDAR 2016, 10–13). The task force concluded that, despite its efforts, some Massachusetts growers would likely exit the industry (MDAR 2016, 26).

The task force gives recommendations on ways to renovate and also on ways to help cranberry farmers exit the industry, according to the report (MDAR 2016, 14–23) and informants (interviews, Massachusetts, July 2019). We were led to understand that only a few parts of this agenda have so far been funded by the Massachusetts government. The main funding has gone to a virtual innovation center and tax breaks for R&D and renovation efforts to upgrade bogs. Informants noted that renovation requires matching funds, which are beyond the means of most small growers. Some suggested that revised current efforts are aimed at ensuring that smaller growers have equal access to funds. Informants suggested both the task force and the recommendations originate from industry, primarily through the Cape Cod Cranberry Growers Association. Attempts are also being made to monetize the environmental services provided by the wetlands functions of cranberry bogs, which also prevents their conversion to other uses—in turn reducing growers' ability to exit the industry, as the land cannot be resold for other purposes, a common refrain throughout the industry.

However, informants stated that the ability to convert bogs to wetlands, for families who want to exit the business, is limited and "extremely slow" in terms of state regulations. Renovation includes reshaping the landscape, such as creating a smoother bog surface, lower to the ground, to reduce water pump and usage costs, and potentially introducing the new, significantly higher-yield and larger varietals developed by Rutgers University and used elsewhere, such as in Québec and Wisconsin. Tax breaks are suggested for renovation efforts. The report also recommends funding the creation of an economic development coordinator and new extension courses. Efforts are also under way to fund health and pest management research through the University of Massachusetts. Finally, funding alternative energy sources on cranberry farms has also been suggested.

The bottom line is that land in Massachusetts is more limited, and more valuable, thus acting to push up production prices. Nonetheless, informants suggested that cranberry farmers are family-oriented businesses, in place for multiple generations, and reluctant to exit the business, so most favor renovation. In fact, informants said that the formula for a $1 million state bond for cranberry bog renovation, under discussion in 2019, would likely attempt to favor smaller growers, in order to help them survive the downturn. However, some growers estimate a bog renovation cost of at least $20,000 per acre, thus the amounts dedicated by the state are likely to be inadequate. Only one of those interviewed indicated that they have been able to take advantage of Massachusetts state support for renovation. In fact, many stakeholders suggested that most bogs in the state are now too small to be independently viable, requiring owners to diversify their crops or take on additional economic activities (second jobs). One large East Coast grower offers visitors a range of tourism activities, from participating in harvests to cranberry festivals. It also has diversified into other businesses, including custom soils and real estate, both of which have helped it thrive in a period of low prices. Overall, there is a real concern in some of the family businesses in Massachusetts that the next generation will be unable to succeed. Informants stated that the importance of the industry goes well beyond economic contributions. The fierce loyalty of multigenerational family businesses and the historical place of the industry in southeastern Massachusetts are intangible but valued attributes. This is reflected in a strong unity of diverse growers around the Cape Cod Growers Association, who informants said is the main source of industry ideas. Even with the limits of state support, the Massachusetts Growers Association seems to have gained significant policy support; no other state supports bog renovation or easing growers out of the business.

In New Jersey, some growers suggested that the state would like them to exit on their own, so that the land can be reconverted to wetlands, but offers no support, reflecting the greater power of the state environmental department versus the agricultural department, according to locals. Informants on the West Coast suggested a situation of general neglect from the states, though Oregon growers did get some help with irrigation from the Natural Resources Conservation Service. The growers in these other states, when pressed, stated that in a reeling industry, no one has time or resources to support lobbying, even in coordination with other agricultural industries. Perhaps not coincidental is the fact that most states, unlike Massachusetts, have a voluntary levy for their state growers' association. The Oregon association, for example, includes just 30% of the grower population. Its options are further limited by the $150 annual fee for membership. Also notable is the legacy value of Massachusetts cranberries, where a deep history creates a cultural value (including the Thanksgiving mythology), unlike other locations.

The state-level stakeholders reported that they do *not* coordinate directly with the USDA or other states around policy. The former cranberry caucus in the US Congress no longer seems active, and thus it is not surprising that USDA is not proactive on cranberries. Moreover, there are no signs of coordination with other agricultural industries. These are missed opportunities for the cranberry industry to push for more federal and state help, both for reducing barriers to exit and bog renovation and for promoting exports. For example, one logical answer for oversupply would be for states or the federal government to pay cranberry farmers to convert their land back to wetlands for environmental preservation, but outside of the limited Massachusetts program, there is nothing available along these lines.

As far as innovation and extension, Massachusetts growers expect University of Massachusetts or Rutgers to undertake such efforts. There is general support among Massachusetts growers for volume limitations, as long as the playing field is level. One informant mentioned the possibility that some growers on the West Coast were skirting rules as a potential flare. Nonetheless, informants remarked repeatedly on how unified the Massachusetts industry was, with generations of growers cooperating back years, even from the functional perspective of coordinating water use.

Informants in New Jersey revealed similarly daunting obstacles. While New Jersey plots are larger than those in Massachusetts, they are largely concentrated in the Pine Barrens region of the state, where they are native, due in part to growing conditions and in part to exceptions in state regulations allowing for the use of protected land in that region for cranberry cultivation. However, the area is increasingly warmer and more humid and thus subject to worsening pestilence related to climate change. Informants suggested little legislative support from the state outside of the highly valued services of the Rutgers extension station. Taking all the factors together suggests a likely consolidation of the cranberry industry in both states, as well as on the West Coast, a fact supported by the observations of numerous interviewees in all three locations.

This leads us to our second question: *Why, given the differences in productivity over time, do we have less productive regions still in the game?* Informants gave a variety of reasons for the persistence of cranberry growing in states outside of Wisconsin. The growers in Massachusetts and New Jersey are fiercely proud, multigenerational cultivators of cranberries, with very strong social ties. Cranberries help define their way of life. Even if they face setbacks, they bask in the optimism that prices will eventually rebound. Moreover, interviews with large handlers suggested that the productivity gap does not have to be completely closed. Because of the supply chain situation described in chapter 2, transport costs give Massachusetts and New Jersey some advantages in terms of proximity to markets and the location of cleaning and processing facilities. In theory, the Massachusetts and New Jersey growers could move farther north, to Québec or Wisconsin, but in practice, families are wedded to their local regions. When asked the same question in Washington, Grayland growers pointed to the fresh fruit market as a niche that has allowed them to remain competitive, as it requires a different set of knowledge and techniques and greater labor intensity. Oregon and Washington growers also cited the high reputation value of West Coast fruit, with a darker color, due to growing conditions. Some noted, however, that such advantages were eroding with the new varietals, and that growers were simply making do with smaller margins. As the market shifts from concentrate, where West Coast fruit was used to darken the juice, to SDCs, where a more neutral color is favored, this differentiation advantage has diminished. In contrast to the other coastal clusters, some Oregon growers seem to be in a sweet spot—some are small enough to enter into niche markets, such as pure concentrate for local health-conscious consumers or industrial frozen food ingredients, but large enough to have created their own processing facilities (mostly cleaning), that allow for some aggregation in order to sell to larger retailers, such as juices competing with Ocean Spray nationally. As the industry begins a long shakeout, the challenges for the current model of Ocean Spray's harmonization of disparate cranberry clusters are only going to ramp up, accelerated as Québec's industry begins to mature, as we discuss in chapter 5.

Chapter 5
The Emerging Giant in Québec: A Challenge to Ocean Spray Leadership?

We have so far focused on overall industry organization, and the attempts of industry to both influence and respond to market evolution, but there is another layer that can best be seen through the prism of each unique regional cluster. In this section, we offer two mini case studies that provide such a view. The two main Canadian cranberry-growing provinces, British Columbia (BC) and Québec, illustrate the differences between an Ocean Spray–dominated area and one that is fiercely independent in its industrial organization. Although the Atlantic provinces region is historically important, the volume produced there is insignificant. Because of proximity to the lead researcher of this study, BC is reported here as a mini-case reflecting challenges similar to those faced in other smaller clusters in Massachusetts, New Jersey, and Washington state the rely very heavily on Ocean Spray. We spend more time on the Québec case because of its pivotal role in shaping the future of the industry.

BRITISH COLUMBIA
History

British Columbia emerged as a cranberry trading center in the middle of the nineteenth century, because of seafarers' need for a ready and long-lasting source of vitamin C to prevent scurvy, essential for those traveling primarily by ocean vessel to reach the remote province. The Fraser Valley became the central growing location after World War II (BC Cranberries 2018). Growers stated that the industry took off during the 1980s. They cite the financial capital proactively offered by Jim Branta, the head of the Royal Bank of Canada's agricultural division, who saw the opportunities for stable high returns from Ocean Spray contracts. Record high interest rates slowed things down until the 1990s, when the cranberry price spike fueled expansion in BC as elsewhere. During this period, independent purchasers led several farms to take some acreage out of Ocean Spray–designated production, taking advantage of higher independent prices. Therefore a number of farms have mixed acreages—some designated for Ocean Spray and some for independent sale. Estimates of the value of the BC cranberry crop in 2020 place it at C$43.6 million in annual farm receipts (Ference and Company Consulting 2020, ii). Like Washington state, BC is an Ocean Spray–dominant region.

Virtually all the BC interviewees noted familial ties to agriculture, beginning in other industries such as dairy, livestock, or other berries, before their family started with cranberries. Some mentioned more recent forays including limited conversions of land into blueberries, though others believed blueberries are also likely to reach surplus production. A general increase appears to have occurred in the 1990s when prices were higher (see statistical analysis below). The average farm size is 88 acres, and most are family owned. Growers with more than two acres are required to get a provincial license. The farms sell to three agencies; Ocean Spray takes 95% of cranberries; Pacific Canadian Fruit Packers and Coast Cranberries take the rest (BCCMC 2020). According to one expert, approximately 90% of BC's crop goes to SDCs, 5% is sold fresh, and the other 5% is processed, frozen, and sold to overseas markets. Almost all of it (90%) is exported to the United States (*Inside Vancouver* 2013).

Market trends

As in other growing regions, most interviewees suggested that there is unlikely to be significant new growth in the number of cranberry farms, though new varietals are expected to increase productivity significantly. One expert mentioned the exit of a few very small farms that had entered about twelve years ago and did not have Ocean Spray contracts. Land costs, even for areas reserved for agriculture, are far too high to justify cranberries, according to most interviewees, and thus selling the land is theoretically attractive. As in older growing areas in the United States, the lack of exit is explained by many interviewees, who noted that most have already paid off their land, so they do not feel enough pressure from currently low prices to exit. Several growers also noted their levels of debt reduce the chances of exit. However, parallel concerns about the ageing cranberry farmer population were mentioned; many families do not have successors to take over the farm, and BC's agricultural land reserve restrictions (similar to those of Québec) prevent conversion of farms into more lucrative sales opportunities, though some growers cited possible loopholes.

Concerns in 2011 that BC cranberry farms were 50% as productive as US ones seem outdated now (BCCMC 2011, 21). Table 5.1 shows the remarkable increase in Canadian production as represented by growth in the largest provinces.

As seen in table 5.1, the number of growers showed initial increases, but has reverted to the same number as in 2009. The number of growers in

Table 5.1: Growth in B.C./Québec Production, 2006-2021

	2006	2007	2008	2009	2010	2011	2012	2013
Growers				70	75	72	73	72
Acreage	5,846	5,870	5,916	6,129	6,508	6,505	6,539	6,566
Barrels	764,106	792,132	693,290	788,418	643,851	607,520	944,051	941,277
Yield	131	135	117	129	99	93	144	143
Quebec Cranberry Statistics								
Growers				66	74	76	80	81
Acreage				4,354	4,878	5,880	7,070	7,657
Barrels				963,617	918,896	1,193,306	1,854,680	1,621,764
Yield				221	188	203	262	212

	2014	2015	2016	2017	2018	2019	2020	2021
Growers	72	72	76	70	74	75	75	70
Acreage	6,541	6,483	6,483	6,411	6,382	6,297	6,556	6,374
Barrels	837,538	988,903	1,007,684	858,941	1,347,753	631,045	1,003,998	1,012,786
Yield	128	153	155	134	211	100	153	159
Quebec Cranberry Statistics								
Growers	84	82	82	80	78	78	81	80
Acreage	8,516	9,247	9,504	9,828	9,965	10,145	10,682	10,777
Barrels	2,410,472	2,085,387	2,758,937	1,602,672	2,513,928	2,558,094	2,306,906	2,201,382
Yield	283	226	290	163	252	252	216	204

Source: Patty Hira from BCCMC reports. Yield = barrels/acre; our calculations.

Québec increased until 2016 and has declined slightly to eighty since then. Acreage increased slightly (9%) over the period in BC, but increased monumentally (148%) in Québec. While the number of barrels increased by 33% in BC and 128% in Québec, the increase in yields seems to have peaked in 2018 but then declined during the COVID-19 period, reflecting perhaps less crops harvested. The yields are considerably higher in Québec. Many growers and experts in BC suggest an accelerating adoption of certain "first-generation" new varietals, such as Mullica Queen and Crimson Queen, based on reassurances from local test farm results funded by the BCCMC.

Some BC growers and researchers noted that the new varietals are still "a work in progress." in the sense that best practices are still being developed for them. So far, harvest times have not changed dramatically, which would be problematic, given that most fields now contain a mix of traditional and new varietals. A few growers, however, would appreciate varietals with a later harvest time, to happen closer to the peak Thanksgiving and Christmas seasons for cranberry sauce. Some growers expressed concerns about the new varietals' greater susceptibility to rot and less firmness. The bottom line is that, even if acreage does not change, production is going up as fields are converted to the new varietals.

A major concern in BC during the early 2020s has been "cranberry field decline," under which portions of farms start to die and stop producing fruit, though concerns seem to be dissipating by 2023 (IAF 2019; Someya 2019). There are more general concerns around climate change, including surprisingly cold temperatures in 2020 and the "heat dome" in 2021, which caused a few growers to lose their crops, though other experts suggested that these were isolated incidents. At present, there does not appear to be any clear provincial or federal-level strategy for climate change adaptation in agriculture for the United States or Canada.

Most growers rely heavily on temporary workers, often hired through labor contractors, during harvest time, since the local labor supply is inadequate and wages are high. Many growers cited the pain of new months-long processes to hire the "same laborers" that they had been using for the past decade from Mexico. One large grower sponsored a frequent worker from Mexico, who was bilingual, along with his family, to manage the farm. The grower suggested that this could be part of a future solution package for succession in farms where younger generations do not want to take over.

Governance and R&D

In terms of formal governance, BC's industry is run via a marketing board, BC Cranberry Marketing Commission (BCCMC), set up under provincial law in 1968 (BC Laws 2022). As explained by one expert, under provincial law, marketing boards can be created at the request of the industry, to manage supply, similar to the USDA marketing orders for cranberries in the United States. The expert pointed out that there are only eight boards across the province because it is extremely difficult to get industry farmers to agree to a unified board. In the case of cranberries, a surplus in 1968 precipitated the action. Beyond supply management, the mandatory levy that comes with such a board allows the industry to create collective goods, including R&D. The cranberry marketing order was revised in 2021, according to one interviewee. The BC-CMC board has six members: a chair appointed by the lieutenant governor in council, a member appointed by the board, and four elected representatives from the growers. The commission has regulatory powers over "the transportation, processing, packing, storing and marketing" of cranberries; it can fix license fees for the ability to participate in such activities in BC. As with other marketing boards in BC, it can regulate the quantity and quality of a product

Table 5.2: BCCMC Levies (US $/lb.)

	2014	2015	2016	2017	2018	2021
Grower's levy	0.0048	0.0048	0.0048	0.0048	0.0048	0.0028

Source: Patty Hira from BCCMC Annual Reports and for 2021, https://www.bccranberries.com/wp-content/uploads/2021/09/General-Orders-08Sep2021.pdf, pp. 12-13, accessed June 6, 2022. Levies for 2019-20 were not available.

that it is marketing (BC Laws 2023); in short, it has powers similar to that of the USDA marketing order (discussed below). The BCCMC is supported by a levy, as reported in table 5.2.

A supplemental levy was charged from 2012 to 2014 to pay for the research farm. The BCCMC can also create fees on cranberries coming into or leaving the province. There is an industry advisory committee, designed to help provide input from growers to the commission (BCCMC 2011, 16). BCCMC sponsors local research projects, responding to farmers' needs. For example, it supported an experimental farm to test the viability of new varietals from Rutgers. The results from the farm are widely known and of interest to growers around BC, whose comments about the utility of the farm are universally positive. Also important was a study commissioned by Dr. Kim Patten, professor emeritus of Washington State University, who produced a business assessment of the new varietals showing they would pay for themselves in ten years; the report was delivered at the 2019 NACREW meeting. The BC Cranberry Growers' Association, run by a part time manager, was established in 1989 to create an alternative, more independent voice for growers from the BCCMC, including lobbying and responses to regulation, according to interviewees. The growers' association is supported by a voluntary levy based on acreage. Members work with the BCCMC as part of the committee that selects research projects for funding from the BCCMC levies. Some experts point to the BCCMC as "an insurance policy" for the local industry, should anything happen to Ocean Spray. One interviewee suggested that the approximate annual research budget is between C$50,000 and C$80,000 in BC, relatively small compared to other clusters but vitally important for conducting research that is locally relevant.

The Canadian federal system cedes most economic activities to provincial jurisdiction, and management of the cranberry industry is no exception. The federal government does provide research scientists to the agricultural industry. In BC, the Agassiz Research and Development Centre, run by Agriculture and Agri-Food Canada, runs a horticultural research station that covers a range of research on berries. Overall, the government's level of commitment to the local cranberry industry is more limited than in other regions. One could argue that this reflects the relatively small size of the industry in BC. More problematic is the fact that the federal government is oriented toward basic research, and thus does not provide regular extension services. However, some experts use the federal labs to evaluate soil and pest samples.

As elsewhere, cranberry-specific training takes place primarily through a winter "cranberry congress" organized by the BCCMC, which, during the COVID-19 pandemic, was replaced by a biannual online Pacific Northwest Congress with Washington and Oregon growers, with short presentations from funded researchers and invited guests. The congress received a mixed reaction from BC growers. The bottom line is a heavy reliance on Ocean Spray for both applied R&D and extension services. Ocean Spray is able to leverage its research and extension network across North America to share information. Echoing their US counterparts, BC growers did not report any regular interactions with provincial or federal agricultural researchers, though they were very positive about their support from Ocean Spray. The lack of government support in any concerted way to develop new local demand or overseas markets, or to aid in extension, are major concerns for local industry. Related to these, but more comparable to growers across the continent, are concerns about pesticide regulations, important in BC's relatively warm and humid climate.

Challenges

The challenges for BC are similar to those seen in Massachusetts, New Jersey, Washington state, and Oregon, with each having relatively limited growing regions and all except Oregon heavily dependent on Ocean Spray for getting their crops to market. As one grower put it, BC does not produce enough to warrant large-scale processing or marketing on its own. So, the most important thing for growers is to support Ocean Spray and ensure good relations with their partners to the south. Nonetheless, a handful of growers also sell independently, filling contracts when they find them or selling to small local retailers or though farm stores where they can. A few growers/handlers reported some modest success in selling to the Chinese and EU markets, through their own initiative. A marketing office of the BC provincial office is designed to help farmers with export opportunities, through a team of overseas BC government marketing representatives. The provincial government offers the possibility for customized reports by industry and help at the individual company level. However, none of the growers or handlers interviewed knew about any government support. Most growers are limited by their smaller independent volumes (in contrast to the larger independent Québec growers) in accessing possibilities for consistent independent export contracts; they would need to pool together to meet overseas contracts. BC has only one independent SDC producer; the other independents produce frozen berries or juice. The resulting DIY culture, similar to that in Massachusetts, New Jersey, Washington, and Oregon, is reflected in the fact that growers rely on their own wits and sometimes local craftsmen to customize equipment.

One grower who does so said that it was a very hard road to learn and do all the marketing work necessary to establish independent outlets. Farmers recognize that a different skill set is required to move up the value chain, and most are not motivated enough to do so, perhaps with warranted skepticism, given the effort that would be required. According to growers, the roller-coaster ride of cranberry prices has pushed a large number into diversifying their income beyond cranberries, to include other activities, such as blueberries and dairy, or farm-to-table sales in exceptional cases. However, diversification is a hard road, and many noted that neither blueberries nor dairy provide respite from low prices. Establishing retail operations requires processing and cleaning equipment, freezers, retail space, and food regulations, all of which require considerable capital and time investments; these would not be affordable for most of the small-acreage farms in BC. One expert pointed to the Investment Agriculture Foundation of BC (IAF, https://iafbc.ca) as a potential source of funding for growers to pivot to farm to table or farm retail or export operations. The IAF receives contributions from the federal government and is run by representatives of nine agricultural industries in BC; a cranberry representative was recently added to the board. The provincial government also offers training programs in business marketing skills, market research, and strategic planning, including linking farmers with mentors. One expert identified a particular gap in provincial support for the challenges of moving from one market segment to another, for example, moving from fresh to juice or frozen. However, none of the growers seemed aware of any of the government programs, or of any other potential support programs, such as the Canada Small Business Financing Program (https://www.ic.gc.ca/eic/site/csbfp-pfpec.nsf/eng/home). Additionally, a few experts expressed the possibility for cross-investment between other berry operations and cranberries. For example, some growers are selling their own juice, processed by companies in the Fraser Valley who do the processing for other products. In theory then, the blueberry industry, with its greater vertical integration, well-developed processing facilities, and export expertise, could serve as a backup or alternative to Ocean Spray for independent growth, through its mastery of export markets.

Another expert pointed to the high concentration of ownership among the large retail chains, who prefer to simply make one global order for all their markets—for example, from California, from where they can count on volume and quality, ignoring the hassles of the local market. Experts point to the fact that local groceries such as Thrifty's have been bought out by large chains such as Sobey's, eliminating long-standing relationships with local farmers. While many have heard of possibilities for the Chinese market, it is not of immediate concern, as Ocean Spray takes all their production. The same is generally true for marketing, which reinforces a general sense of stability or complacency in the BC cluster, depending on how you look at it.

While the Ocean Spray relationship provides stability, some interviewed growers felt remote from decision-making concerning the overall strategy for the cooperative, reinforcing their sense of lack of agency for dramatically changing their circumstances. Others are happy about BC representation on the Ocean Spray board and grateful for the strong brand presence the cooperative provides them. Several remarked on the luxury of being able to simply load their fruit on trucks and leave the rest to Ocean Spray, in sharp comparison to other farmers. Nonetheless, most growers would like to see more provincial support on marketing to grow local markets. The general agricultural marketing program called "Buy BC" (funded by the Investment Agriculture Foundation) could be a source of matching funding for further marketing of cranberries. Buy BC also offers funding for industries to undertake specific marketing campaigns, offering further opportunities for BCCMC. Some growers offer a harvest tour; some sell modest amounts directly at their farms, including juice and fresh berries; and there is one annual cranberry festival around harvest time in Langley. The BCCMC also hosts occasional marketing events, such as a cranberry culinary contest in 2020, regular presentations to Canadian and international dieticians, joint marketing events with other agricultural producers, and educational programs for the public. However, no concerted campaign around cranberry consumption in BC or the rest of Canada outside of Québec currently exists.

In general, BC growers, like their counterparts elsewhere, foresee consolidation in the future of the cranberry industry. The smaller family operations generally feel too burdened by debt and the vagaries of price swings to undertake any major initiatives or expansion; Ocean Spray provides them with a stable situation that does not require such. They suggest outside financiers looking for investment vehicles are starting to buy up agricultural enterprises and hire local managers. Most growers therefore see bigger consolidated farms as an inevitable outcome. A major shift seems to be required for family farms, which are used to providing most of their own labor, to move to larger operations. Most find it very challenging to develop reliable seasonal labor. Some suggested that larger corporations acting as investment vehicles are starting to buy up land, both for diversification and to take advantage of tax loopholes. If a shift to larger ownership continues, the lack of local cranberry training and extension capacity will become a more acute concern. Several also expressed concerns about streamlining pesticide and labor regulations. Most of these concerns are shared across agriculture sectors, thus raising the challenge of better institutional coordination across the federal and provincial levels toward concerted action. While things are stable in the BC cranberry industry, the rising tide of supply for new varietals speaks to the need to be proactive in identifying additional local and global market diversification opportunities.

QUÉBEC: THE CREATION OF A NEW CLUSTER THROUGH ENTREPRENEURSHIP, GOVERNMENT POLICY, AND SUPPORT FOR INNOVATIVE RESEARCH

Our second case study, Québec, provides a strong contrast with BC and, along with Wisconsin, reflects the impending exigencies of market consolidation, economies of scale, and the will, and potentially, the means, to challenge Ocean Spray's supply chain dominance, with huge implications for the industry (as we spell out in chapter 7). We spend some time here detailing a very unusual case study, the opportunity to document how a new cluster was formed and matured. We find that a combination of entrepreneurship and consistent, long-term government support, including access to finance, are crucial for explaining how a new cluster becomes successful.

Profile

Despite the spectacular growth of cranberry production in Québec, few documentary sources exist to help us understand how, beyond the considerably lower prices of land, a new cranberry industry was created largely from scratch. Its growth has been impressive. Poirier suggests that, though cranberries have been grown in Québec since at least the 1930s, the more recent growth has its origins in the 1980s (2010, 5–6, 10–11). She notes that the area cultivated with cranberries grew 22% between 1995 and 2006, while the volume produced increased by 26%. Meanwhile, the number of producers increased from thirty-five to sixty-six between 1999 to 2009. Québec has the additional advantage of colder weather, like Wisconsin, which means fewer pests (Poirier 2010, 23). In Washington state, stories circulate of nascent organic producers being wiped out by Québec's lower production costs. Some in Oregon report experimenting with organic production, with outside investors seeing a ready local market for such. Interviewees in these markets discussed the huge challenges to organic caused by warmer temperatures anywhere but Wisconsin and Québec. On the other hand, Québec has other issues related to winter freeze, which can damage vines, and very intense short and humid summers (like Wisconsin), which can increase the chances for pests or rot.

The Association of Cranberry Producers of Québec (APCQ), located in the heart of the main growing region in central Québec, was founded in 1994. It operates based on member fees based proportionately on the overall size of each producer's harvest. New producers, processors, and producers from New Brunswick pay a flat $350 annual fee. Interviewees noted that it operates on a consensual basis, and helps by providing agronomist advice, representing the industry to government, and reporting on industry statistics. It holds a biannual meeting, alternated with a congress wherein growing issues and new research and techniques are discussed. Speakers from outside the region are often invited to present.

About 77% of cranberries grown in Québec are processed there. The three main growing areas, according to interviewees, are the central areas around Victoriaville and Drummondville, south of Québec City and east of Montreal, which is currently the dominant production region; the northern area around Lac St. Jean; and a third mini cluster to the northeast of Montreal, in the direction of Joliette, toward the Laurentian mountains (Lanaudière region). Deloitte (2020) estimated that 89% of cranberry production was in central Québec; 6% in the Joliette region; and just 2% around Lac St. Jean in 2020; another 3% took place in other parts of the province. From 2009 to 2019, it estimates total growth in cranberries by land area as 9%; with conventional growth at 74% and organic at 402%. The total cranberry acreage was just over 10,000 acres in 2019. Because of concerns about environmental wetland regulations, the area of Lac St. Jean is the most likely one for future growth, according to some interviewees, as less development and a greater availability of wetlands there cause regulators less concern. However, the central Québec region retains natural advantages of a longer growing season, generally more flat terrain, and a finer sand than the other locations, according to interviewees. Alongside the advantages of proximity to supply chain nodes, as explained in chapter 2, this gives the region "sticking power" as a cluster.

As discussed in chapter 4, productivity has increased impressively over time, going from 24,000 lb./acre in 2015 to 27,000 lb./acre for conventional in 2019 and from 17,500 lb./acre to 18,500 lb./acre for organic in the same period (Deloitte 2020). Godin's calculation puts the breakeven point at $0.2756/lb., which would make Québec the lowest cost producer, and able to withstand sustained price downturns beyond most counterparts except for Wisconsin (2013, 9). As of 2008, approximately 38% of the crop went to concentrate, 59% to SDCs, and around 3% to fresh (Poirier and Painchaud 2010, 9, 13). Painchaud (2017) estimated that 31% of the crop would be organic by 2018. Québec is the largest producer of organic cranberries in the world. Cranberries are now the number one fruit crop by value in

Québec (Poirier and Painchaud 2010, 9). A 2021 government document cites eighty-one cranberry growers in the province, with an estimated growing area of 4,047 ha. The report states that the industry a little more than doubled from 2009 to 2021 in terms of land for production (Ministère de l'Environnement 2021, 18). Between 2006 and 2021, the area under cultivation increased by 7% per year on average. It currently employs approximately a thousand people. A 2019 Deloitte Report sponsored by APCQ offers rosier numbers, including 2,168 employees, up 30% from 1,673 in 2015. The sector contributes $149 million to GDP and $36 million in public revenues. Organics represent 40% of total production. Organic yields are 18,500 lb./acre in 2019, up 6% from 2015, while conventional harvests are 27,000 lb./acre, up 10% from 2015. Fully 75% of the cranberries are processed locally. The report also suggests that cranberries are the fastest growing fruit in terms of local consumption.

Organic cranberries reportedly fetch up to double the conventional price; however, they are far more capital- and labor-intensive and risky to grow. The higher selling price for them limits the overall market size. Interviewees suggested that the market share of organics is probably at its ceiling, given present limitations to market demand. Indeed, several interviewees stated that Ocean Spray and others recently agreed to switch organic back to conventional cranberries; one interviewee estimated that 1,200 acres were switched back in 2020–2021 because they simply cannot sell enough organic cranberries. At the same time, some interviewees suggested that fruit rot (from fungus) is a serious problem in Québec, and thus a team from Université Laval had been working on solutions. Others suggested insects (fireworm) are the primary issue.

The leading independent handler is Fruit d'Or, which is the largest organic producer in North America (Alston, Medellín-Azuara, and Saitone 2014, 6). The processing sector appears to be an effective oligopoly, with Ocean Spray (through its purchase of Atoka), Fruit d'Or, Citadelle (another cooperative), Emblème, and Canneberges Québec (which also sells conventional fruit to Ocean Spray) dominating. Emblème does not process, but sells frozen cranberries around the globe, with local sales accounting for only 5% of sales. Processors have been innovative in seeking out new markets and developing new products. For example, one features whole SDCs (versus sliced). Citadelle has a juice contract with Coke. Several interviewees cited contracts with China and the EU as signs of the success of their diversification efforts.

Origins

A complete story of the origins of the Québec industry is too complicated to cover within the scope of this book. However, the recent spurring of the industry, together with conversations with key interviewees who were part of the founding, offers a fascinating insight into the origins of clusters.

Since 1939, a limited crop of cranberries was grown by the Larocque family for local consumption and, later, sales to Ocean Spray. Not much happened in the industry until the 1980s, when pioneer Monsieur Bieler decided to start his own cranberry farm. Why Larocque's efforts did not result in a nascent cluster in the 1950s, when it became profitable, remains mysterious. Perhaps the best answer is given by Bureau, who states simply that there was a lack of knowhow and technicians, despite provincial and federal interest. He also states that growing techniques were modeled on Massachusetts, when Wisconsin is a better parallel for soil and climactic conditions (1970, 383). Bieler had an MA in regional planning from the University of Montréal. Entrepreneurship seems to run in the family, with relatives in Aix-en-Provence running a winery. Bieler worked in grain management in Vancouver and Winnipeg in the early years of his career. He came back home to work as a regional planning consultant for the Québec government and so had experience with policy. He longed to start an agricultural business and sold a family farm in Vermont, which helped provide seed money for an apple juice venture.

According to several interviewees, Bieler had been receiving agricultural advice for his apple orchard from Joe Pelis. Pelis operated as a self-taught agronomist across the US-Québec border in the 1980s and was familiar with the cranberry industry from work in Massachusetts. He was an expert in fertilization, known as "the cranberry doctor" for his work in Cape Cod, though his reputation is mixed according to some in Massachusetts. As he saw Bieler struggle to make money in apples, he suggested trying cranberries. As Bieler tells it, he had been selling unfiltered juice in New York City from his apple orchard, and it was very popular, particularly in natural foods/health stores. The distributor suggested Bieler start adding cranberry juice, to enhance perceived health benefits. However, Bieler was unable to purchase cranberries from Larocque because all their production was going to Ocean Spray. According to Bieler, this planted the seed of growing his own cranberries. As we relate below, cranberry prices were increasing from the late 1980s, so the timing was propitious, and Bieler's calculations showed a viable enterprise was clearly possible. He purchased some cheap land close to the Larocque operation, which had similar conditions.

Québec growers repeatedly stated that they have "perfect" natural growing conditions in terms of temperature, with cold conditions reducing pest issues, lots of sandy soils, and plenty of access to water. Several interviewees mentioned that the cranberry growing area around central Québec was marginal agricultural land, with sandy soils that were perfect, however, for cranberries.

The few attempts to create farms there in the 1940s and 1950s were largely abandoned because of the poor soil. Therefore, the land around this area was cheaper. Michel Gardner, a consultant to Bieler, was an agronomist who also had a background in financing; he played a crucial role, through his English-language capability, in helping to lead teams to visit Massachusetts and Wisconsin to learn growing techniques. Pioneers across the board said it was soon apparent to them that Wisconsin was the best model for Québec, and they focused their attention there.

While Bieler had enough wealth to make the initial investment in cranberries, the connections that Gardner and several other pioneers had to the local banking industry were crucial. The Royal Bank also included several officers with training in agronomy who, seeing the positive results of Bieler's efforts, started to form credit lines for other entrepreneur growers. Several interviewees noted that the Royal Bank already had ties to the BC cranberry industry and thus were easily convinced of the potential viability of a Québec-based industry and ready to provide financing. Soon other sources of finance came in, including local unions and other banks, such as Caisse Populaire. Several interviewees cited the key role of Jacques Painchaud, of MAPAQ (the provincial government agricultural and fisheries ministry), as a major champion of the industry who advocated hard for government support in the early years. While there are several support programs by MAPAQ for agriculture across the board, it was Painchaud who pushed the ministry to back cranberries. Painchaud was an agronomist by training and had worked in pesticide R&D; he was also a fan of entrepreneurship and so the perfect champion from the government side. Painchaud, Bieler, and others were able to make the case to the Québec government that the marginal land in central Québec, which had proven unsuitable for other types of agriculture, would be a perfect place for a new viable industry in cranberries. Thus, he became a crucial catalyst in promoting knowledge transfer from US practices and development for the local industry. He pushed Université Laval professor Léon Etienne Parent to set up an MA program to help with fertilizer management in agriculture, with a focus on cranberries. Caroline Turcotte of MAPAQ, a researcher, helped initiate summer programs for agronomy students to start working in the cranberry industry. This helped create a pipeline of students who could enter the industry with a basic background and start to promote improved techniques.

Slowly a small group of pioneering growers started to expand. Some interviewees suggested that they were spurred to create their own processing plants because of the example of Bieler's Atoka, and since Ocean Spray limited the amount of organic cranberries they would purchase. The Larocque family was part of Ocean Spray at this point; however, one interviewee notes that

Monsieur Larocque was instrumental in directing Ocean Spray agronomists to open knowledge to the Québec pioneers. MAPAQ official Jacques Painchaud pushed hard to create shared documentation from this opening. Ocean Spray may have been more open because of the perceived shortage of cranberries on the market during a time of high prices in the 1990s. As with other cluster origins (see Hira and Swartz 2014 on Napa wine), a small group of families knew each other and shared knowledge; most of these are now the owners of the large processing plants. Several interviewees suggested that the family orientation of the pioneers was crucial to its early expansion; as the initial businesses succeeded, they were able to draw siblings and extended family into the business, thus ensuring both expansion and knowledge-sharing. Bieler also hired top-notch consultants from Wisconsin, and thus it is not surprising that the Québec industry closely resembles that state and its efficiencies. Several interviewees mentioned the key role of Bieler in promoting cranberry growing to local contemporaries and his openness to sharing knowledge; this created a culture, at least among this first generation of pioneers, of regular sharing and promotion of cranberry technologies. Bieler was the first president of APCQ and has also served on the Cranberry Institute boards; he is thus a crucial catalyst in the cranberry industry. In fact, the APCQ reported that it had not needed to take a vote in years, because the industry operates by consensus. Moreover, his decision to create his own processing plant created a demonstration effect for other independents to follow, to control their product outside of Ocean Spray, which was not willing to take on all of Québec's production. Moreover, interviewees pointed out that prices in the 1990s were higher for growers who would sell to independents, leading some to leave Ocean Spray, as was the case in Oregon. In 2018, Ocean Spray bought Atoka from Bieler, reportedly with the intention of getting a foothold in Québec for favorable tariff conditions for exports to Québec, and for Québec's enormous organic potential.

Ocean Spray's Entry

Ocean Spray came late to the game in Québec, after Atoka had already established an independent culture in the cluster, and thus missed the window to expand the cooperative to another region. Wisconsin served as a model for creating the large economies of scale and modern techniques (such as large square farms, automated irrigation, and the use of booms) present in Québec. Gardner worked with some Université Laval researchers early on to develop a new varietal, but it did not take off as expected; however, this shows the engagement of researchers early in the industry. Moreover, growers noted the importance of having local equipment manufacturers who could custom make and help maintain cranberry equipment. However, most of the standard equipment, such as tractors, is still imported. Perhaps the most important shift was to promote organic growing, the high proportion of which distinguishes Québec's industry. Painchaud in MAPAQ also pushed for efforts to find organic fertilizers, funded in part by the Cranberry Institute; chicken manure provided the main solution.

Growers interviewed in late 2021 stated that, with such comparative advantages, they are still able to make money even in low price periods, and thus see no real likelihood of anyone leaving the industry, though prospects for growth are limited to the Lac St. Jean area, because of both price and natural lands available because of environmental regulations. They stated that there is less concern for wetland preservation north of the St. Lawrence, so government policy is determining future growth of the cluster there. As in Oregon, there is fierce competition between growers who are members of Ocean Spray and the quickly growing group of independents. Bieler, the pioneer, created the Atoka processing plant to provide an alternative to selling to Ocean Spray. As prices increased in the 1990s, other local processors followed suit, particularly Fruit d'Or, Canneberges Québec, Emblème, and Citadelle, who have now become major players in the global cranberry market. The different cranberry companies offer an interesting contrast in business strategies. Canneberges Québec sells primarily conventional cranberries to Ocean Spray and has its own organic business on the side. Emblème wholesales frozen (fresh) cranberries across the world. Citadelle, a long-term maple syrup co-op, moved into honey and, more recently, into cranberries. Like Ocean Spray, its growers own shares of the central processing and marketing business. Citadelle has an unusual structure of using one business platform for all three product lines; it sells its products at the retail level, under a variety of brand names (unlike Ocean Spray).

Fruit d'Or is by far the largest so far and has its own land, as well as purchasing from independent growers. It offers a full line of retail products but mostly occupies emerging niches, such as 100% cranberry juice and supplements. It is fairly innovative in its marketing, such as introducing sour (dried) cranberries. Several interviewees attributed its impressive growth to founder Martin LeMoine's entrepreneurial vision and management capacity. Fruit d'Or's website states that they were the initiators of the organic movement in Québec in 1993, something backed up by other interviewees (Fruit d'Or, nd). LeMoine was a former pig farmer. Interviewees noted LeMoine was assisted by hiring consultants from the Institute Nationale de L'Agriculture Biologique (National Organic Agricultural Institute) in Victoriaville, which is designed to promote organic growing across products and is the largest R&D and training center in Canada. This assistance helped ensure large enough yields, reducing the gap with conventional cranberries, ensuring that organic growers would be able to compensate for their additional risk. Of course, the sale of Atoka to Ocean Spray removed what would likely have been an independent company as large as Fruit d'Or. In 2020, Fruit d'Or announced a C$17.5 million investment in expanding its processing facilities to meet additional demand (Isabel 2020).

The large independent Québec companies purchase from local independent growers but also create their own fruit. They seem quite innovative in entering into nontraditional markets, such as "sour" SDCs and 100% cranberry juice (for health-conscious consumers), as well as making inroads into European markets through their cultural ties. Cranberries were Canada's third-largest fresh fruit export in 2019, after blueberries and cherries (Government of Canada 2019). A press release from 2017, regarding the Canada-EU free trade agreement under negotiation at the time, stated that it would substantially reduce tariffs for cranberry imports to the EU. Some mentioned success in penetrating Asian markets, and particularly the ability to sell in China.

Explaining Québec's Success: Natural Conditions, Knowledge-Creation, and Policy Support

Québecois interviewees insisted that their yields were superior to those of Wisconsin, and far above those of the other US producers, suggesting that natural comparative advantage is in good part responsible for growth. Unlike BC, Québec's colder weather and the presence of sand are major advantages, along with cheaper land, though land prices in the area around Victoriaville have supposedly doubled in the last twenty years, again pushing future growth northward. Growers stated that they are mostly using the Stevens variety, but that the new varietals from Wisconsin and Rutgers are gradually making their way in, leading to a potential doubling of the size of harvests. A number of other interviewees suggested that improved techniques, including new irrigation techniques that better manage water levels, and larger and more extensive and precise equipment, are more responsible for the increased yields and returns on investment, linked to Caron's research at Université Laval. According to one interviewee, water management research was spurred on by new environmental regulations for wetlands and, particularly, phosphorous runoff into water from the early 2000s. Wisconsin interviewees also pointed to the work of Leroy Kummer of Ocean Spray, who had been working on water management and supposedly assisted Caron with data reinforcing his research. Caron helped found a water management company, Hortau, which is now involved in projects across agricultural sectors. Hortau is well known in Wisconsin for help in improving water management, according to interviewees there, though they noted that there are a number of competitors as well.

More important still, the interviewees stated, is the enthusiasm of Québec growers to embrace a scientific approach to cranberry cultivation, which is the universal response to how they learned agricultural techniques so quickly. Researchers described a ready audience, with industry leaders such as Atoka and Pampev willing to devote farms to experimentation and growers more generally interested in learning the latest research. The growers have been receptive to hosting PhD students who have developed a thick knowledge of cranberry growing conditions and thus effectively act as extension agents, though they lack formal training. In response to grower requests, Université Laval built a website app that can advise them how much irrigation is needed based on recent rainfall patterns. This culture of learning is reinforced by the willingness of some producers, such as Fruit d'Or, to impose new techniques on their grower members, something Ocean Spray's scientists are challenged to do. Farmers are naturally risk-averse, but Québec's recent entry appears to be initiated in part by agronomists and economists who were likely better trained than the legacy growers in the United States. This advantage, along with simply starting later, might explain the greater willingness to adopt new technologies. The Québec pioneers appear to include a number of champions who were formally trained in agronomy and finance, which is clearly another advantage and could help explain their willingness to more readily adopt new techniques, such as water management. One interviewee summarized the state of the Québec industry as "everyone is still making good money, so no one is looking to exit. However, they are not making enough money to attract new growers or the big finance that was involved in the gold rush years of the 1990s."

Once cranberries were established as a viable sector, the Québec government made a conscious effort to support the cranberry industry, pouring in resources to attract technology transfer, such as inviting Massachusetts growers to buy land and establish businesses there through tax breaks. The Québec government provides project grants to farmers if they have obtained loan guarantees through its financing arm, Financière Agricole. Cranberries are an "emblematic crop" for Québec, along with maple syrup and blueberries, and so are favored for public funding. There are also specific programs aimed to support young farmers (Appui financier à la relève agricole), and an agristability program to help stabilize incomes. Moreover, according to Poirier (2010, 25), from 1998 to 2008, the government invested C$2,159,160 into university-based research, with 83% oriented toward cranberry production, another 13% toward health, and 4% toward processing. The Government of Québec estimates public investments of C$4.9 million between 2007 and 2015 (MAPAQ 2018a, 9).

The two important programs are the Agri-Stabilité and Agri-Investissement. The former provides growers support when prices decline beyond a certain historical threshold (30%) for sustained periods, while the second provides matching support for farmers wishing to upgrade their operations. Separate funds are available for organic conversion as well (we leave aside the details for the sake of brevity). Some growers also cited federal agricultural loan support, though it has been challenging to document the amounts given for these various support policies. Growers are circumspect about government support, stating that subsidized loans and insurance were helpful, but that the private sector really made things work. They mention their struggles with developing export markets and with having enough migrant labor as ongoing challenges. However, another interviewee suggested that the labor shortage was a temporary one related to COVID-19, and that there are regular intermediaries and channels that can bring in migrant workers from Mexico and Guatemala for the labor-intensive chores of weeding and harvesting. One interviewee mentioned a research project by a grower and the Centre de Recherche Industrielle Du Québec, an arm of the provincial government (Investissement Québec), which is testing new ways to electrocute weeds, which mostly stand taller than cranberries, in order to kill them.

According to the Government of Québec (MAPAQ 2018a, 6), the industry had to change after prices declined in 2008. One response was to invest in freezing equipment, which was done by three independent processors between 2010 and 2016, the start of continuing efforts to improve processing capacity and efficiency. This support appears ongoing, for example, in 2017, the Canadian government provided more than C$9.3 million in funding to Fruit d'Or through its AgriInnovation Program to expand its facilities, including building a new plant. Furthermore, a 2019 news report stated that the provincial government was making C$1,755,319 available, including a loan of $621,550 to the company Emblème Canneberge, to help improve equipment for the preparation, packing, and freezing of cranberries (La Nouvelle Union 2019; *Fruit Growers News* 2017). Here are some other examples of the extensive support given to industry by the government:

- The Québec government made a $11,673,500 grant to Emblème Canneberge to expand its facilities and acquire innovative technological equipment for the cleaning and freezing of small fruits and vegetables. The project is valued at more than $28 million and will lead to the creation of twenty jobs (June 2021). https://www.quebec.ca/nouvelles/actualites/details/levier-strategique-developpement-economique-regional-embleme-canneberge-cooperative-grand-bleu-32194.

- The Québec government provided a grant of $2.45 million in financial assistance to the Citadelle Maple Syrup Producers' Cooperative for the acquisition of equipment to modernize its cranberry processing plant in Aston-Jonction and its tertiary maple syrup processing plant in Plessisville (April 5, 2019). https://www.quebec.ca/nouvelles/ actualites/details/developpement-economique-du-centre-du-quebec-quebec-accorde-245-m-a-la-cooperative-de-producteurs-de-sirop-derable-citadelle.

- The Government of Québec is providing financial assistance of $63,535 to Diana Food Canada to support the development of an engineering plan to help the company increase its production capacity. The funding for this project comes from the Fonds de diversification économique du Centre-du-Québec et de la Mauricie. Diana Food Canada specializes in the powdering of fresh and frozen berries (cranberries, blueberries, and strawberries) for the marketing of thirty to forty finished products to food and health product manufacturers (August 6, 2018). https:// www.quebec.ca/nouvelles/actualites/details/fonds-de-diversification-economique-du-centre-du-quebec-et-de-la-mauricie-quebec-accorde-plus-de-63-000-a-diana-food-canada-pour-laider-a-optimiser-sa-capacite-de-production.

Besides provincial support for APCQ efforts, research is ongoing at Laval and McGill universities, l'Institut national de la recherche scientifique, la Chaire de recherche industrielle CRSNG-Hortau in irrigation, le Club Environnemental et Technique Atocas Québec (CETAQ), l'Association des producteurs de canneberges du Québec (APCQ), the growers' association, and l'Institut de recherche et de développement en agroenvironnement (IRDA), all receiving at least partial public funding in a way one cannot find in the United States. Research funding between 2012 and 2016 totaled C$4.6 million (MAPAQ 2018a, 12). Another project, by IRDA (completed in 2022), examined the effects of organic fertilizer on nitrogen levels and cranberry production (Landry nd). Interviewees also cited funding for improving local demand, such as the local cranberry festival. Overall, the Government of Québec views cranberries as a "growth vector," and they are featured in the overall strategic plan it has for food industries. It particularly sees a specialization in organic cranberries as a comparative advantage (MAPAQ 2018b, 19). The strategic plan mentions a number of avenues for the support of organic food generally, from insurance for farmers to subsidies for conversion from conventional production to subsidizing certification programs. Regional strategic plans have also been developed for increasing agricultural production in certain areas, including projects that would benefit a variety of sectors and joint projects with growers' associations, including APCQ. There are even specific programs for reducing bee mortality.

In 2017, a report noted C$9.3 million in federal funding from Agriculture and Agri-Food Canada for expansion and a new plant at the Québec handler Fruit d'Or, as well as C$183,127 to be invested in pollination studies. Much of Québec production is independent of Ocean Spray, and thus it presents a profile different from BC, with Ocean Spray taking perhaps 25%–30% of production, according to interviewees. Independent growers stated that they fear being squeezed between Ocean Spray and the giants of local industry, who may continue further vertical integration by buying more land of their own, though the processor co-op Citadelle's model is based on five-year contracts with independent growers. Non-grower interviewees also observed some degree of consolidation over time, with the number of growers declining while overall acreage has increased substantially. One interviewee suggested that few new farmers entered the industry after 2010, and that the overall size of farms has increased. While the person thought the handlers might buy more land, they believed that there will be a limit because of the price of land and the desirability and relative facility of buying fruit from independent growers (for now).

Despite a Slowdown, the Future Is Bright for Cranberries in Québec

Indeed, several interviewees noted the likelihood of limits on new land being tilled for cranberries in Québec, citing increasing constraints from environmental regulations by the Ministry of Environment and Fight Against Climate Change, which require a certain ratio for farms to infrastructure/housing to land that must be conserved for wetland preservation (Avard, Larocque, and Pellerin 2013). In general, it seems urban Québécois populations are at odds with their rural counterparts, and there does not seem to be an effort to weigh environmental against social and economic benefits and costs in any clear way. In short, there is a bifurcation of purpose between MAPAQ's support of further sector growth and the Ministry of Environment and Fight Against Climate Change's constraining approach. Either way, the net effect is to slow but not halt new cranberry farm construction.

Some noted that land prices in central Québec have doubled in the last decade and that several growers have been bought out by neighbors. On the other hand, another interviewee noted that the industry started in this region because it was marginal agricultural land, which was its attraction, and so land prices are still lower compared with other more attractive growing regions. Moreover, there is potential for cranberry cultivation to take over other currently more-marginal agricultural operations, such as some local corn or dairy farms that are small and so less profitable. Some mentioned New Brunswick as a growth area, because it is not too far from Québec processors, unlike Nova Scotia, and the environmental regulations are less stringent there. Most believe that cranberry production will continue to grow, but at a dramatically slower pace than in the past. All of this reinforces the likelihood of further consolidation through horizontal and vertical integration, as through path dependency the early incumbents have advantages of lower/paid-off land costs, built-up capital, and know-how.

Independent growers are concerned not only about vertical integration but also about the lack of agricultural extension support. A group of agronomists supported by growers and the APCQ, called CETAQ (Le Club Environnemental et Technique Atocas Québec), provides the main support services. CETAQ provides a summer training service for agronomy students who go out to the cranberry fields and conduct measurements, leading to advice on issues such as fertilizers and pests. This summer program seems to be very valuable for training personnel in the field, with several cranberry professionals having started in the industry there. These two associations work closely and provide some extension services. Growers stated that the universities are not involved in extension work, so the link depends more on personal contacts and knowledge between the university researchers and CETAQ/APCQ personnel. Some interviewees expressed concerns that the member dues are so low that the budget for research is very modest; in fact, there is only one dedicated agronomist researcher at APCQ.

The degree of support received from the government seems to depend on whether there is an active MAPAQ agent in cranberries. Many cited the departure of Jacques Painchaud, whose retirement was a major loss. There is no formal training program for cranberries; the agronomy and agricultural programs in Québec, however, particularly at Laval and McGill universities, appear to create a well-educated workforce that is behind much of the cranberry sector's success. Moreover, many of those interviewed had formal training and, sometimes, experience in finance as well. This resonates again with the triple helix theory of innovation, involving cooperation among researchers, government, and industry. However, now that the cluster is established, there is clearly less need for the shepherding that Painchaud provided.

Why would Ocean Spray promote cranberry growing in Canada, when it competes with US producers, and most of the supply is exported out of Canada? The most obvious reason is that it is cheaper to produce the crop there. Timing is important as well. According to interviewees, production was ramped up there in the 1990s, when there was a perceived long-term shortage of cranberry supply. The other part is that Québec has differentiated its production by becoming a leader in organic growing, reflecting its deep investment in R&D that will benefit the whole sector. However, this may be reaching a saturation point, as Ocean Spray has frozen any further growth in organic, leading to some dissonance (as elsewhere) with independent growers who would like to become members.

Finally, Canada offers additional trade opportunities, stemming in part from Québec's long-standing ties and personal networks with Europe and from lower sugar prices due to US protection for domestic high-cost sugar growers. For example, the new Canada-EU free trade agreement reduces duties on SDCs and juice by 17.6% (Government of Canada 2022), with the same advantages maintained for the UK post-Brexit via a continuity agreement. It is being applied on a provisional basis while awaiting full ratification by EU member states. Canadian growers were also shielded from US president Trump's trade spats with China and the EU, which led to temporary tariffs. Nonetheless, Poirier describes an equal oversupply crisis in Québec, related to the collapse of demand in the United States (2010, 12, 15). The price of organic cranberries in Québec went from $.40/lb. (versus $.11 for conventional) to $.60/lb. (versus $0.16 for conventional) in 2016, according to the Government of Québec. However, the price of conventional cranberries declined from an average of C$1.08/kg between 2007 and 2011 to 0.68/kg from 2012 to 2016 in Québec, while it declined in BC over the same period from C$1.26/kg to $1.09/kg. The price difference is of obvious concern to Québec and may reflect the price premium given by Ocean Spray, which is predominant in BC but not in Québec (MAPAQ 2018a, 8, 12).

Growers in Québec, as in Oregon, are dichotomous in their attitudes toward Ocean Spray, with independents wanting the freedom to chase higher prices when possible, but frustrated at discriminatory prices paid by Ocean Spray to members (which, according to them, do not reflect market prices). They see Ocean Spray as offering potential stability; however, they stated that they have not been given the choice to become members. Processors seem even more ambivalent about Ocean Spray's entry. They believe that they are innovating and occupying markets where they do not compete directly with Ocean Spray. They see Ocean Spray as the giant, still able to pay higher grower prices because of its vast retail reach. Moreover, because Ocean Spray has stable demand, since it bought Atoka, local processors say it has not really increased local competition for cranberries.

Overall, Québec can play a very positive role in the industry, helping to open new product innovation and overseas markets alongside offering fierce competition to higher cost growers. The real question is whether and how Ocean Spray and the Québec processing oligopoly can cooperate around industry-wide issues. Québec processors seem generally positive about these possibilities, citing the importance of Ocean Spray in historical terms and how its still much larger size means it can continue to provide industry leadership in developing new products. Some stated that Ocean Spray's brand and retail footprint give it a lasting advantage, far above the ability of most local producers to directly reach customers; Fruit d'Or has made some inroads in retail but still has a long way to go. The next big challenge for the Québec industry is to improve its retail profile. Somewhat ironically, smaller independents or growers seeking to develop their own products complain that they have limited options for selling their products and that developing their own distribution channels is exceedingly difficult, reflecting oligopolies in other segments of the supply chain, including large grocery chains. Some in Wisconsin point to the disappearance and diminishment over time of outlets such as Northland, Cliffstar, and Graceland, as reducing their choices and leverage, a path not taken away from Ocean Spray that Québec has followed.

From the perspective of cluster theory, Québec shows that active policy support can make a clear difference. By contrast, US policy at both the federal and state levels, largely limited to supply management, lacks severely in imagination and thus tends toward ad hoc and haphazard efforts, such as marketing orders, rather than a long-term strategy. Ocean Spray has, by default, provided the public goods needed for industry success in the United States, but, as we have documented, its ability to do so into the future is under duress. While Wisconsin has a robust R&D system, as described in chapter 2, its support of industry in terms of financing and development of overseas markets is far more limited than that of Québec. Of all the clusters across North America, Québec comes closest to the triple helix ideal, though it lacks the element of extension and of export development. A partnership between Ocean Spray and the largest Québec producers could jointly support shared strategic initiatives for the industry with great benefits, and indeed may be necessary to preserve industry collective action (as we discuss in the conclusion).

Chapter 6
Comparing Ocean Spray to Other Large Agricultural Cooperatives

COOPERATIVES AS A POTENTIAL SOLUTION TO COMMODITY CYCLES: A COMPARATIVE PERSPECTIVE

The cranberry industry, including growers, handlers, and Ocean Spray, is understandably concerned about market conditions, which are significantly challenging, as we have illustrated throughout this book. With a wider perspective, however, we can see that the conditions facing the cranberry industry and the solutions we have discussed, and expanded upon in the conclusion, are not unique, but part of a pattern of experimentation throughout the US agricultural sector. In this section, we provide mini cases of four of the most well-known and dominant agricultural cooperatives: Sun-Maid (raisins); Welch Foods (grape juice and jams/jellies); Land O'Lakes (agricultural inputs, dairy, and feed); and Sunkist (citrus fruits and juices).

Through these examples, we see the common problems inherent to agriculture—volatile supply conditions, including from weather, improvements in productivity, and overreaction to increases in demand with lag effects; the lack of power and returns for the farmer/grower from the final product; and the challenges with marketing a generally undifferentiated natural product. These cooperatives offer a solution parallel to Ocean Spray's by creating a membership group, which is able to pool its resources in order to capture some aspects of vertical integration, including processing and distribution and, perhaps more importantly, branding. Moreover, like Ocean Spray, they offer the additional value proposition of providing member services, including R&D, technical assistance, and some efforts at quality standards. While there is important variation in terms of the ways that the central questions of managing cooperatives is addressed—from avoiding free ridership to governance to dealing with oversupply and international competition—the central point is that the cooperative solution is flexible across sectors and should be considered more widely as a viable model of industrial organization in agriculture.

SUN-MAID RAISINS

Sun-Maid is another remarkable case of agricultural producers working together as a cooperative to try to tackle commodity cycles and engage in common marketing (Uhle 2007). Sun-Maid currently has approximately 1,200 members, or 30% of California raisin growers. It has a fifteen-person board of directors, elected to three-year terms from each of the five districts (Sánchez, Boland, and Sumner 2008, 361). It has 550 employees and is owned by 750 families who farm 50,000 acres in central California, producing over 200 million lb. of grapes per year, according to its website (Sun-Maid nd).

As with cranberries, raisin marketing and distribution are also regulated by federal marketing orders; however, supply issues are not. Since grapes could be used for table grapes, raisins, or wine concentrate, the grower has to continually monitor prices in more than one market. Approximately one-third of US grapes are used for raisins. Raisin production is highly concentrated in California, which produced 45% (622 million lb.) of global supply in 2008. Until 1975, half of all raisins were sold directly to consumers; however, paralleling the use of SDCs in the cranberry industry, now almost two-thirds are sold in bulk, for use in other products. As of 2008, Sun-Maid controlled about 35% of California raisin production (Sánchez, Boland, and Sumner 2008, 360–362).

Sun-Maid Growers of California is perhaps the most well-known raisin company in the United States. Raisins came into fashion as a cash crop during the late 1800s. M. Theo Kearney provided a vision of cooperation in the raisin industry as early as 1893, starting the California Raisin Growers' Association in 1898. He promoted cooperation among growers to start their own packing houses in order to capture more value, at a time when prices were in freefall. However, dissension among members, including tensions between Armenian and other growers, led to the demise of the organization in 1906 (Woeste 1998, 81–90).

The precursor to Sun-Maid started in 1912 as the California Associated Raisin Company (CARC), created as a cooperative based on inspiration from earlier companies such as Sunkist and Welch's. It was organized by member-farmers, led by a group of twenty-five trustees, including bankers and community leaders, and issued $1 million of stock, available for purchase by anyone. Growers sold their raisins to CARC for a guaranteed price and then shared in the next profit, after paying a fee of $0.25/lb. for organizational and dividend costs (*Wall Street Journal* 1923). Like Ocean Spray did for cranberries, CARC packaged and marketed their product around the United States and provided technical support to growers. The organization improved on Kearney's efforts in important ways. First, it recruited bankers to help provide the capital for vertical integration, and sought out alliances with other business partners rather than relying solely on the growers. Second, it refused to operate on behalf of farmers until 75% of the farmers had joined, creating an imperative membership drive. Third, it was able to enforce membership deliveries, and cut down on free-rider sales when prices went temporarily high, suing such growers for breach of contract. Last, but not least, it created a strong sense of community peer pressure for growers to join, supported by social institutions such as churches (Woeste 1998, 115–116, 127, 135).

By 1913, the cooperative had grown to include 4,400 of the 6,500 (68%) California raisin growers. In 1918, it opened a large Fresno-based processing plant. Though an antitrust suit against the cooperative was filed in 1919, the matter was settled by the Capper-Volstead Act in 1922, which exempted agricultural cooperatives from antitrust (Woeste 1993, 28). The cooperative changed its name to Sun Maid Raisin Growers of California in 1922, to reflect its successful branding. In 1924, it declared bankruptcy and was restructured (*Wall Street Journal* 1923). In addition, stories circulated about nonmembers being intimidated to join, as well as an inability to enforce production cutbacks at the time (*New York Times* 1925). Sun-Maid vertically integrated, setting up its own processing industry and marketing system. According to Woeste, Sun-Maid punished packers who refused to work for it by restricting their supply of raisins (1993, 28). It also required growers to sell 100% of their produce, at times physically threatening farmers who did not comply. In 1927, the company issued $5 million in bonds; however, as prices continued to decline, it declared bankruptcy again. In 1930, it paid off its debts and reestablished as a cooperative. The H.J. Heinz company took over distribution from 1942 to 1952, until Sun-Maid resumed this function. Based on growing demand, Sun-Maid opened a new $12 million plant in Kingsburg, California, in 1964 to replace the Fresno plant. Challenges in the 1970s stemmed from weather-related losses as well as growing labor activism among farmworkers.

Like cranberries, raisins are governed by a marketing order. The Raisin Administrative Committee (RAC) has thirty-five growers, ten handlers, one cooperative bargaining association member, and one public member, and is charged with gathering and examining information on raisin production statistics. As in cranberries, the RAC can, with two-thirds of the board's support, limit the amount of raisins that can be sold in open markets, with the rest going into reserves or noncompetitive outlets, such as school lunch programs. Unlike cranberries, this commodity also has a Raisin Bargaining Association (RBA), established in 1966 to negotiate an annual field price. The RBA represents about 40% of California volume (Sánchez, Boland, and Sumner 2008, 365–366).

Also similar to Ocean Spray, Sun-Maid unsuccessfully attempted to diversify into other product lines. In 1980, Sun-Maid joined Diamond Walnut Growers and Sunsweet Prune to form Sun-Diamond Growers, an umbrella marketing organization. In 1995, Sun-Diamond purchased Dole Food Company's dried fruit operations. In 1998, Sun-Diamond was dissolved, leaving Sun-Maid and the newly formed California Raisin Marketing Board (state government), which succeeded the former California Raisin Advisory Board, to promote raisin consumption (the board was shut down in 2021). Nonetheless, Sun-Maid continues to offer a variety of dried fruits. The raisins it produces are about equally spread between direct sales and sales to cereal and baking companies.

The 2000s were marked by both organizational changes and oversupply issues. In the early part of the decade, Sun-Maid decided to start retaining some of the earnings (previously sent back to growers) for reinvestment; it gave up its tax-exempt status as well. In 2002, the California Raisin Marketing Board decided to ban any replanting of vineyards that had been out of production for three years, and growers were further encouraged to dispose of raisins through selling them for cattle feed or as a biofuel additive. During this period, mechanized drying systems became widespread and were used on 20% of the crop as of 2004; some 40% of growers used mechanical harvesting as of 2005 (Boland 2006).

The target market for Sun-Maid is women between ages twenty-five to forty-four with children between the ages of three and thirteen, which explains why they emphasize wholesome goodness and health benefits and feature an iconic image of a farm maiden on the box (Barrientos 2006). In 2003, A. Lassonde, Inc., licensed the Sun-Maid brand to use it on a line of fruit juices in Canada. This same company is active in the cranberry industry, illustrating the value of the brand.

Recent reports (Allen 2019) indicate that Sun-Maid is facing flat demand and oversupply conditions similar to Ocean Spray. Its current CEO suggests the need to "change and increase demand" to resolve the issues. Indeed, raisin prices have been highly volatile in recent years; for example, they went from $1,290/ton in 1999 to $491 in 2002, before recovering to $1,210 in 2004 (Boland 2006).

WELCH FOODS INC.

Welch Foods Inc. is the manufacturing and marketing arm of the National Grape Cooperative and is based out of Concord, Massachusetts. The founder of the original firm was Thomas Bramwell Welch, an Englishman who immigrated to New Jersey and became a dentist and physician. He sought to bottle grape juice and preserve it in a way that would avoid fermentation, in line with his religious convictions. He focused on locally grown Concord grapes, which were developed through ten years of breeding experiments in 1849 by Ephraim Wales Bull in Concord, Massachusetts. In 1869, after much experimentation, he invented a preservation technique by dropping the bottled juice in boiling water, which killed the yeast microorganisms that produce alcohol. Thomas's son, Charles, then took over the business. Growers were paid $10/ton during the period between 1873 and 1893. Dr. Welch's Grape Juice was sold in local grocery and drugstores from 1890, becoming a big hit at the 1893 Chicago world's fair. After the fair, the product was renamed Welch's Grape Juice, in line with the newly (1897) publicly incorporated stock company, the Welch Grape Juice Company. Production moved from 40 lb. of grapes in 1869 up to almost 500 tons in 1878. The company moved its pressing operations from Vineland, New Jersey, to Watkins in Western New York, to be closer to grape-growing regions and in response to black rot problems with the local grapes. The Chautauqua-Erie area, comprising Western New York, northwestern Pennsylvania, and northeastern Ohio has ideal climate and soil for growing the types of grapes Welch's needed for its juice (Dinger and Haahr 2019; Chazanof 1977).

Supply chains played a role similar to that of Ocean Spray in spurring the formation of the cooperative. A major challenge for grape growers going into the twentieth century was to develop the storage and transportation systems for transporting grapes via railroads that would minimize spoilage en route to the East Coast, one that Welch's helped resolve through smoothing out inventory and logistics tracks. Eventually, this included insulated cars to protect the grapes and juice from freezing during winter. The need to shift to economies of scale in the logistics and transportation aspects, along with the usual disruptions of supply booms and busts due to weather, demand, and increasing planting, started to push the growers in the region toward cooperation. In 1886, they formed the Chautauqua Grape Growers Shipping Association. Besides coordinating shipping, the association began to demarcate quality standards. In February 1892, the newly expanded Chautauqua and North East Grape Association controlled about 75% of grape production in the region. The group was incorporated in New York and was run by a board of nine, with one member elected from each of the eight districts and one at-large member. The company required growers to sign contracts guaranteeing their fruit and compliance with grading and inspection standards. In return, the association engaged in marketing under a common brand name. In 1897, independent growers in the area formed a second association, the Chautauqua and Erie Grape Company. It also encompassed eight districts, with inspection and record-keeping done at that level, and a central committee of eight elected representatives. For a variety of reasons, principally related to oversupply, the challenges of quality grading, and dissonance about board salaries, the Chautauqua and Erie Grape Company association fell apart as members slowly left, until just fifteen remained by 1901 (Chazanof 1977, 50).

Welch's was incorporated in New Jersey in 1903. It engaged in heavy advertising, particularly in medical and religious publications, touting the health benefits of grape juice. These merged with the growing temperance movement and were endorsed by the prominent politician and secretary of state under President Wilson, William Jennings Bryan. The establishment of the Fredonia (New York) experimental station by the state legislature in 1909 greatly improved grape harvests and quality over time. In 1910, Welch's bought the plant of the former rival Walker Company, which had gone bankrupt, in the town of North East, Pennsylvania, effectively doubling its capacity and giving it 75% of the juice market share. Growers were essentially beholden to meet the prices and quality standards of the company. It introduced its first jam product in 1918, called Grapeade. In 1919, it built additional plants in Lawton, Michigan, and Springdale, Arkansas, to keep up with increasing demand partly caused by perceptions of health benefits. In 1926, one of Charles's sons, Edgar, took over the business and began to produce non-grape products, including tomato juice. In 1927, his brother, Paul, took over as the CEO, and continued in the position despite the company being bought out by investors from the American National Company. The sale was related in part to family squabbles over who would control the company. The new owners helped expand the product line to include tomato juice, fountain syrup, Grapeade, and a variety of fruit jellies (Dinger and Haahr 2019; Chazanof 1977).

The development of Welch's business model is explained by the same motivations that cranberry growers had in establishing mutually beneficial joint supply chains and marketing efforts. In 1943, the Federal Trade Commission charged Welch Grape Juice Company with making unsubstantiated health claims. In 1945, Jacob M. Kaplan took over the company after acquiring 40% of the stock. He was the former president of Hearns department store and established a lucrative business in wine and liquor sales there. In 1933, he had bought a Brockton, New York, grape-processing plant from the Chautauqua and Erie cooperative and formed the National Grape Corporation, to ensure a steady supply of grapes for wine production. In 1945, he helped create the National Grape Cooperative Association, which created the National Grape Corporation to package, process, and market grape juice, spurred in part by the motivation to avoid taxes. Formed by a group of 891 members across several states, including New York, the corporation expanded over time to reach 4,600 members in ten states by 1955. Kaplan innovated by setting an advanced price ($40/ton) before harvest, thus helping stabilize conditions for growers. The cooperative shared profits on sales by Welch's minus a 10% fee (to Welch's) (*New York Times* 1956). Kaplan set aside some of his own wealth to buy shares of Welch's, and he introduced a number of innovations, including a cold storage plant, larger stainless steel storage tanks, and processing equipment. The efforts to sell Welch's wine failed. He also expanded operations to the West Coast, principally through acquisitions. By 1952, Kaplan had increased his ownership of Welch's to 90%; he then sold it to the National Grape Corporation (which had become the National Grape Cooperative Association in 1945). National Grape completed the takeover in 1956, paying some $28.6 million. The company at the time was generating $37 million in annual sales, boosted by extensive marketing efforts including children's TV programs and ties to Disneyland (Dinger and Haahr 2019; Chazanof 1977). Since then, Welch's has been the processing and marketing subsidiary of the National Grape Cooperative Association, currently representing some 1,054 family farmers across the United States and Ontario, Canada (NCFC nd).

In 1964, Raymond T. Ryan took over as Welch's president. He expanded the product line to include other fruit spreads and drinks, increasing revenues to $70 million by the time he stepped down in 1970. His successor, R. Craig Campbell, continued to expand product lines into red and white grape juice and powdered drink mix in the 1970s, and sparkling grape juice and squeezable jellies in the 1980s. The company shifted its headquarters from Westfield, New York, to Concord, Massachusetts, in 1983, to be closer to the large markets. However, consumer tastes toward lighter breakfasts started to kick in, eroding markets such that revenues dipped through the 1980s, prompting a new strategy in 1991 (Dinger and Haahr 2019; Chazanof 1977).

Welch's new strategy included acquisitions of rivals, such as BAMA, a brand popular in the South, and new food categories, such as Cascadian Farm, an organic food manufacturer (subsequently sold in 1996). In 1996, the company introduced a new line of juice concentrate called Juice Makers that did not require freezing, increasing revenues by $572.7 million in 1997. In the same year, it also built a new technology center in Billerica, Massachusetts, to develop new products. It has particularly focused on working with universities, such as Cornell, University of Illinois–Urbana-Champaign, and Wisconsin to document the antioxidant health benefits of grapes (Amanor-Boadu et al. 2006, 41–42). It also was able to expand its distribution to other outlets, including convenience stores and diversified retailers such as Walmart. Nonetheless, revenues began to decline again in the early 2000s as consumers moved away from fruit juices toward healthier alternatives. The company has sought to rebound through introducing organic juice, dried fruit, fruit snack lines, low-cost base filler for wine products, and nonalcoholic sparkling and energy drinks. Welch's also moved toward a global strategy, principally focused on East Asia, through a new push in the late 2000s for international growth.

Over time, to help cultivate leadership, Welch's developed a three-tier governance structure: committeemen at the local level in each district; delegates at a regional level; and directors on the board. Representatives are elected (Chazanof 1977, 337). National Grape and Welch's each have their own board. National Grape has four regions, thirteen production districts, and 103 geographical sections. Each member has one vote, with thirteen members on the board, one from each district; there are also delegates at the district level (Amanor-Boadu et al. 2003, 40). Welch's board includes four growers from National Grape who are elected; two hired managers (CEO and the CFO), and four outside directors, hired on the basis of their expertise in the packaged food industry (Amanor-Boadu and Boland 2005). While the current webpage for the National Grape Cooperative, of which Welch's is a subsidiary, is not publicly available, other sources (Marketline 2012; Welch's nd) indicate that the company is based in Westfield, New York, with 952 employees as of 2012, representing 1,282 grape growers in Michigan, New York, Ohio, Pennsylvania, Washington, and Ontario. Welch's website states that it is owned by nine hundred farmer families and is headquartered in Concord, Massachusetts. Dun & Bradstreet's 2019 report on the company notes that it has a thousand total employees.

Welch's farmers currently seem to be suffering from the same problematic conditions as those of Ocean Spray. In a 2018 article, West notes that grape prices have remained flat for ten years, with growers getting between $120–$250/ton in recent years. Grape juice is "in a slump," with sales down 5% from the previous year. The multiple-generation farmers who are part of the co-op hope product innovation and internationalization will help them overcome growing consumer wariness about the harmful effects of high sugar content.

LAND O'LAKES

Land O'Lakes is reportedly the largest agricultural cooperative in the United States, with more than 1,140 member associations covering all fifty states.

According to the company website (Land O'Lakes, nd), Land O'Lakes currently has 3,667 members, including 1,851 dairy producers, 749 "ag producers" and 1,067 retail-owners; it has ten thousand global employees. The co-op offers technical assistance and research, as well as providing branding for retail dairy products, including its iconic butter brand and Purina animal feed (acquired in 2001). It also has a strong presence in dairy manufacturing of butter, cheese, and dairy powders (Carper 2016).

The board of directors of Land O'Lakes has twenty-four members: dairy members nominate twelve directors; agriculture members nominate another twelve. The directors are elected by each group by region, with the number per region based on the volume of business conducted there (Boland, Cooper, and White 2015, 654).

Unlike the other mini cases we have profiled, Land O'Lakes has its hands in a variety of businesses, from seeds to dairy to crops to animal feed. The company was created on June 7, 1921, when 350 farmers from across Minnesota created a statewide dairy cooperative called the Minnesota Cooperative Creamery Association, Inc. One of the original founders, John Brandt, became president in 1923. He promoted a vision of cooperation leading to higher individual profits through shared distribution and quality standards. In 1924, the cooperative held a $500 contest for a new name, and Land O'Lakes was born, the beginning of a powerful brand. In 1928, the cooperative began to diversify, by venturing into eggs and poultry. In response to lower prices during the 1930s Great Depression, the company began to develop more diverse distribution, including smaller retail outlets, and began to further diversify its products, including cheese, dried milk (in response to World War II), feed, seed, and other supplies for farmers. In the 1950s, it moved into ice cream. From the 1960s to the present, the company has continued to expand, principally through acquisitions in the dairy industry, but also including beef, soy, and petroleum. By the 1980s, the excessive expansion began to threaten earnings, thus leading to divestments of petroleum, turkey, and beef. In the 1990s, it started its International Division, expanding overseas and working as a subcontractor to US AID; it also extended its range to the West Coast through a variety of acquisitions. Through acquisitions, the company deepened vertical integration, thus becoming able to provide a full range of agricultural support, from R&D to seeds, fertilizer, and crop protection. It operates WinField United, a subsidiary, to conduct R&D, develop talent, and offer a wide range of technical solutions to agriculture (Salamie 2007).

Boland, Amanor-Boadu, and Barton (2004, 63–66) divide Land O'Lakes into two main segments: dairy (both industrial and retail) and agricultural services. As with cranberries, significant productivity increases in dairy from a variety of sources, including genetics, has resulted in a major increase in supply. Land O'Lakes has responded through consolidating its processing plants, overseas expansion, and diversification of its portfolio to include feed manufacturing, eggs, crop input and protection products, and business services. The number of cheese-processing plants declined 49%, from 737 in 1980 to 376 in 1999. The number of plants processing butter fell by 68%, and those processing nonfat dry milk by 58% over the same period. The company operated its services division in more than fifty countries. In this sense, Land O'Lakes offers an unusual example of both internationalization and diversification of product within a cooperative structure.

SUNKIST

Sunkist was formed in the late nineteenth century as California's citrus industry started to boom, in response to the food needs of miners coming for the gold rush of the 1860s and spurred, further, by the completion of the transcontinental railroad in 1870 (Boland, Pozo, and Sumner 2009, 629). Citrus fruit was introduced to California and Arizona by Spanish missions in the late 1700s (Kirkman 1975, 6). In 1873, a group of American missionaries brought a Brazilian seedless variety of orange to Riverside, California. Between 1880 and 1893, citrus acreage in the state increased from 3,000 to more than 40,000 acres. As production increased, depressing prices, growers moved to organize themselves, to counteract the packing and distribution segments. The early period was volatile, based on demand and supply conditions and subject to a variety of pests. Shipment of fruit to St. Louis could take as long as a month in 1870. Growers were subject to freighter's prices, and inadequate refrigeration frequently led to rotting fruit and subpar prices. Coordinated efforts by policymakers at local, state, and federal levels moved to support the industry and create quality standards; moreover, high tariffs helped eliminate competition from imports (Boland, Pozo, and Sumner 2009, 629; Kirkman 1975, 6–7).

Sunkist is headquartered in Valencia, California, and has 223 employees. Approximately 45% of its current fresh fruit sales and more than 20% of processed sales come from overseas; gross annual revenues exceed $1.2 billion. The company operates a processing plant as a joint venture with Ventura Coastal in Tipton, California (Hoovers 2019).

As with Ocean Spray (see chapter 2), transportation and distribution networks play a crucial role in the citrus industry. The central means of transporting oranges from California was by railcar; the central innovation in this transport mode was the ventilated rail car (1887), followed by the insulated ice-bunker car (1889) (Sunkist Growers 1994, 4) and, eventually, refrigerated cars, which preserved fruit until it reached eastern markets, allowing California, with its longer growing seasons and drier climate (less pests) to compete with Florida. Agents purchased the fruit from growers and then took care of the transporting and marketing, engaging in large fruit auctions at the East Coast terminals. The crucial role of the railways was underscored in 1891, when agents decided to end the FOB terms and switched to consignment payment, whereby growers were paid only when the fruit sold. This squeezed growers' margins and vastly increased their risk, such that "a grower could receive nothing for his fruit and still have to pay his agent a handling charge of 50 cents a box" (Sunkist Growers 1994, 6, 10). In a wider sense, all of California agriculture came from man-made large-scale efforts to bring water to irrigate the natural deserts of the southern part of the state (Boulé 2013, 88). Riverside became the center of citrus harvesting, packing, and distribution machinery industry (Boulé 2013, 107). The natural result was to promote grower collective action.

In 1885, growers formed the Orange Growers Protective Union of Southern California. It sent salaried agents to help distribute fruit in eastern markets, but it lacked control of transport and thus disbanded in 1893. However, a number of other locally based associations succeeded it, such as the Claremont California Fruit Growers Association (Kirkman 1975, 7). Claremont was one of the first to use a common packinghouse, to which growers dedicated all their fruit, giving them bargaining power with wholesalers, who then accepted FOB terms. It also opened the way for common marketing. More importantly, growers were receiving $1/box, versus $.30 to .50/box for independent growers (Sunkist Growers 1994, 17, 19). In 1893, sixty growers formed the California Fruit Growers Exchange, a cooperative representing 80% of the orange growers of the region. Growers continued to have local packinghouses; three of these then participated in district exchanges, which could offer at least five hundred railcar loads/season. The exchange included eight districts, each with a local association and their own packing and labels. The districts then worked on the cooperative's marketing efforts and participated on its boards. Quality was monitored and exhorted. Fruit was prorated to ensure equal chances for sales of each growers' fruit (Covell and Feldman 2009; Siebert 1998, 3; Sunkist Growers 1994, 28).

Over time, the exchange lost its one-time coverage of 89% of growers; it is hard to tell exactly why, but Kirkman (1975, 7) suggests that a lack of business knowledge by growers led to poor practices, and a backlash by existing distributors harmed the ability of growers to develop their own reliable wholesale networks. By 1897, the exchange represented just 23% of growers. Moreover, directors who know the growing business did not understand marketing or distribution. For instance, exchanges did not coordinate on shipments, so they sometimes competed against each other in eastern markets. Established dealers also sought ways to undercut the exchange, using the transparency of its prices to their advantage (Sunkist Growers 1994, 29–30). In parallel, independent shippers created the California Fruit Agency in 1903, combining attributes of the Southern California Fruit Exchange and the California Citrus Union. However, antagonism spread between growers and fruit brokers, so that the agency was dissolved in 1904. In 1906, the Mutual Orange

Distributors was formed, later known as Pure Gold, Inc. Pure Gold, formed as an agricultural cooperative, was much smaller than the exchange, consisting of only a few packinghouses and a distribution system. It played a minor role in the exchange, controlling only about 10% in 1933, and closed in 1989. As with the exchange, and later Sunkist, Pure Gold lost market share over time to independent handlers, including large companies such as Dole and Sun World (USDA 1994, 21–22).

In 1905, the exchange expanded to cover the whole state, changing its name to the California Fruit Growers Exchange. It regulated shipments of products, held bargaining power, and represented 45% of the state citrus industry through its five thousand members. In 1907, it created its own timber supply company, to ensure a steady supply of packing crates. The initial campaign cost $7,000, and a blitz was organized to promote "Orange Week" in Iowa. Sales increased significantly, underscoring the value of advertising and leading to ramped-up efforts. In the same year, the exchange began an advertising campaign, launching the Sunkist brand. In 1914, it introduced marmalade and orange juice. In 1915, the exchange bought a marmalade factory in Ontario, California, transforming it into a plant to produce citric acid and orange and lemon oil. In 1916, it began its "Drink an Orange" campaign, promoting orange juice, including selling juicers for ten cents, for the first time; the response was overwhelming, and juice became a mainstay product and advertising focus (mostly for its purported health benefits). The campaign is attributed to Don Francisco, an advertising manager, who saw the possibilities for marketing oranges as a breakfast food and for advertising Sunkist oranges in ways that linked them with the California dream of a garden paradise (Boulé 2013, 58). Over time, ads directed at housewives associated orange juice with a mother's duty to take care of her infants through good nutrition. In 1917, the exchange pushed the California legislature to provide a maturity standard to regulate orange quality. In 1918, the exchange began selling grapefruits as well. Its sales force included 150 men in fifty-nine offices across the country. In 1920, its advertising budget reached $500,000 per year, and its campaigns began to emphasize vitamin C. By the end of the 1920s, it included more than thirteen thousand fruit growers and 75% of the state crop. In 1930, it introduced teletype to keep continual track of prices around the country. During this decade, the exchange began to sell canned orange juice, an innovation it had developed over time. In 1951, it introduced frozen concentrates for juice. The exchange changed its name officially to its Sunkist brand name in 1952. However, with the entry of new rivals, membership declined to five thousand, and to 56% of the California citrus crop, by 1983. Further challenges were encountered in the 1990s as the federal marketing order (1994) on citrus production ended, and new competition from Argentina and Spain entered the market. The marketing order repeal was based on a growing set of complaints by independent producers that it impinged on their ability to compete, as Sunkist engaged in "block voting." Sunkist sells a range of citrus fruits, juices, peels, and oils. In 2007, it introduced a 100% natural line of juices and smoothies and a Premium Sweet line of fruit packed in juice. A majority of its farmers work 40 acres or fewer. It imports fruit from around the world to sell to the US market (Covell and Feldman 2009; Siebert 1998, 3; Sunkist Growers 1994, 44, 52, 55, 61, 75, 77).

Similar to Ocean Spray, Sunkist shows consistent efforts at innovation. For example, in 1907, it began the first national campaign for a perishable product. In 1916, it helped establish the orange juice industry through a national campaign. In 1922, it began advertising the presence of vitamin C. In 1926, it pioneered stamping its trademark directly on fresh produce. In 1951, it began selling frozen juice concentrate. In 1953, it developed corrugated cardboard boxes to handle its fruit; these were cheaper, lighter, and not subject to the timber shortage issues previously experienced. As domestic markets seemed saturated, Sunkist launched a major international campaign in 1960, increasing exports to Europe and Japan, including lobbying to open up the latter's import restrictions. This effort yielded major increases in sales and paved the way for cross-marketing of products such as soft drinks. In the same year, the company introduced a fruit-lemon punch and frozen fruit bars (Siebert 1998, 2; Sunkist Growers 1994, 113, 117, 129, 133). It began selling Sunkist orange soda in 1977 (Marketline 2018).

Returning to our cluster theme—why growing conditions alone do not explain location—it is interesting to note that, in 1909, Florida orange growers had sent a delegation to California to study the exchange, its new competitive rival in eastern markets. That same year, a hundred growers formed the Florida Citrus Exchange on June 1. The name was later changed to Seald Sweet Growers in 1969. It followed Sunkist in setting up packinghouses as regional nodes, but did not set up district exchanges, reflecting the closer proximity of Florida growers. In 1912, it began national campaigns, and in the 1930s set up an export division. Although the company is a rival to Sunkist in the fresh market, it never followed Sunkist's example to enter the processed market (orange juice), which accounts for some 90% of sales (USDA 1994, 24, 34).

Like cranberry producers, California orange producers have also struggled with marketing orders. In the 1930s, oversupply prompted strong battles over prorating, whereby growers were assigned certain volumes they could sell, reinforced by California state regulations. Independent distributors also chafed at the rules, as with cranberries. In 1938, the industry distribution committee was unable to agree on a prorate plan. Also in parallel with cranberries was the juice stocks issue. In 1949, 75% of oranges were consumed as juice. Because juice could be canned, stocks began to build up across seasons (Sunkist Growers 1994, 88, 105-106).

Sunkist has also had to periodically deal with antitrust lawsuits, suggesting that it was not operating properly under the Capper-Volstead Act as a cooperative. In 1967, it lost its case before the Supreme Court, and in 1968, it was forced to reorganize. It created a federated cooperative, one that did not own all packinghouses, though they would maintain an affiliation. It also sold a large processing plant in Yuma, Arizona. By the late 1970s, syndications, partnerships, and large corporations began to invest in citrus fruit growing operations, attracted by tax incentives and depreciation allowances, which further undercut Sunkist's position. This period was marked by consolidation of citrus growing, leading to a decline in the number of growers and Sunkist's membership (Sunkist Growers 1994, 139, 147, 164, 166).

Sunkist is organized into sixteen district exchanges, with some six thousand citrus growers in California and Arizona. Each district has an exchange that fills regional orders. The twenty-seven-member board is elected by thirty-one districts, though the exact number of board members is based on the volume of fruit sold. All members are elected by member local associations, which in turn are organized by the packinghouse to which they send fruit. The packinghouses—affiliated with, but not owned by, Sunkist, an unusual arrangement for co-ops—are free to take fruit from other growers as well (Mueller, Helmberger, and Paterson 1987, 85). This freedom creates more competition and flexibility at the level of distribution than that provided by Ocean Spray. Each grower has a proportional percentage of their fruit accepted for shipment weekly, providing in theory equitable opportunity among growers and helping stabilize supply, though the system has been controversial among growers (Siebert 1998, 2-3). The existence of some level of competition among the packinghouses arguably incentivizes cost reduction (Kim 2013, 298). While each grower has one vote for director, other votes are based on one vote per a predetermined volume (one thousand cartons in 1994) (USDA 1994, 74).

Similar to Ocean Spray, Sunkist provides technical assistance, branding, and distribution to its members, including extensive lines of processed fruit products. Sunkist is a dominant presence in R&D in the citrus industry, accounting for the largest number of patents, from which everyone benefits. They also operate an orange and lemon juice processing facility. Members sign up annually, pledging a certain amount of their crop to Sunkist, which they are then obliged to fulfill. Members receive percentages of annual earnings minus an amount retained for working capital by the board. Earnings are enhanced through brand licensing. Over 80% of Sunkist's oranges are sold in the fresh market. Consumption of citrus fruits is growing at a slow pace along with population growth, with per capita consumption flat at 12 lb./capita. As of 2006, Sunkist controlled 48% of the market share of oranges, and 54% of that of lemons in California and Arizona. Sunkist also has led the way in opening overseas markets to exports, including lobbying for reduced barriers and increased access; such efforts were highly successful in developing the Japanese market from the 1960s to the 1980s (Boland, Pozo and Sumner 2009, 630–633; Siebert 1998, 4; Mueller, Helmberger, and Paterson 1987, 83, 187).

The decision to move toward importing fruit appears, not surprisingly, to be controversial among members, but management defends it as inevitable, as imports would reach markets anyway, increasingly through US free trade agreements, and the strategy gives the company the chance to use its brand (Smith 2004).

CONCLUSION: DO COOPERATIVES MAKE SENSE FOR AGRICULTURE INDUSTRY ORGANIZATION?

Through these cases, we see the common solution of agricultural cooperatives forming as a result of a sense of shared problems by growers/farmers in each industry. To begin with, one needs economies of scale, including pools of capital and highly trained personnel, long-term commitment, and an ability to not only respond to but also to anticipate R&D and extension that will be helpful to growers. In every case, the cooperatives' ability to create common distribution and processing nodes in the supply chain is the crucial mission it fulfills for grower members.

At the same time, we have seen that the continual turmoil surrounding membership and contributions is not unique to cranberries. As noted, Sun-Maid's attempts to crack down on free riders and intimidate nonmember growers and packers to join its cooperative raised challenges from the US government and ill will among others. Moreover, there does not seem to be any easy answer for the oversupply issues facing all the products we have reviewed, including cranberries for Ocean Spray. Simply put, there may be a limit to the types of product innovations that a certain agricultural product can undergo to stimulate demand. On top of that, all the products reviewed have been subject to increasing international competition, as production and branding techniques naturally disseminate.

It is near impossible to limit the spread of basic innovation, but R&D, extension, and training are, by definition, collective public goods, requiring a larger organization for support. Most significant is the desire to establish control over vertical integration. In doing so, growers are able to establish some modicum of capture from the processing and distribution end, where they would otherwise be held hostage. For example, we have discussed the challenges orange growers faced in the early 1890s, when they had no vertical control. Of course, when prices are high and supply tight, the situation is not so dire, but over the long run, it seems most growers see the wisdom of being part of a more stabilizing organization. As we see with each of the above brands, the growers are effectively delegating this portion of the supply chain to a hired agent (acting on their behalf), thus internalizing a transaction, one in which they as individuals would otherwise have very limited bargaining power. This allows for potential economies of scale in processing and distribution that would otherwise be available to only the largest growers. Welch's innovation in bottling and packing, Sun-Maid's in drying, and Sunkist's in refrigeration are soon matched by others, as with Ocean Spray's innovation, but it is the large organization itself that is able to invest in developing the R&D and its applications in the first place. Arguably, the most important value farmers receive for their joint efforts is marketing, that is, the brand, which helps create consumer awareness, increasing demand and the size of the market through using it for horizontal innovation of new product lines. As with Ocean Spray, Sun-Maid's brand and iconic illustration are synonymous with its product.

Similar unresolved issues apply across these cases in common with Ocean Spray. The issue of how to set the purchase price is foremost. If a cooperative sets too high a price, it will gain members and loyalty, but also create incentives for surplus production and independent free riders. If the cooperative company sets prices too low, it will create internal dissonance and lose members. More importantly, even if it remains a dominant presence, no large company can ignore market forces. Supply has to adjust to meet demand. Even if a company like Ocean Spray can provide temporary "shock absorbers" for downturns, it cannot continue to lose money. For example, in the previous marketing order during the 2000s, Ocean Spray had to absorb the majority of the dumping of concentrate. Happily, it has been able to pay down much of its debt during the recent price spike. Mueller, Helmberger, and Paterson state that Sunkist's goal is to be a "barometric price leader"; it does not seek to set prices but "to *discover* market-clearing prices" (1987, 115; emphasis original). Like cranberries, Welch's jams, jellies, and juices (along with Sunkist) are buffeted by slack juice sales and concerns about sugar content; adding a line of sparkling juice is only a salve. The lesson is that Ocean Spray should stay away from using superior prices as a loyalty inducement for its members, which is a losing game in the long run. It should rely on its contributions to R&D, value added (including creating new products), and market development featuring its brand to make its value proposition. That means in the short run it might have to engage in "supply correction," as painful as that might be. Ocean Spray's recent raising of quality standards is an indirect way of doing this, but is likely to be relatively ineffective and create distortionary resentment among members. Quality does seem to be improving, but it should be driven by buyers. For example, fresh fruit growers in Washington mentioned the need to meet "global gap fresh" quality standards required by large buyers such as Kroger and Walmart. Moreover, some informants state that Ocean Spray is introducing new minimal amounts for contracts; this could eliminate some of the smaller growers who are hanging on to legacy bogs. Demand growth is an obvious, but not a sure, solution. As in cranberries, Sun-Maid has moved into greater diversification in health snacks and cereals, as a way to move beyond its fresh segment, but this makes capture of the distribution more challenging, as diverse companies control these secondary or derivative products. None of the brands seem to have resolved in a satisfactory way differences in quality, with growers paid by quantity as long as they meet certain standards. In combining fruit for sale, it seems hard to avoid this, unless one raises quality standards across the board, as Ocean Spray recently has.

By far the largest and most diversified company, Land O'Lakes, stands out from the rest in regard to its seeming ability to keep members aboard amid low price conditions. We have reviewed at least three strategies that allow for this. The first is a continued horizontal diversification, acquiring other competitors, such as the dairy producers on the West Coast and Purina feed line, in the last few decades. This increases potential economies of scope, diversifies earnings to potentially ride out low prices in one segment, and might give one the levers to manage supply, as well as free riders, better. The second is a serious effort at vertical integration, including becoming an R&D, seed, fertilizer, and agricultural consulting firm as well as a distributor. This gives the company a knowledge base across its industries that is hard for individual farmers or distributors to compete with. The third is the embrace of internationalization, to the point where the company now operates in fifty countries and competes for government international development contracts. Thus, instead of reacting to the threat of internationalization, it seeks to turn the challenge on its head, to use its advantages to become a global company. As we see in the discussion of Sunkist's decision to start importing fruit, moving in the direction of Land O'Lakes is extremely complex—the governance issues multiply manyfold from those of Ocean Spray, across members, industries, and countries, and may provide insights into a long-term evolutionary path for cranberries, at a time when they are produced in greater quantities outside of North America. Clearly, all these cases deserve more investigation.

Chapter 7
Conclusion, Recommendations, and Implications for Agricultural Industry Organization[1]

SURVEY PRESENTATION AND ANALYSIS

From December 2021 to February 2022, we conducted a survey of cranberry growers and handlers. The survey was anonymized, though participation was encouraged by offering random draws of sixteen $50 Amazon gift cards. The CMC, APCQ, the BCCMC, and the Wisconsin Cranberry Board all sent an e-mail with the link for the survey to their members. The survey was translated into French for Québec growers. Unfortunately, only forty-six responses were received, and therefore it is not possible to reach any clear conclusions about growers' perceptions, or to do cross-tabulations to tease out possible explanations for differences in opinion about the state of the industry. Nonetheless, we present some highlights from the survey, which overall reinforce the points made through the rest of this analysis.

- Approximately 80% of the responses were from individual business owners (growers), rather than individuals working for companies. The average acreage size was 1,145 acres, and average annual barrels was 74,230. About 70% of respondents said that they belonged to Ocean Spray; however, 43% said that they also sold independently, indicating that a significant percentage sell to both Ocean Spray and independently.
- The average number of years in the business for individuals was twenty-nine and for their families fifty-two years, reinforcing the intergenerational nature of most respondents as family enterprises.
- Just 20% of the respondents sell directly to customers, reinforcing the importance of supply chain partners made in chapter 2, and the central role of the cooperative.

---

[1] Opinions expressed are those of the authors alone, on the basis of the previous analysis, and do not express any factual claims.

In terms of profitability, 35% said that their businesses were always profitable; 54% said sometimes; another 11% said not yet. The "always" proportion is larger than one would expect, given the commodity cycles of cranberries, and perhaps reflects a stronger staying power in the industry than indicated by the more pessimistic patterns in the interviews. The relatively high number may also reflect the high proportion of Ocean Spray respondents. Even if we accept these rough estimates, it suggests that over half the industry suffers from the commodity price cycle curse.

Respondents' opinions on whether there is an oversupply situation were almost evenly split, with 49% agreeing that there is. One person commented, "The industry needs to be regulated by the CMC or entity that can have a forward-looking view of supply and demand the new varieties of vines are being planted at an incredible pace in Wisconsin which in approximately 3 to 5 years will result in catastrophic over supply situation yet the planting is not regulated."

Participants were asked what the most important factors for success are in the industry, ranking a set of factors on a zero-to-ten scale, with ten being the most important. The highest ranked factors (with average scores) were growing conditions (9.1); marketing and branding (8.3); product price (8.2); and access to new knowledge and technologies, and access to national and global markets (both 8.1). This ranking reflects the fact that cranberry growers are not generally responsible for the downstream parts of the supply chain.

When asked about what remedies should be used to deal with oversupply, respondents rated a series of choices along the same ten-point scale. Very few are in favor of taking acreage out (3.5), while, in line with our recommendations, the most favored solutions are to expand overseas markets (9) and to work on new cranberry-based products (8.5). These responses suggest that downsizing the industry to a more healthy supply equilibrium will be a painful process.

In regard to R&D priorities, the highest-ranked priorities are pest (9) and bed management (8.7), which could be concerning for the long term, considering the ability of the industry to invest in activities that would provide resources to expand overseas markets and develop new products. These priority rankings underscore the tension that Ocean Spray management faces in balancing the short-term priorities of growers against long-term industry interests.

When asked from where they receive support, respondents were again asked to rank different actors on a zero-to-ten scale, with zero being unimportant and ten being vital. The actors receiving the highest recognition for support were local fellow growers (8.1) and university extension agents

(8). Ocean Spray received a favorable but weaker score (7.6), while the CI received a rating of just 6.7, the CMC 5.8, and the USDA or AAFC (the Canadian counterpart) just 5.5. Another question asked about the importance of meetings with various actors. Here again the most highly ranked were other individual growers (8.5) and extension agents (8). When asked to rate the importance of geographical location, the average score was 7.4. This reinforces cluster theory's premise about the advantages of colocation—access to and sharing of locally tailored and tacit knowledge.

Question 21 asked about how the industry should be organized; there was no real consensus, with 43.5% suggesting no mandatory industry association, and just 11% favoring one national or global industry association.

When asked about how knowledge spreads across the industry, the highest rated items on the zero-to-ten scale were industry conferences (8.3), agricultural extension (8.2), and industry journals or newsletter (8.1). The lowest ranking items were public sector outreach (5.2), and equipment suppliers and contacts with other industries (both at 5.8).

Finally, respondents were asked about climate change. It is paradoxical to note that 74% said they saw evidence of climate change, but the average rating of its importance was only 4.1. This is in line with other large surveys of general public opinion about climate change.

We cannot take it for granted that the responses of the survey are representative of the industry as a whole, but it is important to note that they largely reinforce the conclusions of the rest of our analysis and of the value of cluster theory to explain the advantages of colocation beyond growing conditions. We turn now to some general implications from chapters 2–6, analyzing the state of the industry.

OCEAN SPRAY'S ROLE UNDER DURESS

The ethos of cooperation in the cranberry industry, built up through historical experience, reinforced by loyalty to a dominant cooperative and major payoffs in terms of product and market innovation, is under threat. The basis of cooperation continues for now. Knowledge is widely and freely shared, though there are some obstacles to cross-border Canada-US cooperation; growers help each other on a regular basis; and most stakeholders work hard to build consensus in the industry for common aims. As discussed in chapter 2, the requirements surrounding processing conditions, as much as the growing conditions and culture of cooperation, help explain geographical clustering. The unique value proposition of Ocean Spray to take all the fruit grown by members and find ways to brand, market, and sell it has helped smooth out normal agricultural cyclicality, mainly through demand innovation, and requires steady investment and effort. As discussed, signs of consolidation of land are found in all the clusters, which signals increasing economies of scale are likely to reduce the number of small family growers. Such transformations would likely have happened sooner were it not for Ocean Spray.

Economies of scale clearly abound in both juice and SDCs, the two main markets, and limit the possibilities for individual growers to become large players in downstream markets. Competitors such as Pappas Lassonde, Refresco (previously Cott), and, until recently, J.M. Smuckers (through its R.W. Knudsen label) have come and gone in attempting to compete with Ocean Spray for many years without affecting its dominance. The same is true in SDCs up to now, such as Wisconsin-based Mariani (among others) creating a niche market share. Similar to Pepsi's play for Ocean Spray in the 1990s, one can also see the possibility of a large SDC buyer such as Nature's Valley or Kellogg's considering backward integration by buying up farms or making competitive offers alongside Ocean Spray's, as had begun to temporarily happen under Northland in the 1990s, before its efforts fell apart. It is also possible that an overseas competitor could eventually begin to compete in the cranberry market, as has been the case with apples. But Ocean Spray has withstood all such challenges through more than half a century.

As discussed in chapter 3, most member interviewees suggested that Ocean Spray has historically built up a great track record as a cooperative, explaining its longevity. The cooperation is most closely reflected at the local level, particularly in Massachusetts and New Jersey, where Ocean Spray started, and the culture of cooperation and knowledge sharing abounds. As in New Jersey and Washington state, several BC growers expressed a fierce loyalty to Ocean Spray. They compared their situation with that of blueberry farmers, who are "at the mercy" of independent processors. They feel like the company represents their interests well, and they express optimism for its future direction. They suggest complaints are from growers not looking at the long-run picture. As one said, "Cranberries are a crop that you have to be in it for multiple generations. . . . You won't get the same returns as other investment vehicles, but they are consistent over the long run." The grower noted that, even while they did not make the "big returns" that independents do during boom periods, Ocean Spray helped stabilize prices for them. Moreover, the grower was happy to "see the trucks loaded" after every harvest and to not have to worry about it afterward, allowing them to do what they are passionate about—farming. The person, like other Ocean Spray loyalists, suggested that they found the spirit of cooperation unique in agriculture, so "we're not competing with each other" like other farmers and "we're in it together." This means they are open to sharing information and feel a sense of community as part of a larger operation.

At the same time, our conclusion is that it is good to have some share of independents, to keep Ocean Spray honest and to react more flexibly and innovatively to market opportunities. In fact, many interviewees pointed out that, even as Ocean Spray is challenged by independents, it is still the dominant force in the market. They pointed out that the oversupply conditions come from decisions during the high prices of the 1990s. The result happened in good part because Ocean Spray sought to expand production by some 5,000 acres, underestimating the yields of the new varietals and of independents' equal response to expand acreage. This means that, beyond their dominance in marketing, R&D, and industry institutions, Ocean Spray's lack of a clear plan for managing supply actually contributes to the roller-coaster conditions. Part of this may be its challenges with holding back its own growers who want to expand during high prices, even though they are happy to be part of the organization's stability when prices are low. This is another paradox of a grower-run management team.

Québec's entrance to the market in the 1990s has provided the largest growth in the independent segment ever seen. As discussed, Québec provides evidence of how supportive policy, including crucial financial and R&D support, helped stimulate industry growth even when Ocean Spray showed faint interest.

It is not clear at what point the growth of independent production supersedes the ability of Ocean Spray to continue to provide industry leadership. More pointedly, there are concerns for the future regarding the industry's ability to find the next new product or market for cranberry demand growth to resolve the oversupply issue. Given the post-COVID-19 cranberry supply issues and spike in health-related demand for cranberries, many growers in the industry are basking in the high prices of 2021–2022, forgetting about the long history of roller-coaster prices. Even as prices have spiked, so have prices for inputs, so the industry is not making more money. Similarly, "short crops" over these two years have reduced supply, meaning that, even while prices are higher, there are fewer cranberries to sell. In fact, the temporary supply constraints are likely to induce faster consolidation of growing areas. So, the key question for our analysis is how to evolve industry organization to deal with the need for Ocean Spray to coexist with emerging large independent growers and handlers.

Most independent growers and handlers acknowledge the central importance of Ocean Spray for the industry, even as they cherish their freedom to work as individuals. It has been the provider of public goods for cranberry processing, demand growth, and lobbying efforts. It is the central figure in marketing cranberries and expanding overseas markets. Ocean Spray provides its own R&D and extension support, in addition to being a crucial funder to state-level efforts. It also helps stabilize the incomes of cranberry grower-members, sometimes to its own long-term detriment. One Massachusetts grower, echoing what we heard in all of the clusters, relayed how he had tried for many years to get into Ocean Spray, and felt a sense of relief at "finally getting in," because it provided price premiums and a greater sense of stability. Tensions seem to arise principally from independent growers not being able to "get in" to Ocean Spray, as well as some resentment at its market power.

As discussed, Ocean Spray does the bulk of cranberry marketing, but its very size means it has limitations. It has been slower than independents to develop niche products such as 100% juice and supplements, to develop overseas markets, and to find a coherent strategy regarding the health benefits of cranberries. As of this writing, independents seem to be distinguishing themselves from Ocean Spray in a number of innovative niche products, such as developing unsweetened dried cranberries. One low-hanging opportunity is to consider how to better promote cranberry consumption in North America. Wisconsin, Québec, BC, and Massachusetts all have fledgling local marketing programs, but they are underfunded and do not seem tied to any coherent strategy. There is, moreover, a lack of hard data or studies on how to market cranberries in other areas of lower consumption, such as the Southeast. The CMC could in theory play a leading role, but some claim it has not had the resources or capability to step up to the task. Others suggest it is the internal organization of the CMC that is the problem. Several growers express doubt about reform of the CMC. Ocean Spray still dominates in resources, and so it will tend to focus them on its own internal strategy, according to interviewees.

The flip side of having a very large industry cooperative, one that has undergone a number of management shifts, is that it is difficult to reach consensus around industry efforts with potential and long-term payoffs, making decision-making and innovation challenging. Smaller niches, such as fresh cranberries, may be neglected. Overall, we should see the current interplay of Ocean Spray and independents as a generally healthy industrial ecosystem, one that allows for collective goods and innovation through competition—the best of both worlds. The arrangement of Ocean Spray dominance with independent input is a tenuous balance reflected in current US-based industry institutions, from the CMC to the CI.

But this balance is very fragile, and the likely further diminution of Ocean Spray's relative position means that new institutions are needed to create collective action, particularly ones that improve joint efforts between the large Québec producers and Ocean Spray. Multiple interviewees stated flatly that the CMC is dysfunctional, unable to reach agreement on a strategy, and underfunded. The rivalry between independents and Ocean Spray appears to have hamstrung the CMC. As one interviewee stated, "The people on that board [of the CMC] are not collaborative. They are fighting over things that happened twenty years ago. They can't take their hats off at the door and say what's best for the industry." On the other side, some claimed Ocean Spray (understandably) does not fully commit to CMC and CI because they have their own significant marketing and research arms. Regardless of the ultimate cause, the CMC has not been able to really develop overseas markets beyond consulting reports that begin to explore them.

One can see, furthermore, the potential benefits of a cross-border coordinated research and marketing effort, as well as lobbying to mollify the barriers to cross-border supply management, which is an accepted agricultural principle in both countries. We are not so naïve to think such institutions will arise organically. Why would Québec producers contribute to a joint effort in the short run when they see other producers, including Ocean Spray, as competitors and have developed their own R&D and marketing systems? Moreover, they can free ride on any innovations that Ocean Spray develops. But both parties would gain by cooperating on long-term collective goods, such as developing new markets and joint funding and cooperation in R&D.

Perhaps the most important catalyst for cooperation is the fact that supply management via USDA marketing orders is no longer possible, even though both the United States and Canada have individual supply management policies. What is missing is the policy push to develop a workaround, which, after all, is in the best interests of both countries. Beyond this immediate challenge is the need to rethink the cranberry support institutions beyond Ocean Spray so that they can more effectively reflect industry interests across borders. This includes the Cranberry Marketing Committee (CMC), the Wisconsin Cranberry Board, and the Cranberry Institute (CI), as well as all the cluster-based support institutions, including growers' associations.

UPDATING INDUSTRY INSTITUTIONS TO COORDINATE QUÉBEC AND OCEAN SPRAY

As a starting point, there are some positive reviews of recent activities of the CI, which includes participation of handlers in Québec. Interviewees could not explain why the CI functions more smoothly than CMC, other than being a function of personalities and handlers "checking their hat at the door." It is, of course, much easier to manage a smaller group of handlers than the larger group of growers and handlers who are part of the CMC. Even so, the CI and Cranberry Research Foundation come nowhere near fulfilling the needs of the industry at present. Informal coordination does already occur in horticulture and agricultural research; however, a more formal and concerted effort in new products and marketing is needed that may be beyond Ocean Spray's capability to tackle industry issues at this point, such as expanding overseas markets and defining health benefits.

At present, most of the research has focused on improving growing techniques and new varietals, reflecting the grower-heavy management of the CI and CMC and, behind them, of Ocean Spray. It is understandable that growers would like to bet on sure things, and they know improved productivity will pay off for them right away. That Ocean Spray growers focus on investments that will benefit them as individual farmers is understandable, but it reflects a fundamental contradiction at the heart of Ocean Spray, which simultaneously seeks to maximize prices for growers and minimize prices for processing. This explains the debt Ocean Spray found themselves in during the early 2000s, by paying prices above those of the market. More fundamentally, do growers, who run the board, really understand product development and marketing, or can they see long-term potential in product development, marketing, and research that might require a decade or more of funding? Most industry observers say no, and imply that a grower-run organization is inhibited from thinking of long-term strategy or providing the space for marketing and production innovation, which inherently require risk. They point to the dissension and underfunding within cranberry industry institutions that results in underinvestment in long-term industry collective goods. However, a few interviewees noted that, in spite of the inherent contradiction of a cooperative management team running Ocean Spray, the growers had been quite capable of finding enough smart representatives among themselves to manage the company. The recent volatility of management changes at Ocean Spray, as well as the longevity of, and fierce loyalty to, the company, reflects such contradictions.

To realize efforts on the marketing side and to raise sufficient funding to develop new markets would require coordination with independents in Québec. This step requires both the independents and Ocean Spray to recognize that there are benefits to partnering on generic marketing of cranberries, especially to develop new demand in overseas markets. According to interviewees, the culture and governance of the CMC would need to be reformed to develop the levies and deeper investments to do the job properly. More importantly, serious reforms in the contribution system would be needed to raise an adequate budget for serious global marketing efforts. This has been stymied thus far by Ocean Spray's priority to market its own products. This is where marketing to develop new demand and new products needs to be distinguished from marketing existing products. One interviewee noted that the raisin and prune industry spend ten times more on marketing, and several mentioned the almond industry as a potential example of how industry came together to provide more collective funding. Several Wisconsin interviewees suggested that the state could serve as an example of how to create harmony between Ocean Spray and the independents. A note of caution is in order, before completely abandoning the CMC, which does bring together US-based independents and Ocean Spray under a common umbrella to discuss supply issues and, perhaps more importantly, is the main data source of industry trends. Such functions need to be in place through a substitute.

Research coordination, on the other hand, is not inhibited, but it requires a much more agile and well-funded CI that can spur cranberry researchers to coordinate across borders, and perhaps some concerted lobbying to get large funding agencies and universities' attention. CI could seek grants in the US that build on and coordinate with the more generous support systems in Québec. One can imagine National Science Foundation grants, for example, providing a lot of public funds alongside private-sector ones on health issues; if matched with Canadian funding sources, a lot more could be accomplished. There are obstacles, in the sense that Canadian and US funding agencies generally discourage funding of international (nondomestic) teams. Some efforts to create cross-border funding agencies/grants would go a long way, as would potential pooling of industry funding, such as a joint APCQ-Québec-Cranberry Institute research ground, which might help to bridge such gaps. The industry clearly does *not* take advantage of all the opportunities offered to it at the national levels in Canada and the United States, including NSERC and NSF, respectively, funding sources that would vastly multiply research possibilities. The same is true for joint marketing efforts between Ocean Spray and the independents, which are nonexistent. Arguably, the time is right for a slow shift from Ocean Spray providing collective leadership toward a more institutional framework. The process will be evolutionary and still require Ocean Spray leadership, but Ocean Spray should not have sole responsibility for industry R&D, marketing, and innovation.

More generally, while overall industry cooperation is holding for the moment, there does not seem to be a long-term strategic vision for the industry, as reflected in the turnover in Ocean Spray management and the unclear plans around the persistent oversupply situation in the 2000s. As shown in chapter 4, production and productivity differences across the North American clusters are growing; these are bound to increase the strain on Ocean Spray as an actor who can combine interests. Moreover, perhaps because of Ocean

Spray's past success, policy support at both the state and federal levels is weak. As discussed above, Massachusetts has not enacted most of the support requested by the revitalization task force. New Jersey interviewees lauded their close relationship with Rutgers and directly support its activities but report a distance and even negative impacts from state policymakers. USDA supports the industry through the marketing order, but its export promotion assistance seems haphazard, and CMC is too poorly funded to make enough headway in an efficient manner to develop overseas markets.

The success of Québec in developing exports highlights the deficiencies of US efforts, but also speaks to the potential for joint efforts to do much more than deliver consulting reports. Most concerning is the low level and disconcerted efforts to fund R&D in the industry, with no significant ongoing industry support from federal agencies whose mission is to fund research, such as NIH (National Institutes of Health). In health research, such efforts would require far more resources than are presently available in the CMC and CI.

NEW WAYS TO MANAGE COMMODITY CYCLES IN BOTH SUPPLY AND DEMAND

The long-term oversupply situation is related in good part to fast productivity increases in Wisconsin and, more particularly, to the massive increases in Québec. Most growers in Québec are independent, thus Ocean Spray has limited ability to influence the fastest-growing source of supply, with the province moving toward becoming the second-largest cranberry producer. Thus, future marketing orders and the influence of Ocean Spray on supply is increasingly circumscribed. One observer stated, "Ocean Spray was the big gorilla that you needed approval from, to do anything. These guys (in Québec) said, we don't need it." As another long-term industry insider put it, "The industry has shifted and will [continue to] shift [in location]." In their opinion, locational supply chain advantages related to processing and transport costs will not be enough to revive the fortunes in Massachusetts and New Jersey, though growing will continue there, in consolidated form. Moreover, Québec has its own independent handlers as well as an Ocean Spray facility, so processing is not an impediment.

Several experts stated that if the same water and fertilizer management and farm renovation techniques were applied to Massachusetts and Wisconsin, their yields would start to approach those of Québec, thus positing that it is technology and adoption, and not natural comparative advantage, that is responsible for success. But this does not jibe with the basic issue around growing conditions and economies of scale discussed in chapter 2. Moreover, other experts are skeptical about long-term prospects for New Jersey, Massachusetts,

Washington, and Oregon, because the temperatures are too warm and will increase due to climate change. Problems are even worse in New Jersey and Massachusetts thanks to higher humidity levels. Interviewees from all regions reported increased volatility of weather and extreme weather events. In Wisconsin, for example, interviewees reported an alternation of cold snaps and earlier warm temperatures and intense bursts of precipitation that bring plants out of dormancy too early over the past few years. A few mentioned the possibility of climate change also affecting pollination; this aligns with general concerns in agriculture surrounding pollination, including the costs and activities of using bees. Many growers suggested that weather volatility is linked to the "short" (lower) production crops of 2021–2022.

The newer varietals are sure to increase the overall supply even if acreage remains largely stagnant. One 2020 study suggests that Ocean Spray's volume will likely increase from 7.1 million to 8 million barrels soon (Ference and Company Consulting 2020, 109), though variations are normal. On the other side, several growers in these lagging regions see the new, higher-yielding varietals as a saving grace that will allow them to stay in the black on the financial side. Moreover, as discussed previously, for most of them, land is paid off and its sale for other uses is restricted by agricultural preservation and wetlands regulations. Thus, it is understandable that families who have been growing cranberries the same basic ways for generations would be harder to convince. Yet, demonstration effects within the cluster through expanding use of the test farms in each of the clusters could go a long way toward improving productivity in the United States (outside of Wisconsin, where it's already high). However, policy support for such experimentation in the lagging states is lacking. Such support could include policies for exit and consolidation to make larger and more economical farms.

One clear path on price consistency would be to shift the basic operating principle of Ocean Spray away from paying for any amount of crop produced on a certain amount of acreage toward agreeing to purchase only a certain amount of volume per farmer. This, however, would be a huge shift in the industry and have negative effects on productivity and innovation incentives for growers. Interviewees note that Ocean Spray is increasing quality requirements as well as lowering its price. Some say that this is due to lower quality of new varietals, while others suggest that it is a way for Ocean Spray to reduce supply. Either way, it is creating resentment in the industry, and perhaps a broader conversation about a potential chronic oversupply situation is in order. Perhaps more alarming still is the fact that the much higher productivity of the new varietals will further increase supply, thus pushing toward consolidation along with many other discussed factors in the industry. Across the states where subjects were interviewed, with the exception of New Jersey, where land is limited, consolidation is a fact, with a few large growers buying out the smaller ones leaving the business, and many others simply leaving their farms fallow. An interviewee in Oregon said he estimated that there were at least thirty farms for sale now, "and those are just the ones advertised." The ones consolidating in Oregon are the independents who went early into processing (thus allowing them to fill larger orders) and paid off the capital for such equipment while prices were high. Any number of growers stated that they would sell immediately if they could get a fair price, as their kids did not want to take over the farms. One said, "We grew cranberries to raise our kids, and we taught them that doing anything else would be [pay] better." Many are so close to retirement age that they have no options, and they are hanging on as long as they can. Interviewees across the clusters noted ominously that lower prices lead to more farm renovation and introducing new varietals, to increase productivity, which, ironically leads to even more supply. As one Washington grower remarked, in noting that a recent freeze had reduced BC production, "We are one crop away from another crisis."

In terms of developing new markets, especially for higher-cost producers such as Massachusetts and New Jersey, there are still the cluster advantages of proximity to the large East Coast markets to reduce their transportation costs and already-paid-off land and sometimes equipment. Indeed, some growers there are trying to diversify beyond Ocean Spray, to perhaps find a niche in the farm-to-table movement, for direct sales. During our visits, we saw some working in fresh/frozen, and some producing new types of products such as cranberry honey. While cranberry wine does not have much traction, we have seen very successful berry-based liqueurs in Scandinavia, and that might be worth the effort.

Where would significant additional demand potentially come from? This is the central question for the future of the industry. Other products such as milk and almonds in the United States have general industry promotion. Some suggested that market growth will come primarily in the dried fruit category, but there are no good data to back up this claim, and many interviewees suggested an oversupply in this category as well. There are some laudable efforts to promote exports and to facilitate them. One Wisconsin handler suggested that about half of their production was going overseas, but they had no help from government or the CMC in developing such markets. Québec handlers also said that they operated largely on their own. As one large East Coast grower noted, they have frequent tourists to their farms; many are from overseas, such as the UK, and are always asking why can't they find the same variety of cranberry products on their shelves as they found on the tour? In short, on both the domestic and global levels, a polished and targeted marketing campaign to improve cranberry demand is called for. The CMC should look to coordinate better with USDA, Ocean Spray, the growing states, and the Canadian government, around a coordinated demand-enhancement campaign. It is not clear why the CMC decided to focus almost exclusively on China and India, markets that are large but extremely complicated to enter and thrive in and, in the case of the former, are fraught with geopolitics. It makes sense to look beyond the shiny object of China and toward a larger global marketing strategy, including Latin America and other parts of Asia with sizable consumer markets. All these smaller markets together would outweigh the one large prize in China. Frankly, a lot more marketing data around untapped markets, particularly consumer demographics and cultural and culinary predispositions, are needed to create a proper global strategy. Ocean Spray has these, but they do not share them to inform global strategy. It might well make more sense to grow existing markets such as Japan or the EU, where cranberries are already consumed in significant quantities, through extending types of consumption, a depth versus breadth strategy, in the short run, when the industry desperately needs more demand growth. As one interviewee from the handler community noted, "The industry tends to be reactive to consumer demand, rather than proactive in seeking new growth."

Since Canadian producers are not subject to the Chinese or EU tariffs, their market share is likely to continue to increase. Yet, Canadian producers state that the Canadian government does not do much beyond allowing them to present their goods at trade shows. This suggests the possibility down the road that Ocean Spray may have differing internal interests among US and Canadian members, so ensuring harmonization will take some effort. It is interesting to note here the loyalty of most Wisconsin Ocean Spray growers to their counterparts on the coast. So far, Ocean Spray and the industry generally are unwilling to invest enough into academic research that could potentially validate health claims and hugely expand the market. They could be afraid of negative results, but they are also ignoring the most logical path to growing the market.

Some projections suggest the SDC market alone could grow from $170 million in 2018 to $256 million by 2027 (Ference and Company Consulting 2020, 128). Yet, here again, the industry does not have a coordinated global strategy. Unfortunately, Ocean Spray's current financial condition appears to prevent a major new marketing push, and the changeover in management, according to interviewees, has led to prevarication in terms of an overall marketing strategy. While the famous TikTok viral video of a person singing "Dreams" by Fleetwood Mac in 2020 while drinking an Ocean Spray product is widely lauded in the industry, its importance reinforces the conclusion: there is no clear vision for how to market the strategy or the overall brand identity. This is reflected in the so far unsuccessful forays into a vitamin-water type product under previous CEO Papadellis. Interviewees suggest that market penetration is fairly complete in the EU, but we could not find adequate data to check this claim. According to interviewees, the CMC's previous efforts led to some market gains in Mexico, and more recent efforts have focused on China and India. Neither market accepts any significant amount of exports (see table 4.4), but interviewees cite sales in China that were enabled by CMC efforts and are hopeful for the same in India. The CMC, and the industry as a whole, has high hopes for the Chinese market, as health concerns, particularly about *H. pylori* (a digestive tract disease) is a larger concern. Moreover, Chinese consumers are reportedly more open to tart flavors and favor deep red fruit, as is the reputation of West Coast cranberries. One Oregon handler who exports there says there is no way that China will be able to satisfy domestic demand even if they start growing their own. He sees big possibilities for markets in India as well. However, the Trump trade war led to retaliatory tariffs on cranberries, both in the EU and in China. The Chinese tariffs have been reduced, but are still a major impediment, even though partly dampened in the short term by compensation from the US government.

Another logical alternative would be to diversify to other crops and income sources. As noted above, Ocean Spray made earlier forays into the grapefruit market, but seems to have truncated further development. Co-op members seem to be resistant, based on the grapefruit experience. This is understandable, as the growing conditions and locations are quite different for the crops. Lowbush blueberries, however, are grown in most of the cranberry cluster locations. However, they are not a common farm crop, and, as we discussed in chapter 2, each unique cluster, plant, and product requires detailed and ongoing efforts to acquire information and advance improvement. Moreover, interviewees pointed out that developing a cranberry farm requires a unique transformation of land and heavy sunk investments, conditions not easily transformed into a blueberry environment. Once the cranberry bog gets to a certain size, maintenance is a full-time job. Many farmers nonetheless have a second income, either through a spouse or through a second job. The nature of cranberry land makes it unsuitable, according to many growers, for other crops. But that wouldn't prevent them or larger cranberries companies from diversifying by buying suitable adjacent land. As noted earlier, Ocean Spray had previously attempted to diversify to include grapefruits, and their current lines also include blueberries. One could see them therefore acquiring other dried fruit lines, as has Mariani, or even developing their own product lines such as granola cereal and bars that use cranberries, but this would require growers to think outside the box, and give more leeway to Ocean Spray management.

Many struggle to simply diversify to local retail cranberry products. So, while it certainly makes sense for both farmers and Ocean Spray to consider crop diversification, their caution is also understandable. After all, only cranberries are mostly limited to North America, and therefore offer the supply control and collective action discussed throughout this report, at least up to now.

Agritourism is also being pushed by some growers, with positive results so far in Massachusetts and New Jersey, though a few are resistant to the idea, stating that it is outside their area of expertise and would interfere with their ability to harvest efficiently. There are ads for participating in cranberry harvests in Massachusetts and New Jersey. However, there does not seem to be a concerted effort to organize public campaigns around this. A public campaign such as that which occurs in the wine industry would posit a cranberry farm visit as part of a tourist package. It might include a retail tasting store with various cranberry-based items, fresh cranberries, and other souvenirs. More importantly, both the Massachusetts and New Jersey growers are quite close to tourist destinations along the coast, so there could be possibilities of conducting tours during the summer peak tourist season. These things sound good in theory but in reality are very hard to execute. Most of the growers interviewed are loath to enter the tourist industry; it's not part of their personality type. As one Oregon handler suggested, the (independent Oregon) "cranberry grower nowadays needs two hats, one to farm, and one for marketing. And most people can't handle the marketing part." Another told the story of a local grower who started to pack her own fruit and sell it at local farmers' markets around the state. "She got so tired of doing the marketing part, she finally decided to go back to report keeping." Another pointed out that a grower could not sell fresh fruit to a local Safeway, "because he would have to have enough to sell to all the Safeways in the region." Besides the huge volumes and ultra-consistent product that large retailers require to achieve economies of scale, numerous regulations pertaining to food product sales at the retail level create another effective deterrent for most growers and handlers trying to capture more of the downstream supply chain. Simply put, there are no real opportunities in the middle, between individual or small-batch sales and large retail outlets.

Ocean Spray could do much more to take full advantage of growing consumer concerns about large corporations and the desire to have some connection with producers, reflected by the growing fair/sustainable trade movements. Growers are now featured on the back of bottles, but the message is not coming through that they are part of a co-op. Ocean Spray is the premier example of grower cooperation, rather than corporate dominance, and its status as a co-op could be a major selling point, as reflected in past campaigns depicting farmers in farms. The campaigns could reflect the arduous loyalty of many multigenerational Ocean Spray growers. In general, more marketing research is needed to better hone the message for the millennial and subsequent generations of consumers. These consumers are increasingly ethically conscious about production methods, and an anticorporate message could resonate if paired with a health message. It could be that the lane markers against less sweet cranberries held, by common industry wisdom, in both juice and SDCs might soften, given the general health consciousness of younger generations. Moves in that direction are needed to cash in on the health message of the industry.

FINALLY PROVING HEALTH BENEFITS

The industry now needs to decide whether it is willing to take that next step in promoting cranberries as a health product. The upside is huge, but uncertain, and a de-emphasis on the juice blends central to the Ocean Spray product line would be painful. This is where the independents come in. Their lesser interest in blended juice means they are more likely to innovate in trying to develop healthier juice and SDC products, with less sugar (and calories). Even if such efforts succeed in creating great new products, unless the industry is united on the same marketing page, it will be very difficult for the average consumer to truly distinguish between the healthy, more healthy, and traditional cranberry products. Some juice blends reportedly have 5% or less of cranberry content. The industry should shift toward more standardized labeling if it wants to enhance the health appeal of higher or 100% blends. Many health-conscious consumers (including the authors) are willing to adapt to a more tart flavor if it comes with significant personal benefits. By personal observation, one can see that the introduction of sugar-free chocolates and candies and sodas has become mainstream. The same strategy could work absolute wonder in supplements as well, a growing market where the average consumer is in the dark as to product quality.

Many interviewees would like to see a reset of the investments into health research, which could act as a demand trigger. They would like to see Ocean Spray become the champion for arm's-length research that would dispel what they see as unfair criticism of the health benefits of cranberries, which they say have a proven record in reducing *H. pylori* and urinary tract infections. Health experts working on cranberries similarly decry the unregulated use of cranberries in supplements, as well as attempts to use concentrate by-products from sweetened dried cranberries, as they likely lack the key anti-infection ingredients of cranberries that could, if properly sourced, reduce the current overuse of antibiotics. Whether true or not, a large number of interviewees said that the health market reports—that SDC-derived juice does not provide the same health benefits as fresh cranberry juice—taint the branding of cranberry juice in general. Interviewees suggested that Ocean Spray's previous sponsorship of health research backfired amid negative media coverage of the fact that new health claims were tied directly to Ocean Spray sponsorship of the research and placement of personnel as authors, creating the appearance of a conflict of interest. This swirl of claims deserves more independent scrutiny, as it currently has the potential to undercut research studies as well as the health brand of cranberries more generally.

Much of this strategy, in turn, depends on health claims, which require much more research. The CMC sponsored a recent study in China on the effectiveness of cranberries in reducing *H. pylori*, but early assessments are that the studies may have flaws and the results are otherwise not definitive. According to the NIH website, there is potential for cranberry to help with "bladder, stomach, and liver disorders, as well as diabetes, wounds, and other conditions," and "urinary tract infections." However,

> There's still some uncertainty about the effectiveness of cranberry because some of the research has not been of high quality. Also, studies in certain populations at increased risk of UTIs, such as elderly people in long-term care and pregnant women, have had inconsistent results, and studies in other high-risk populations, such as women undergoing gynecological surgeries or people with multiple sclerosis, have not found cranberry to be beneficial. (NIH nd)

Thus, the same website notes that the Food and Drug Administration, as of 2020, now permits producers to claim there is "limited evidence" of health benefits in cranberries. In a recent article, Zhao, Liu, and Gu (2020) state that cranberries could potentially help with a variety of ailments beyond UTI and digestive health, including cardiac issues and cancer; however, "clinical trials with improved study design are urgently needed to demonstrate cranberries' benefits on urinary tract health and cardiometabolic diseases. Hypothesis-driven studies using animals or cell culture are needed to elucidate the mechanisms of cranberries' effects on digestive health."

FINDING NEW WAYS TO FUND AND CHANNEL INDUSTRY R&D AND MARKETING

We could not find an exact funding breakdown for the extension centers in Massachusetts, Wisconsin, and New Jersey, or for projects funded by the Cranberry Institute or Cranberry Marketing Committee. However, the number of personnel and the descriptions of the activities and projects given suggest a woeful shortage of funding for the industry, exacerbated by reported cutbacks by Ocean Spray of their research budget. Having CI operate on a voluntary sponsorship basis obviously leads to inadequate funding. Conducting annual fundraisers on the state level, in addition to local levies and stringing together small amounts of grants from CMC, Ocean Spray, and the Cranberry Institute, is simply not being adequately matched by public funding to conduct the long-term research needed to renovate the industry. Because Ocean Spray conducts its own product and marketing R&D, the knowledge produced there is proprietary, though knowledge tends to diffuse over time. Nonetheless, interviewees across clusters are concerned about having more funding for the Cranberry Institute, in order to engage in larger research projects, including health. It should be easier, in theory, for the CI to gain matching public funding as a neutral nonprofit institute. It would be useful for it to more proactively seek out long-term funding alliances, for example, with NIH and major universities beyond its current partners. At the moment, there appears to be limited ability to take advantage of major revolutions in genomics or GIS (geographic innovation systems) innovations or to deal with long-term threats such as climate change that would provide systematic data beyond breeding to identify varietal performance, including mapping out susceptibility to pests on the basis of micro-conditions (e.g., weather, climate, temperature, precipitation, and the like).

While individual researchers in Rutgers and Wisconsin are working on genetic mapping of the cranberry, this is not proportionate to the potential offered by such technologies, such as the ability to produce less acidic varietals. Early attempts appear to produce berries without the cranberry taste, of which "tart" is a key element. Climate change could be a gradual factor affecting growing practices because of the changes it might bring to cranberry cycles, which are highly dependent on temperature, from ripening to freezing to breaking out of dormancy, all of which must take place in a certain temperature range. Moreover, cranberries require ready access to fresh water; climate change could affect water levels. For instance, interviewees in Washington state reported drier growing seasons, and New Jersey growers increasing pest and rot issues. Oregon growers are concerned about prolonged dry seasons and earlier rises in temperatures. Higher temperatures will also bring greater incidence of rot, though no clear data yet links climate change with these claims. New Jersey has had rot problems for many years. Québec experts say that their harvest time is starting to come earlier. Wisconsin researchers state that increased volatility of weather conditions can stress plants, and that developing more temperature-variation tolerant varietals may be needed. Growers are always concerned about excessively warm summers and heavy precipitation events, which can increase fruit rot, and early warm spells in winter, which can bring plants temporarily out of dormancy, but then make them susceptible to freezing.

Despite these signs, Gareau et al. (2020), in a survey of Massachusetts growers, find little evidence of cluster discussion or adjustments to growing techniques; the industry is focused on immediate priorities. When asked about climate change, most growers and industry experts said that weather conditions are always changing, and there are not enough observational patterns to reach any conclusions. The same can be said about the blindness among policymakers and the lack of research projects on climate change in agriculture more generally, as growers' concerns, like election cycles, are focused on much shorter-term issues. Researchers in the key centers in Wisconsin, Laval, and Rutgers all seem to focus on growing conditions, which provides an immediate benefit to the key lobbying group for R&D, cranberry growers in their states and province.

But scientific research focused purely on agriculture does not address the long-term supply and demand challenges we have discussed. All it does is improve productivity, exacerbating supply imbalances in the absence of attention to the other forces in the industry. Universities and their scientific researchers are too well-connected to change the conditions of the game whereby they capture the bulk of cranberry funding. Scientific researchers at Ocean Spray and the leading universities repeatedly stated in interviews that the funding should continue to focus on growing conditions, such as rot and water management and varietals. Several offered conclusions that Wisconsin and Québec were ahead solely because of greater R&D funding into their local university experts. In fact, the leading research is arguably being done at Rutgers, in a state where the industry is reeling, thus obviating the superficiality of the idea that scientific research alone solves all industry issues, not even considering all the other issues discussed in our analysis, including marketing, supply chains, and commodity cycles. Beyond an understandable myopia common to specialized researchers, this trajectory shows that little effort or interest has been made by any actor in understanding the economics of the industry in order to develop a long-term strategy for industry success. A greater vision and push for research diversification are needed to change funding allocation and push the industry beyond its reactive mode of hoping that Ocean Spray will sort things out with a new market-grabbing product or innovation.

Indeed, we could not find any researchers or long-term funding dedicated to cranberry product innovation and marketing, or overall industry strategy, outside of Ocean Spray's internal efforts, which it did not share with us but which seem rather limited, as reflected in the lack of new product or market success over the last twenty years. One person at Rutgers and two at Wisconsin seem to be managing most of the research on breeding new varietals, a dangerous overreliance. Many of the other personnel at other centers are involved in daily extension activities—an important function, but one that creates tension with the ability to do long-term research. The main pressure for university activities seems to come from state growers' associations, whereas a combined approach, pooling resources, and establishing dedicated cranberry research positions would be more effective, with the understanding that the location of the researcher would not undermine their dedication to the industry as a whole. As one current researcher put it, "We spend most of our time responding to the needs of our local growers, helping them to solve the problems they face on a daily basis. We simply don't have any more bandwidth to undertake long-term research." There are five USDA regional specialists who are supposed to work on cranberries, but they tend to focus on the clusters to which they are assigned. On the other hand, the substantial royalties that Rutgers University and the University of Wisconsin are reaping show that investment in R&D can pay off, and that there needs to be pressure mounted to ensure a reasonable proportion of those royalties are circulated into more research, ensuring a virtuous circle of industry investments and benefits. Particular interest has been directed toward finding biological controls as substitutes for pesticides, which obviously would reduce the costs of organic production.

One solution to consider would be to institute an industry-wide "check off" levy, based on size/profitability/production data from the marketing order, that would fund a joint marketing and research board, which would include representatives from industry, academia, and policy and signal a more serious approach to research and development. This board would effectively combine some of the operations of the Cranberry Institute and the CMC in these areas. This joint organization could be modeled on the triple helix model, as with the wine boards of Australia and New Zealand discussed by Hira (2013b). The difference would be that the dominant presence of Ocean Spray would require an adjustment to the arrangements, to allow its leadership the ability to conduct such activities for its own brand while funneling more resources and efforts into projects that share a common interest, such as researching cranberry health and developing new demand through new product innovation. One big, but surmountable, challenge would be to get the industry to abandon the marketing order, so that Canadian producers can be brought into the fold. This would not be easy, given the reliance for many years on the CMC and the continuing dominance of Ocean Spray, but as we have discussed, the marketing order is no longer effective. More challenging still, Ocean Spray would have to acknowledge that its ability to solve all the problems of the industry is now more limited—not an easy step. Ocean Spray's market share over the past three decades has reportedly declined from 85% to 65%, an estimate shared by multiple interviewees. Ocean Spray needs to adjust its strategy to match this emerging reality, though one suspects it will try to reverse this decline. It is hard to see how a Northland-type scenario would unfold, given the difficulties present in purchasing the quickly growing competition from Québec, where interviewees state acreage is continuing to increase.

The "holy grail" for varietals, as one researcher put it, would be to develop new strains of cranberries that are less acidic and naturally sweeter. Researchers at both Rutgers and University of Wisconsin–Madison are working on this.[2] Natural sweetness would help counter the current anti-sugar sentiment among consumers, though such attitudes ignore all the natural sugars of other juices. If combined with health benefits, in a dual campaign, one could see more palatable versions of cranberry being taken up by the growing numbers of consumers who are concerned about diabetes. After all, non-sweet products have done well in markets over the past decade based on health benefits, such as green tea, maca tea, beet juice, kale, wheatgrass, and spinach, all part of the fresh juice craze. Consumers will adopt all kinds of ingredients if they are tied to health benefits. In fact, 100% cranberry juices (unsweetened) are now available in grocery stores, demonstrating that a market does exist, but so far it is limited.

Long-term research in health to back up product claims requires considerable expense, not only for identifying promising compounds, but also for carrying out large-scale clinical trials. The lack of a health-care team for the industry is concerning, with just one dedicated person at Rutgers who could be identified. There does not appear to be a clear research agenda for the industry, one that could work toward leveraging needed matching funds from NIH or other potential funders. Reinforcing the lack of funding strategies is a lack of coordination. While a biannual meeting (NACREW) brings horticultural cranberry research personnel together, there do not appear to be any large-scale research efforts. Interviewees in the Canadian clusters mentioned the importance of knowledge flows through attendance at other clusters' winter cranberry congresses, the main event for the industry in each cluster for discussing issues and sharing knowledge, including short classes, presentations of recent horticultural research (funded by Ocean Spray and the various growers' associations), and visits to farms and demonstration farms. Québec growers highlighted the importance of knowledge flows from Wisconsin, while BC growers participate in a biannual Pacific Northwest

---

2 On UW efforts, see NAMA (nd).

Congress. Similarly, interviewees noted that the CMC funded research separately from the Cranberry Institute, and that Ocean Spray, while participating in both institutions, also has its own research agenda. What is missing is a way to organize the research into long-term strategic directions and move beyond horticulture to health and marketing.

It may be worth researching other possible uses for cranberries as well; one interviewee suggested potential uses for animal feed or in fish farms. Some interviewees suggested Ocean Spray is not as receptive to new research as it should be, and that its desire to develop proprietary knowledge may get in the way of new product development. Ocean Spray faces the classic "innovator's dilemma," as described by Christensen (2000), wherein, because of its large size, previous success, and pressure from shareholders (growers) to preserve and significantly grow revenues in foreseeable ways and in predictable time frames, it becomes reluctant to enter into blue sky research, even as those product breakthroughs are the foundation of its own historical success. Emerging market niches are generally not of interest to giants, as Christensen explains, because their risk is high and reward is uncertain; however, by the time they grow into sizable markets, the giant may have missed the learning and branding opportunities necessary to gain a dominant position in the new categories. In the case of Ocean Spray, for example, management is naturally reluctant to undercut its dominant, if shrinking, presence in the juice market, where its brand is known for sweet blends.

The same is true for the quickly growing organic market, where Ocean Spray seems to hope that a largely unknown existing Québec brand, Atoka, will give it entrée without disrupting existing markets. The danger with this conservative if understandable position is that the younger generation of sugar-wary and health-conscious millennials and overseas consumers may find their way to cranberries via a different route. Ocean Spray's launching of Pact, cranberry-infused water, is an interesting if limited step. It is unclear whether it is still being sold. While Ocean Spray sells "diet" and "lite" versions of cranberry juice, these are not featured in its marketing strategy, though they do solve the problem of concerns associated with juice more generally. Yet, bringing awareness to its low-sugar products would effectively undercut its still strong business in blended juice. It has recently made cautious forays into the supplement markets and chocolate-covered fruit markets, and there is now a light low-calorie juice blend, which show that the giant is moving. Even aside from these brand dilemmas, there is nothing to stop Ocean Spray from investing in R&D for new products. However, moving away from sugar presents some major challenges, according to interviewees. Aspartame and the usual sugar substitutes are often viewed skeptically, as well, by both consumers

CONCLUSION, RECOMMENDATIONS, AND IMPLICATIONS   169

and, increasingly, health experts (American Cancer Society nd). During the drying process, sugar is used as a substitute for the juice taken out. Several interviewees stated that stevia is far too expensive and difficult to use in the SDC sweetening process and would affect the firmness of the SDC too much to be a readily amenable to adoption. Some interviewees are skeptical about whether sugar content has much effect on the SDC market, seeing consumer concerns as limiting sales only in the juice market. Thus, the holy grail of finding a new varietal with higher natural brix (sugar) remains.

Conflicts of interest in research can be resolved through arm's-length relationships, directing long-term large pools of research money to research teams through third-party administrators such as universities or foundations. Such efforts would require considerable investment of time and money, but since the health benefits would be universal, it would make sense for the different regions and organizations to pool their efforts and seek federal funding from the NIH or some other reputable body. Publication through peer reviewed journals creates bona fides around the integrity of the research. Some in the industry are concerned, given past experience, that there will not be definitive proof of the health benefits of cranberries. The logical response would be that the current uncertainty over benefits leads to skepticism in the public. There appears to be adequate research to back up claims of effectiveness in recurrent urinary tract infections, and more generally, cranberries contain antioxidants, which have proven health qualities. The potential upside for health research is simply too great to ignore.

Finally, the Land O'Lakes mini case shows the upside of a more concerted and organized global strategy. It, along with our other cases, reflects the historical importance of personal and collective leadership and vision. By contrast, the cranberry industry seems cautious and lacking in strategic vision about how to manage global supply and demand. The occasional historical reliance on USDA marketing orders to restore stability to the market during times of very low prices appears to no longer be an option, as the general conclusion is that Canadian and US producers cannot collaborate on supply, according to free trade rules (though this should be challenged or a workaround sought). The ability to rely on the USDA is effectively shrinking, and the industry has fallen into arguing about which particular market to target rather than setting up the more vociferous approach required to increase demand through spreading across markets. Such an approach would require not only more marketing efforts, but greater efforts to find local market partners, including perhaps through mergers and acquisitions. The bottom line is that the increased production in Québec represents a higher supply equilibrium, one that could not be corralled by USDA through marketing orders or Ocean

Spray because of the large number of independents. A thorough examination of potential markets, channels, and product distribution beyond the current focus on China is necessary. It will require greater investment in resources. The expenses for developing new markets and R&D can be shared across Canada and the United States, turning the budding rivalry into an industry-wide vector of cooperation.

The sincere hope of the authors is that the unique experiment in agricultural cooperation in the cranberry industry can adapt and continue to provide an alternative model of governance. Whether that happens depends on a combination of market forces and industry decisions, with government support. It seems clear that painful adjustments to supply need to be made, but at the same time, the industry could pull itself together to make the investments in overseas market development and R&D that could grow demand over the long run.

CONCLUSION: UNDERSTANDING THE CRANBERRY INDUSTRY FROM THE PERSPECTIVE OF HOW CLUSTERS CAN RESOLVE COMMODITY CYCLES

Having comprehensively reviewed the history, conducted the economic analysis, and analyzed the perspectives of the stakeholders, we have diagnosed and begun to offer some suggestions for the cranberry industry. It is necessary to complete this exercise by returning once again to the problem of agricultural commodities production and cluster theory.

As we discussed in chapter 1, commodity agriculture has never really been examined from the perspective of cluster theory. It has been thought to be driven primarily by geography, or the broader wine-based term terroir, meaning the combination of climate, soil, and weather that give a particular location's grapes a supposedly unique flavor. Some wine regions have thus been able to move out of the price-sensitive commodities nature of bulk production toward highly differentiated production in which economies of scale become less important than branding and consistent quality. In theory, such efforts could extend to a variety of products, as is occurring in gourmet categories of coffee and cocoa, but in practice differentiation is extremely challenging for many agricultural products. Cranberries fall into this category. While there are niches for organic and fresh cranberries, it is in general hard to sell cranberries to consumers on the basis of higher quality, though, as we discussed, some characteristics such as color and size might matter at the wholesale level (leading to more/better juice or SDCs).

The story told here reveals a different potential solution for commodities oversupply issues. While clearly natural geographic advantages around

CONCLUSION, RECOMMENDATIONS, AND IMPLICATIONS 171

climate and terroir matter, we have also seen the role of Krugmanesque geographic locational advantage related to economies of scale in growing and processing and proximity to transport hubs and large markets. These factors together help explain the stickiness of cranberry clusters as well as the tensions across them as different factors at play in terms of inter- and intra-cluster competitiveness.

But there is so much more to the story beyond competitive forces. In this case, much of the industry came together around a large cooperative organization, with individual farmer "growers" sharing economies of scale in regard to processing and marketing. The organization became a vital source of new product innovation as well as branding, allowing the industry to expand and broaden consumer demand. The industry also used policy levers to engage in supply management at times, with varying levels of success, to reduce oversupply. In the absence of new innovation, the industry could in theory coalesce around a longer-term supply management model that would reset prices to ensure a better return for the bulk of the remaining growers. Dissonance in the industry, with the entrance of new producers, the inability to coordinate supply management across international borders, and questions about innovation strategies by the co-op, have put this almost century-long venture under duress. Thus, the primary lesson, as we saw in comparing cranberries with our other mini cases in raisins, fresh oranges, and dairy, is that industrial organization is a key and generally underestimated factor in understanding agricultural production. One Canadian agricultural expert suggested that the contrasts with other industries that lacked cooperatives was stark. The expert pointed to the volatility of local apple and other berry markets, where the farmers could not agree to cooperate on a unifying institution, such as a marketing committee, let alone to set up a co-op. The expert pointed to two BC dairy cooperatives, Island Farms and Dairyland, who had stability but were offered a buyout—the former from Québec co-op Agropur—and sold out at a higher price. Now there is much discontent among growers at their loss of control and value-added. So, this answers the counterfactual question of what might have happened had Ocean Spray accepted PepsiCo's offer.

Let's turn now to clusters, which bring our focus back to location; what is produced, where, and why, and what makes some locations perform better? As we have noted, cranberry bogs were set up, in a path-dependent fashion, where they naturally grew through geography. In most places, cranberries form distinct clusters of colocation, and the clusters do not spread much beyond a certain zone, despite possibilities in adjacent areas. It is hard to say what precisely defines a cluster's boundaries, but many have a strong sense of community based on geographical proximity. For example, growers in

Clatsop County, Oregon, near Astoria, interact regularly with Washington state growers across the Columbia River and are served by the Washington state extension agent, as the larger Oregon growing area is some five hours drive south of there. Ties are much stronger among growers within, rather than across, the Grayland and Long Beach areas of Washington state, as they lie on different peninsulas. Moreover, Grayland specializes almost exclusively in dry harvesting, while Long Beach is focused on wet harvesting; informants in both areas say conversion would be very challenging given the level of expertise/experience required. Most growers in these clusters know fellow growers on a personal level. A strong and unique culture characterizes every growing region, reflected in long-term personal and cooperative relationships (such as lending a hand during harvest, sharing equipment, and sharing deals). The cooperation extends across growers regardless of whether they are part of Ocean Spray. In Oregon, for example, growers suggested a big part of the break from Ocean Spray in the 1990s was that many who left were fiercely independent, wanting to make their own fortunes; while they cooperated, they also competed. On a larger scale, from the initial base in Massachusetts, they spread to New Jersey, and then on to Wisconsin, and finally to the West Coast, creating a path dependency in each cluster. Similarly, in Canada, the Atlantic Provinces spread the cultivation of cranberries to BC. In the most recent iteration, we have traced the success of a cluster establishment policy in Québec.

Our study allows us to reach five conclusions about agricultural clusters. First, geography and natural comparative advantage do matter. As we have seen, growing conditions are clearly prerequisite and input to not only production but also cost-competitiveness. We have discussed, for example, the net advantage of Wisconsin and Québec, where colder climates and cheaper land provide a solid long-term cost advantage.

Second, however, those factors alone are not enough—the efforts to establish clusters in Minnesota, Michigan, and Maine did not take hold. Without more information (requiring another grant), we cannot discern precisely why, but the best immediate guess would be that policy was insufficient in terms of both time and resources. We present here the few facts we have been able to assemble on these three alternative growing states. Cranberries were grown in Maine during the nineteenth century, yet the industry was "virtually eliminated" in the early 1900s "by a combination of factors, including lack of adequate technology for frost protection, the spread of disease and pests, depressed demand during World War I, the increasing trend toward specialized farming, the replacement of fresh cranberries in the market with the new canned cranberry sauce, and its relative distance to markets," according to the University of Maine's extension service. The first commercial growers in Maine, set up in

1988, harvested their first crop in 1991. Maine produced just 35,870 barrels in 2013, from 210 acres, about half located in Washington County. Cherryfield Foods, one company, owns half of the state's cranberry acres, but decided to stop growing in 2015. As a result of the glut, the number of growers declined from thirty to twenty between 2013 and 2017. The University of Maine offers cranberry growers extension services (Cairn 2012; Milliken 2017; University of Maine, nd). In 2000, the Maine Cranberry Growers Association pushed for state support to test frozen cranberries in a local supermarket, but the state never supported the bill (Cicotte 2000).

In 1998, A. D. Makepeace developed Minnesota's first cranberry crop. Informants suggested that the growing conditions in one area of the state, with large amounts of water being used for wild rice, was suitable for cranberry cultivation. The Forster family followed, in 2001, creating the Minnesota Cranberry company with 100 acres of bogs as part of a diversified farm spread (Enger 1998; Flansburg 2017). A 1971 report by Michigan State University noted that cranberries grow wild in the northern part of the state and, through tests, found that there were suitable conditions for cultivation in the state. The experiment took place in the Upper Peninsula. Michigan offered tax breaks and a commercial team to evaluate sites in an effort to woo the cranberry business to the state when prices were high in 1997 (ERS 1997, 8). In 2009, the state relaxed wetlands legislation for cranberry growers who wanted to expand their farms. This was part of a general push by the Michigan Department of Agriculture to attract cranberry growing into that state, which is already one of the largest producers of blueberries, a crop with similar growing requirements. The state offered the Michigan Agriculture Advantages Plan, including one-on-one advice for site selection and environmental regulation exemptions (Harger 2009; *Fruit Growers News* 2009).

As we noted in chapter 2, none of these experiments panned out, and their example provides a stark contrast with Québec, where the industry was established and grew through a major government push. Moreover, the lack of access to central processing facilities, as discussed, can play a decisive role, overriding natural agricultural comparative advantage. Processing facilities, in turn, are set up once a large enough well-established growing region is in play; the two factors work hand in hand. This reinforces a central tenet of cluster theory: that is, once established, a cluster tends to draw more suppliers for industry infrastructure, policy support, and subcontractors and exhibit staying power even when it starts to become less competitive.

Third, policy clearly matters for establishing and maintaining clusters. Québec, in contrast to Minnesota, Michigan, and Maine, overcame these obstacles through the state and industry working together to establish alternative processing facilities, and through local industrialists' ability to master and develop retail markets. The level of support and organization of policies is clearly a major factor in the fast productivity increases, including support for R&D and equipment. The same sort of planning mentality is needed across the states involved in the industry, including support for exit where warranted. Above all, support for developing the most important overseas markets is vital. Here, one can see the possibilities for US and Canadian/Québec cooperation, while the need for cooperation in terms of supply stability is needed but more fraught. Industry governance, including by the CMC and the Cranberry Institute, as well as other aspects such as supply management and promoting overseas markets, has to bring Québec producers to the table so that shared aims and goods for the industry can be created. Cooperation appears to happen across the border regularly only in research now.

Along with that of Québec, Chile's emergence demonstrates the distinct possibility that industry production can become more global. Ocean Spray now owns bogs in BC, Chile, and Québec; Fruit d'Or owns Decas in Massachusetts. There are other unverifiable rumors of ownership across the US-Canada border, including suggestions that Québec growers were looking to make an acquisition in Wisconsin as of the time of writing in 2022. Thus, reforming the CMC, perhaps combining it with CI into a North American institution, even at the cost of abandoning the marketing order, is an evolutionary step well worth considering. That move depends, of course, on the willingness of Ocean Spray and the large Québec producers to work together.

This route is by no means clear since, given Québec's spectacular growth, it may feel it has a competitive edge in the industry. Fruit d'Or's purchase of Decas indicates it intends to enter the US market, and the deal includes acreage in Massachusetts. Thus, it seems to have common purpose with Ocean Spray to develop the global industry, even as it further develops its own brand. It is interesting to note that, in Wisconsin, Ocean Spray and independent growers and handlers have managed to overcome past animosities related to the Northland incident and cooperate around both research and marketing. The Wisconsin Growers' Association works with the research foundation and Wisconsin Cranberry Board to support the multiple researchers at University of Wisconsin–Madison, secure several USDA ARS positions, and develop an experimental bog. When asked how such different participants reach a consensus for research priorities, informants stated that they "look at it as a problem-solving exercise," during which they spend all day and talk through the options before reaching an agreement. When pressed as to how Wisconsin institutions have overcome long-standing industry tensions, industry informants there state that the long-standing, multigenerational family ties across the different state regions are binding.

While common policy issues regarding wetlands regulations and seasonal labor are found in all clusters, remarkable differences in the level of policy support are found as well. In New Jersey, Washington, and Oregon, a lack of clear policy support at the state level factors in the struggles of growers there, despite the importance of local extension stations. The overall contrast with policy support in Québec could not be greater. Only Wisconsin has a large enough industry to be able to provide some of these public goods.

Our fourth observation is that there are factors beyond growing conditions and policy that clearly affect competitive advantage in commodity agriculture. The cheaper land prices and lower temperatures in Wisconsin and Québec provide major cost advantages. However, costs depend also on technology. The later entry of these two growing areas allowed them to build more efficient bogs and introduce, on a wider scale, more efficient varietals. In this sense, the idea of having a proximate R&D lab for major productivity increases does not seem that important, though local extension would be important. The varietals coming primarily from Rutgers and Wisconsin have benefited the industry as a whole. This clearly suggests that "economies of scale" are relevant in agricultural R&D. While extension is clearly important for maintenance of yield and troubleshooting, it appears that knowledge disseminates regardless of where it originates. In turn, centralization of funding for R&D makes sense, keeping in mind that varietals will need to be adapted to local growing conditions. Over the long run, the industry needs a larger pool of researchers and training programs to widen innovation and the depth of research, particularly addressing the lack of economic and particularly business (marketing) research, which is nonexistent at the moment. Training will be increasingly important, to provide managers as some growers retire and as the forces of consolidation continue.

Our fifth and final observation takes us back to industry governance of clusters. As we saw in both cranberries and our other mini cases, vertical integration is a natural step for growers to reduce uncertainty and capture more of the value chain of production. Yet, membership will never be 100%. Perhaps some healthy competition by independent growers and handlers is necessary, both to spur the larger cooperative organization toward innovation and for cost reductions. The large organization helps to pool tacit knowledge, creating a spirit of cooperation that helps growers ride out storms, in the process creating a fierce sense of loyalty that is probably necessary to survive in the long run in agriculture. Yet, it might also create a sense of complacency or expectations of the larger organization that are unrealistic. Even given the remarkable string of product innovations by Ocean Spray, there is only so much it can do to increase cranberry juice sales. This then brings us to the crossroads: under pressure, does the cluster double down through further vertical or horizontal integration—such as entering into crop insurance, seeds, fertilizers, buying out cranberry growers who want to leave the business, or buying juice competitors—or does it start to unravel?

In the case of cranberries, our evidence suggests that the reasons for clustering go beyond history or loyalty. As with the case of raisins and oranges, the packing and distribution, as well as, more indirectly, the branding, provide nodes for clustering. The logistics involved in shipping fresh products, or in freezing/processing them, and the inefficiencies inherent in every grower trying to do this on their own, create natural clusters. The key question posed by this case is whether a cooperative organization can take these natural forces and marshal them into even greater gains, such as through R&D and conquering international markets, or whether centrifugal forces continue. In this sense, future research on agricultural clusters should look very closely at the supply chain of production, beyond the farm, and start to map out who controls the inputs, such as fertilizers and insurance, and the outputs, including processing, distribution, and retail networks and, perhaps more importantly, whether there is a strong sense of culture and loyalty to a centralized organization that can provide collective shared goods through transparent and capable governance mechanisms. In the end, it is matching physical, economic, and human resources with an effective governance and policy system that allows clusters to succeed, thus paving a potential road out from the commodity curse.

References

Agricultural Marketing Resource Center. 2021. "Cranberries." September. https://www.agmrc.org/commodities-products/fruits/cranberries.
Allen, Lee. 2019. "Little Red Boxes of Sunshine: Sun Maid Disrupts California's Raisin Market." March 13. https://www.farmprogress.com/grapes/little-red-boxes-sunshine.
Alston, Julian M. Josué Medellín-Azuara, and Tina L. Saitone. 2014. "Economic Impact of the North American Cranberry Industry." Report for CMC, Cranberry Institute, and BCCMC. http://www.bccranberries.com/pdfs/Economic_Impact_of_the_NA_Cranberry_Industry_August2014.pdf.
Amanor-Boadu, Vincent, and Michael Boland. 2005. "Dan Dillon, CEO of Welch Foods." *International Food and Agribusiness Management Review* 8 (2): 115–120.
Amanor-Boadu, Vincent, Michael Boland, and David Barton. 2003. "Ocean Spray Cranberries at the Crossroads." Arthur Capper Cooperative Center, Case Study Series No. 03-01. Ames: Iowa State University, Agricultural Marketing Resource Center. https://www.aaea.org/UserFiles/file/AAEA2003casestudy-CranberryIndustryataCrossroads.pdf.
Amanor-Boadu, V., M. A. Boland, and D. Barton. 2006. "Welch Foods." In *Cases in Strategic Management*, 7th ed., edited by Thomas L. Wheelen and J. David Hunger, 35–49. Boston: Houghton Mifflin.
American Cancer Society. nd. "Aspartame and Cancer Risk." https://www.cancer.org/cancer/risk-prevention/chemicals/aspartame.html#:~:text=International%20Agency%20for%20Research%20on%20Cancer%20(IARC)&text=One%20of%20its%20major%20roles,specifically%20liver%20cancer)%20in%20people.
Avard, Karine, Marie Larocque, and Stéphanie Pellerin. 2013. "Perturbations des tourbières de la région de Bécancour, Centre-du-Québec, entre 1966 et 2010. *Le Naturaliste canadien* 137 (1): 8–15.
Badger State Fruit. nd. https://www.badgerstatefruit.com/. Accessed October 1, 2021.
Baffes, John. 2007. "Oil Spills on Other Commodities." *Resources Policy* 32 (3): 126–134.
Barkley, David L. 1988. The Decentralization of High-Technology Manufacturing to Nonmetropolitan Areas. *Growth and Change* 19 (1): 13–30.
Barrientos, Tanya. 2006. "Raisin Queen's Millennial Makeover: Sunmaid Goes Digital: 'Capitalizing on the Iconic Value of Her Image.'" *National Post*, April 21.
Bassett, Keith, Ron Griffiths, and Ian Smith. 2002. "Cultural Industries, Cultural Clusters and the City: The Example of Natural History Film-Making in Bristol." *Geoforum* 33 (2): 165–177.

Bathelt, Harald. 2005. "Geographies of Production: Growth Regimes in Spatial Perspective II: Knowledge Creation and Growth in Clusters." *Progress in Human Geography* 29 (2): 204–216.
Bathelt, H., A. Malmberg, and P. Maskell. 2004. "Clusters and Knowledge: Local Buzz, Global Pipelines and the Process of Knowledge Creation." *Progress in Human Geography* 28:1.
BCCMC (British Columbia Cranberry Marketing Commission). 2011. "The British Columbia Cranberry Marketing Commission 2011–2016 Strategic Plan." September. http://bccranberries.com/pdfs/Cran%20Strategic%20Plan%202011.pdf.
BCCMC (British Columbia Cranberry Marketing Commission). 2019, 2020. *Annual Report*. Chilliwack, BC: BCCMC.
BC Cranberries. 2018. https://www.BCcranberries.com/consumers/cranberries-in-BC/. Accessed September 3, 2019.
BC Laws. 2022. "The British Columbia Cranberry Marketing Scheme, 1968." https://www.bclaws.gov.bc.ca/civix/document/id/complete/statreg/259_68.
BC Laws. 2023. "Natural Products Marketing (BC) Act." http://www.bclaws.ca/Recon/document/ID/freeside/00_96330_01#section11.
Boland, Michael. 2006. "Sun Maid Growers of California." Written for use with the American Agricultural Economics Association's Graduate Student Case Study Competition. July 4. https://www.aaea.org/UserFiles/file/AAEA2006casestudy-SunMaidGrowersofCalifornia.pdf.
Boland, Michael, Vincent Amanor-Boadu, and David Barton. 2004. "Land O'Lakes." *International Food and Agribusiness Management Review* 7 (2): 63–75.
Boland, Michael, Brendan Cooper, and James M. White. 2015. "Making Sustainability Tangible: Land O'Lakes and the Dairy Supply Chain." *American Journal of Agricultural Economics* 98 (2): 648–657.
Boland, Michael, Veronica Pozo, and Daniel Sumner. 2009. "Sunkist Growers: Refreshing the Brand." *Review of Agricultural Economics* 31 (3): 628–639.
Boschma, Ron. 2005. "Proximity and Innovation: A Critical Assessment." *Regional Studies* 39 (1): 61–74.
Boulé, David. 2013. *The Orange and the Dream of California*. Santa Monica, CA: Angel City Press.
Bradley Fertilizer Co. 1892. *The Cranberry*. Boston: Bradley Fertilizer Co.
Bureau, Luc. 1970. "Un exemple d'adaptation de l'agriculture à des conditions écologiques en apparence hostiles: l'Atocatière de Lemieux. " *Cahiers de géographie du Québec* 14 (33): 383–394.
Cairn, North. 2012. "Climate Change May Boost Maine's Take." The Weather Channel. September 30. https://weather.com/news/news/climate-change-maine-cranberry-harvest-20120930.
Caron, Jean, Vincent Pelletier, Casey D. Kennedy, Jacques Gallichand, Silvio Gumiere, Simon Bonin, William L. Bland, and Steeve Pepin. 2017. "Guidelines of Irrigation and Drainage Management Strategies to Enhance Cranberry Production and Optimize Water Use in North America. *Canadian Journal of Soil Science* 97 (1): 82–91.
Carper, Jim. 2016. "Ford Drives Innovation at Land O'Lakes." *Dairy Foods*, October, pp. 38–42.

Carroll, Michael C., Neil Reid, and Bruce W. Smith. 2008. "Location Quotients versus Spatial Autocorrelation in Identifying Potential Cluster Regions." *Annals of Regional Science* 42 (2): 449–463.

Caruso, Frank L., Peter R. Bristow, and Peter V. Oudemans. 2019. "Cranberries: The Most Intriguing Native North American Fruit." American Phytopathological Society. https://www.apsnet.org/edcenter/apsnetfeatures/Pages/Cranberries.aspx. Accessed Nov. 20, 2019.

Chandler, F. B. 1957. *A Survey of... Oregon's Cranberry Industry.* Misc. Paper 38. Agricultural Experiment Station. Corvallis: Oregon State College.

Chazanof, William. 1977. *Welch's Grape Juice: From Corporation to Co-operative.* Syracuse, NY: Syracuse University Press.

Chen, Xiangrong, et al. 2020. "Research on the Development of Cranberry Industry in China [Manyuemei chanye zai zhongguo de fazhan yanjiu]." *Rural Economy and Technology* 20 (19).

Christensen, Clayton M. 2000. *The Innovator's Dilemma.* New York: HarperBusiness.

Cicotte, Carrie. 2000. "Cranberry Prices Plunge: Cherryfield Foods Puts 900-Acre Plan on Hold." July 20. http://ellsworthamerican.com/archive/news2000/07-20-00/ea_news2_07-20-00.html.

Collier, Paul, and Benedikt Goderis. 2012. "Commodity Prices and Growth: An Empirical Investigation." *European Economic Review* 56 (6): 1241–1260.

Cooke, Philip. 2017. "'Eventually Even Attractive Illusions Come to an End': The Death of Monitor—and Demise of Clusters?" In *The Life Cycle of Clusters: A Policy Perspective*, edited by Dick Fornahl and Robert Hassink, 259–275. Northampton, MA: Edward Elgar.

Cooke, Philip. 2013. "Global Production Networks and Global Innovation Networks: Stability versus Growth." *European Planning Studies* 21 (7): 1081–1094.

Cooke, Philip, M. Heidenreich, and H.-J. Braczyk, eds. 2004. *Regional Innovation Systems.* London: Routledge.

Covell, Jeffrey L., and Heidi Feldman. 2009. "Sunkist Growers, Inc." *International Directory of Company Histories* 102:399–404.

D., Andrew. 2021. "Cranberries Hit Record Recognition and Popularity among Chinese Consumers." *Produce Report*, February 27. https://www.producereport.com/article/cranberries-hit-record-recognition-popularity-among-chinese-consumers.

Delgado, Mercedes, Michael E. Porter, and Scott Stern. 2010. "Clusters and Entrepreneurship." *Journal of Economic Geography* 10 (4): 495–518.

Delgado, Mercedes, Michael E. Porter, and Scott Stern. 2016. Defining Clusters of Related Industries. *Journal of Economic Geography* 16 (1): 1–38.

Deloitte. 2019. Estimation des retombées économiques de l'industrie québécoise de la canneberge. Report for APCQ. Victoriaville: APCQ. http://www.notrecanneberge.com.

Deloitte. 2020. Étuede des retombées économiques de l'industrie de la canneberge au Québec. Report for APCQ. Victoriaville: APCQ. http://www.notrecanneberge.com/Nouvelle/Detail/etude-des-retombees-economiques-de-lindustrie-de-la-canneberge-au-Quebec---La-filiere-canneberge-au-Quebec---Creatrice-de-richesse.

Dinger, Ed, and Taylor Haahr. 2019. "Welch Foods Inc." In *International Directory of Company Histories*, vol. 208, edited by Drew D. Johnson, 450–455. Detroit, MI: St. James Press.
Durand, Loyal, Jr. 1942. "Wisconsin Cranberry Industry." *Economic Geography* 18 (2): 159–172.
Eastwood, B. 1859. *A Complete Manual for the Cultivation of the Cranberry: With a Description of the Best Varieties*. New York: A. O. Moore. Nineteenth Century Collections Online. http://tinyurl.galegroup.com/tinyurl/9ghSL1.
Eck, Paul. 1990. *The American Cranberry*. New Brunswick, NJ: Rutgers University Press.
Ellison, G., and E. Glaeser. 1997. "Geographic Concentration in U.S. Manufacturing Industries: A Dartboard Approach." *Journal of Political Economy* 105 (5): 889–927.
Enger, Leif. 1998. "Minnesota's First Cranberry Crop." Minnesota Public Radio. June 1. http://news.minnesota.publicradio.org/features/199806/01_engerl_cranberries-m/.
ERS (Economic Research Service). 1997. "Agricultural Outlook/November 1997." Washington, DC: USDA.
Erten, Bilge, and José Antonio Ocampo. 2013. "Super Cycles of Commodity Prices since the Mid-Nineteenth Century." *World Development* 44:14–30.
Etzkowitz, Henry. 2003. Innovation in Innovation: The Triple Helix of University-Industry-Government Relations. *Social Science Information* 42 (3): 293–337.
Etzkowitz, Henry, and Loet Leydesdorff. 2000. "The Dynamics of Innovation: From National Systems and 'Mode 2' to a Triple Helix of University-Industry-Government Relations." *Research Policy* 29:109–123.
Farm Credit East. 2015. "Massachusetts Cranberry Cost of Production Study 2012–2014 Crop Years." file:///C:/Users/14019/Desktop/ma-cop-report-08-21-15.pdf.
Farm Credit East. 2016. "Massachusetts Cranberry Cost of Production Study 2015 Crop Year." file:///C:/Users/14019/Desktop/cranberry-2015-cop-final.pdf.
Ference and Company Consulting. 2020. *Market Opportunities Assessment for B.C. Berries: Final Report*. March. Victoria: British Columbia Ministry of Agriculture.
Feser, Edward J., and Edward M. Bergman. 2000. "National Industry Cluster Templates: A Framework for Applied Regional Cluster Analysis." *Regional Studies* 34 (1): 1–19.
Flansburg, Rebecca. 2017. "Homegrown/Minnesota Cranberry Company: Minnesota's Only Cranberry Farm." *Lake Country Journal*, October/November. http://lakecountryjournal.com/homegrown-octobernovember-2017/.
Frenken, Koen, Elena Cefis, and Erik Stam. 2015. "Industrial Dynamics and Clusters: A Survey." *Regional Studies* 49 (1): 10–27.
Friedman, Thomas L. 2005. *The World Is Flat: A Brief History of the Twenty-First Century*. New York: Farrar, Strauss, and Giroux.
Fruit d'Or. nd. "Who We Are." https://fruitdor.ca/en/who-we-are/. Accessed October 10, 2021.
Fruit Growers News. 2009. "Michigan Takes a Serious Look at Cranberries." *Fruit Growers News*, August 12. https://fruitgrowersnews.com/article/michigan-takes-a-serious-look-at-cranberries/.

REFERENCES

Fruit Growers News. 2017. "Canada Invests in Quebec Cranberry Industry." *Fruit Growers News*, October 16. https://fruitgrowersnews.com/news/canada-invests-quebec-cranberry-industry/.

Gallardo, R. Karina, Parichat Klingthong, Qi Zhang, James Polashock, Amaya Atucha, Juan Zalapa, Cesar Rodriguez-Saona, Nicholi Vorsa, and Massimo Iorizzo. 2018. "Breeding Trait Priorities of the Cranberry Industry in the United States and Canada." *HortScience* 53 (10): 1467–1474.

Gareau, Brian J., Xiaorui Huang, Tara Pisani Gareau, and Sandra DiDonato. 2020. "The Strength of Green Ties: Massachusetts Cranberry Grower Social Networks and Effects on Climate Change Attitudes and Action." *Climatic Change* 162 (3): 1613–1636.

Gereffi, G. 1994. "The Organization of Buyer-Driven Global Commodity Chains: How US Retailers Shape Overseas Production Networks." In *Commodity Chains and Global Capitalism*, 95–112. Westport, CT: Praeger.

Gereffi, G. 1999. "International Trade and Industrial Upgrading in the Apparel Commodity Chain." *Journal of International Economics* 48 (1): 37–70.

Girard, Kirsten K., and Nirmal K. Sinha. 2012. "Cranberry, Blueberry, Currant, and Gooseberry." In *Handbook of Fruits and Fruit Processing*, edited by Nirmal K. Sinha, Jiwan S. Sidhu, József Barta, James S. B. Wu, and M. Pilar Cano, 399–417. New York: John Wiley and Sons.

Giuliani, E., and M. Bell. 2005. The Micro-Determinants of Meso-Level Learning and Innovation: Evidence from a Chilean Wine Cluster. *Research Policy* 34:47–68.

Glass, Brent D. 1992. *The Textile Industry in North Carolina: A History*. Raleigh: North Carolina Department of Cultural Resources.

Godin, Vincent. 2013. "Stabilisation des revenus dans l'industrie de la canneberge." Working paper for AGC 7004 (Politique Agroalimentaire) class by Msr. Daniel Mercier Gouin. Québec: Université Laval.

Goetz, Stephan J., Steven C. Deller, and Thomas R. Harris. 2009. *Targeting Regional Economic Development*. New York: Routledge.

Gorski, E. 2015. "Denver's River North Neighborhood: The Brewing District." *Denver Post*, February 16. https://www.denverpost.com/2015/02/16/denvers-river-north-neighborhood-the-brewing-district/.

Government of Canada. 2019. "Aperçu statistique de l'industrie fruitière du Canada 2019." Division des cultures et de l'horticulture. Ottawa: Agriculture et Agroalimentaire Canada.

Government of Canada. 2022. "Opportunities and Benefits of CETA for Canada's Agriculture and Agri-Food Exporters." https://www.international.gc.ca/trade-commerce/trade-agreements-accords-commerciaux/agr-acc/ceta-aecg/business-entreprise/sectors-secteurs/agri.aspx?lang=eng#fnb2.

Graves, Mark. 2014. "Oregon Cranberries: A 360-Degree Look at the Industry." November 27. https://www.oregonlive.com/business/2014/11/oregon_cranberries_a_360-degre.html.

Greve, Henrich R. 2008. "Bigger and Safer: The Diffusion of Competitive Advantage." *Strategic Management Journal* 30:1–23.

Halberstam, David. 1986. *The Reckoning*. New York: Avon Books.

Harger, Jim. 2009. "Wetlands Legislation Includes Help for Growing Michigan Cranberry Industry." *mlive: Michigan*, September 28. https://www.mlive.com/news/grand-rapids/2009/09/post_15.html.

Harker, John. 1997. "Cranberry Development in Maine: The First Nine Years." Report. Augusta: Maine Department of Agriculture, Food and Rural Resources.

Hassink, Robert. 2010. "Regional Resilience: A Promising Concept to Explain Difference in Regional Economic Adaptability?" *Cambridge Journal of Regions, Economy and Society* 3:45–58.

Hira, Anil, ed. 2013a. *What Makes Clusters Competitive? Cases from the Global Wine Industry*. Montreal: McGill-Queen's University Press.

Hira, Anil, ed. 2013b. "Special Issue on the Wine Industry." *Prometheus: Critical Studies in Innovation* 31 (4).

Hira, Anil. 2015. "From Industrial Strength to World Class: Gallo and Mondavi's Contributions to the California Wine Industry." *California History* 92 (4): 48–72.

Hira, Anil, and Tim Swartz. 2014. "What Makes Napa Napa? The Roots of Success in the Wine Industry." *Wine Economics and Policy* 3 (1): 37–53.

Hira, Anil, Brian Wixted, and Ricardo Arechavala-Vargas. 2012. "Explaining Sectoral Leapfrogging in Countries: Comparative Studies of the Wireless Sector." *International Journal of Technology and Globalisation* 6 (1/2): 3–26.

Hira, Ron, and Anil Hira. 2008. *Outsourcing America: The True Cost of Shipping Jobs Overseas and What Can Be Done about It*. New York: Amacom.

Hoovers. 2019. "Sunkist Growers, Inc: In Depth Records." October 16. www.hoovers.com.

Huggins, Robert, and Andrew Johnston. 2010. "Knowledge Flow and Inter-Firm Networks: The Influence of Network Resources, Spatial Proximity and Firm Size." *Entrepreneurship and Regional Development* 22 (5): 457–484.

Hyson, Charles D., and Fred. H. Sanderson. 1945. "Monopolistic Discrimination in the Cranberry Industry." *Quarterly Journal of Economics* 59 (3): 330–369.

IAF (Investment Agriculture Foundation). 2019. "Digging Up the Dirt on Cranberry Field Decline." March 26. https://iafbc.ca/digging-up-dirt-on-cranberry-field-decline/.

Inside Vancouver. 2013. "A Guide to Cranberries in Metro Vancouver." *Inside Vancouver*, September 27. https://www.insidevancouver.ca/2013/09/27/a-guide-to-cranberries-in-metro-vancouver/.

Isabel, Carol. 2020. "Fruit d'Or envoie un signal fort à la communauté économique." September 2. https://www.lanouvelle.net/2020/09/02/fruit-dor-envoie-un-signal-fort-a-la-communaute-economique/.

Jabet, Tiphaine, Jean Caron, and Rémy Lambert. 2016. "Payback Period in Cranberry Associated with a Wireless Irrigation Technology." *Canadian Journal of Soil Science* 97 (1): 71–81.

Janzen, Mark Ryan. 2010. "The Cranberry Scare of 1959: The Beginning of the End of the Delaney Case." PhD diss., College Station: Texas A&M University.

Jesse, Edward V., and Richard T. Rogers. 2006. "The Cranberry Industry and Ocean Spray Cooperative: Lessons in Cooperative Governance." Food System Research Group (FSRG) Monograph Series. No. 19. Madison: University of Wisconsin.

REFERENCES

Jones, Barbara K. 2003. "Catch the Cranberry Wave: Ocean Spray's Role as an Important Social and Economic Institution." In *Anthropological Perspectives on Economic Development and Integration*, edited by Norbert Dannhaeuser and Cynthia Werner, 325–344. San Francisco: Elsevier.

Just Drinks. 2004a. "US: Ocean Spray Completes Northland Purchase." September 27. *Just-drinks research news*. https://advance-lexis-com.proxy.lib.sfu.ca/api/document?collection=company-financial&id=urn:contentItem:56SK-CM81-DXD9-X521-00000-00&context=1516831.

Just Drinks. 2004b. "US: Ocean Spray Completes Subsidiary Sale." October 14. *Just-drinks research news*. https://advance-lexis-com.proxy.lib.sfu.ca/api/document?collection=company-financial&id=urn:contentItem:56SK-CM91-DXD9-X01F-00000-00&context=1516831.

Kim, Jin-Young. 2013. "Development of Agricultural Cooperatives for Revitalization of the Rural Community-Focused on the Case Study of 'Sunkist.'" *International Journal of Smart Home* 7 (3): 293–299.

Kirkman, C. H. 1975. *The Sunkist Adventure*. Farmer Cooperative Services, No. 94. Washington, DC: USDA.

Kirwan, Hope. 2021. "Wisconsin Cranberry Research Station Offers New Opportunities to 'Move the Industry Forward.'" Wisconsin Public Radio, September 30. https://www.wpr.org/wisconsin-cranberry-research-station-offers-new-opportunities-move-industry-forward.

Krugman, Paul. 1991. "Increasing Returns and Economic Geography." *Journal of Political Economy* 99 (3): 483–499.

Kuchiki, Akifumi, and Masatsugu Tsuji. 2011. *Industrial Clusters, Upgrading and Innovation in East Asia*. Northampton, MA: Edward Elgar.

Lambert, Matthew, Richard Rogers, and Daniel Lass. 2004. "The U.S. Cranberry Industry: Historical Changes and the Current Situation." Unpublished paper. Department of Resource Economics, University of Massachusetts, Amherst.

Land O'Lakes. nd. "What We Do." https://www.landolakesinc.com/Company. Accessed October 19, 2019.

Landry, Christine. nd. "Impacts de la température et du type de fertilisant organique sur la fourniture en azote du sol et la productivité des cannebergières en régie biologique." https://www.irda.qc.ca/fr/projets-recherche/azote-canneberge-bio/. Accessed October 13, 2021.

La Nouvelle Union. 2019. "Québec soutient la croissance de l'entreprise Emblème Canneberge." August 29. https://www.lanouvelle.net/2019/08/29/quebec-soutient-la-croissance-de-lentreprise-embleme-canneberge/.

Leonhardt, Kris. 2017. "The Biggest Little Guy in Cranberries." *Hub City Times*, April 20. https://hubcitytimes.com/2017/04/20/butch-gardner-badger-state-fruit-processing-cranberries/.

Long, Steve, Derek Jacques, and Paula Kepos. 2017. "Ocean Spray." In *International Directory of Company Histories*, vol. 192, 315–321. New York: St. James Press.

Lorey, Christina. 2022. "How Wisconsin Became the Cranberry Capital of the World." *Up North News*, October 12. https://upnorthnewswi.com/2022/10/12/how-wisconsin-became-the-cranberry-capital-of-the-world/.

Luhning, Jessica. 2014. "Cranberry: Sweet or Sinister?" *Edible Madison*, September 19. http://ediblemadison.com/articles/view/cranberry-sweet-or-sinister/c/full/.

Malerba, Franco. 2002. Sectoral Systems of Innovation and Production. *Research Policy* 31 (2): 247–264.
MAPAQ (Ministère de l'Agriculture, des Pêcheries et de l'Alimentation, Government of Québec). 2018a. "Portrait-Diagnostic Sectoriel de la Canneberge au Québec." Québec City: Government of Québec.
MAPAQ. 2018b. "Politique Bioalimentaire: 2018–25." Québec: MAPAQ.
MarketLine. 2012. "Company Profile: National Grape Cooperative Association, Inc." www.marketline.com.
MarketLine. 2018. "Company Profile: Sunkist Growers, Inc." www.marketline.com.
Markusen, Ann. 1996. "Sticky Places in Slippery Space: A Typology of Industrial Districts." *Economic Geography* 72 (3): 293–313.
Marple, Wesley Jr., and Donald J. Harding. 2002. "Case Study: Ocean Spray Cranberries, Inc." *Journal of Financial Education* 28:78–98.
Marshall, Alfred. 1890. *Principles of Economics*. London: MacMillan. https://www.econlib.org/library/Marshall/marP.html.
Martin, Ron, and Peter Sunley. 2003. "Deconstructing Clusters: Chaotic Concept or Policy Panacea?" *Journal of Economic Geography* 3:5–35.
Mason, Carol Y. 1926. "The Cranberry Industry in Massachusetts." *Economic Geography* 2 (1): 59–69.
Matusinec, Daniel, Andrew Maule, Eric Wiesman, Amaya Atucha, Mura Jyostna Devi, and Juan Zalapa. 2022. "The New Cranberry Wisconsin Research Station: Renovation Priorities of a 'Stevens' Cranberry Marsh Based on Visual Mapping, Genetic Testing, and Yield Data." *International Journal of Fruit Science* 22 (1): 121–132. doi:10.1080/15538362.2021.2014016.
MDAR (Massachusetts Department of Agricultural Resources). 2016. "The Massachusetts Cranberry Revitalization Task Force: Final Report." https://www.mass.gov/info-details/cranberry-revitalization-task-force.
Milliken, Maureen. 2017. "Maine Food Insider: State's Cranberry Industry Striving to Stay above Water." *Mainebiz*, November 22. https://www.mainebiz.biz/article/maine-food-insider-states-cranberry-industry-striving-to-stay-above-water.
Milwaukee Business Journal. 2004. "Northland Sells Cranberry Processing Business to Ocean Spray; Drops Lawsuit." *Milwaukee Business Journal*, September 24. https://www.bizjournals.com/milwaukee/stories/2004/09/20/daily46.html.
Ministère de l'Environnement (Government of Québec). 2021. "Analyse d'impact réglementaire du projet de règlement modifiant principalement le Règlement sur la compensation pour l'atteinte aux milieux humides et hydriques et d'autres dispositions réglementaires." Québec: Ministère de l'Environnement.
Morrison, Andrea, and Roberta Rabelloti. 2009. "Knowledge and Information Networks in an Italian Wine Cluster." *European Planning Studies* 17 (7): 983–1006.
Mueller, Willard F., Peter G. Helmberger, and Thomas W. Paterson. 1987. *The Sunkist Case: A Study in Legal-Economic Analysis*. Lexington, MA: Lexington Books.
National Archives. 1992. "Code of Federal Regulation. Part 929." https://www.ecfr.gov/cgi-bin/text-idx?SID=58c55106641f13f4a2f3144681008c24&mc=true&node=pt7.8.929&rgn=div5#se7.8.929_120.

Natural Products Insider. 2004. "Ocean Spray Sells Subsidiary." *Natural Products Insider,* December 6. https://www.naturalproductsinsider.com/archive/ocean-spray-sells-subsidiary.
NCFC (National Council of Farmer Cooperatives). nd. National Grape Cooperative Association, Inc. https://ncfc.org/member/national-grape-cooperative-association/.
Nelson, Richard. 1993. *National Innovation Systems: A Comparative Analysis.* New York: Oxford University Press.
New York Times. 1925. "Sargent Halts Sun Maid Inquiry." *New York Times,* December 30. Pro-Quest Historical Newspapers. https://www.proquest.com/docview/103452180/8F11D09CC9274DB8PQ/1?accountid=13800.
New York Times. 1956. "Farm Group Buys Welch Grape Co.: 87-Year-Old Concern Sold for Equivalent of 28.6 Million to Cooperative." *New York Times,* August 27. Pro-Quest Historical Newspapers. https://www.proquest.com/docview/11374 1195/67922F9AABA84F18PQ/1?accountid=13800.
Ng, Boon-Kwee, A. S. Magli, Chan-Yuan Wong, and V. G. R. Chandran. 2017. "Localised Learning in the Malaysian Rice Cluster: Proximity, Social Capital and Institutional Dynamics." *International Development Planning Review* 39 (2): 163–185.
NIH (National Institutes of Health, National Center for Complementary and Integrative Health). "Cranberry." nd. https://www.nccih.nih.gov/health/cranberry. Accessed March 6, 2022.
Norton, R. D., and J. Rees. 1979. "The Product Cycle and the Spatial Decentralization of American Manufacturing." *Regional Studies* 13 (2): 141–151.
OECD. 2009. *Clusters, Innovation and Entrepreneurship.* Local Economic and Employment Development (LEED). Paris: OECD Publishing.
Pacific Coast Cranberry Research Foundation. 1997. *Pacific Coast Cranberries: The Cranberry Industry and Its History in Pacific County.* Long Beach, WA: Pacific Coast Cranberry Research Foundation.
Painchaud, Jacques. 2017. "L'adaptation de l'industrie québécoise de la canneberge aux conditions du marché: la grosse part va à la R & D." Powerpoint presentation to Journée d'information sur le bleuet sauvage, Dolbeau-Mistassini. March 15. https://www.mapaq.gouv.qc.ca/SaguenayLacStJean.
People's Daily Online. 2015. "Cranberry Contains Similar Nutrients as Other Fruits: Health Benefits of Cranberries Being Deified [Manyuemei suohan chengfen qita guoshu douyou: Baojian gongneng beishenhua]." *People's Daily Online,* October 26. http://health.people.com.cn/n/2015/1026/c21471-27739856.html.
Phillips, Peter W. B., Jeremy Karwandy, Graeme Webb, and Camille D. Ryan. 2013. *Innovation in Agri-Food Clusters: Theory and Case Studies.* Boston: CABI.
Piore, Michael J., and Charles F. Sabel. 1984. *The Second Industrial Divide: Possibilities for Prosperity.* New York: Basic Books.
Playfair, Susan. 2014. *America's Founding Fruit: The Cranberry in a New Environment.* Hanover, NH: University Press of New England.
Poirier, Isabelle. 2010. "La canneberge au Québec et dans le Centre du-Québec: Un modèle de développement durable, à la conquête de nouveaux marchés." Victoriaville: Government of Québec.

Poirier, Isabelle, and Jacques Painchaud. 2010. "La canneberge au Québec et au Centre-du-Québec un modèle de développement durable, à la conquête de nouveaux marchés." Victoriaville: Ministère de l'Agriculture, des Pêcheries et de l'Alimentation.

Porter, Michael E. 1990. *The Competitive Advantage of Nations.* New York: Free Press.

Porter, Michael E. 1998. Clusters and the New Economics of Competition. *Harvard Business Review* 76:77–90.

Prebisch, Raúl. 1950. *The Economic Development of Latin America and Its Principal Problems.* New York: United Nations.

Procopio, Nicholas A. III, and John F. Bunnell. 2008. Stream and Wetland Landscape Patterns in Watersheds with Different Cranberry Agriculture Histories, Southern New Jersey, USA. *Landscape Ecology* 23:771–786.

Sachs, Jeffrey D., and Andrew M. Warner. 1999. "Natural Resource Abundance and Economic Growth." NBER Working Paper no. 5398. Washington, DC: NBER.

Salamie, David E. 2007. "Land O'Lakes, Inc." *International Directory of Company Histories,* vol. 81. Detroit, MI: St. James Press.

Sánchez, Déborah S., Michael A. Boland, and Daniel Sumner. 2008. "Sun Maid Growers of California." *Review of Agricultural Economics* 30 (2): 360–369.

Saxenian, AnnaLee. 1983. "The Genesis of Silicon Valley." *Built Environment* 9 (1): 7–17.

Schumpeter, Joseph. 1939. *Business Cycles: A Theoretical, Historical, and Statistical Analysis of the Capitalist Process.* New York: McGraw-Hill.

Scitovsky, Tibor. 1954. "Two Concepts of External Economies." *Journal of Political Economy.* 62 (2): 143–151.

Siebert, Jerry. 1998. "Sunkist Case Study: Developing a Strategy for a Changing Production, Marketing, and Regulatory Environment." *Proceedings of Economic and Policy Implications of Structural Realignments in Food and Ag Markets.* Park City, UT: The Food and Agricultural Marketing Consortium Research Conference, July 31–August 2.

Silver Creek Nursery. nd. "Stevens Cranberry." https://silvercreeknursery.ca/products/stevens-cranberry. Accessed June 2, 2022.

Slaper, T., K. Harmon, and B. Rubin. 2018. "Industry Clusters and Regional Economic Performance: A Study across U.S. Metropolitan Statistical Areas." *Economic Development Quarterly* 32 (1): 44–59.

Smith, Claire. 2004. "A Cooperative Evolution: Sunkist Competes in the Global Market." Agricultural Outlook Forum. ageconsearch.umn.edu/bitstream, Accessed October 19, 2019.

Someya, Takuhiro. 2019. "Characterization of Cranberry Field Decline Syndrome in British Columbia." MS, University of British Columbia.

Spencer, Gregory M., Tara Vinodrai, Meric S. Gertler, and David A. Wolfe. 2010. "Do Clusters Make a Difference? Defining and Assessing Their Economic Performance." *Regional Studies* 44 (6): 697–715.

Stang, Elden J. 1993. "The North American Cranberry Industry." *Acta Horticulturae* 346:284–298.

State of Maine. 1988. *Cranberry Forum Background Report: Opportunities and Constraints to Establishing a Commercial Industry in Maine.* Augusta: Maine Department of Agriculture, Food and Rural Resources.

REFERENCES

State of Maine. 1996. "Cranberry Development Plan for the State of Maine." Augusta: Maine Public/Private Cranberry Development Workgroup, Maine Department of Agriculture, Food and Rural Resources.

State of Wisconsin. nd. "Wisconsin Cranberry Board." Department of Agriculture, Trade and Consumer Protection. https://datcp.wi.gov/Pages/AgDevelopment/WisconsinCranberryBoard.aspx. Accessed June 2, 2022.

Statistics Canada. 2016. "Table 32-10-0417-01, Fruits, Census of Agriculture, 2016." Data table. doi:https://doi.org/10.25318/3210041701-eng.

Steinle, Claus, and Holger Schiele. 2002. "When Do Industries Cluster?: A Proposal on How to Assess an Industry's Propensity to Concentrate at a Single Region or Nation." *Research Policy* 31 (6): 849–858.

Stevens, Neil E., and Jean Nash. 1944. "The Development of Cranberry Growing in Wisconsin." *Wisconsin Magazine of History* 27 (3): 276–294.

Sturgeon, Timothy J. 2000. "How Silicon Valley Came to Be." In *Understanding Silicon Valley: Anatomy of an Entrepreneurial Region*, edited by M. Kenny, 15–47. Stanford, CA: Stanford University Press.

Sunkist Growers. 1994. *Heritage of Gold: The First 100 Years of Sunkist Growers, Inc., 1893–1993*. Los Angeles, CA: Sunkist Growers.

Sun Maid. nd. "Get to Know Our Grower Story." https://www.sunmaid.com/about-us/grower-story/. Accessed October 19, 2019.

Turner, S. 2010. "Networks of Learning within the English Wine Industry." *Journal of Economic Geography* 10:685–715.

Uhle, Frank. 2007. "Sun Maid Growers of California." In *International Directory of Company Histories*, vol. 82, edited by Tina Grant, 367–371. Detroit, MI: St. James Press.

University of Maine. nd. "Cooperative Extension: Cranberries." https://extension.umaine.edu/cranberries/cranberry-facts-and-history/. Accessed November 14, 2019.

US Cranberries. nd, a. "Cranberry Varieties." https://reports.uscranberries.com/TheCranberryStory/Varieties/. Accessed March 10, 2022.

US Cranberries, nd, b. "Cranberry Marketing Committee." https://www.uscranberries.com/industry-news/2020-2022-cmc-membership/. Accessed September 27, 2023.

USDA. 1994. "Cooperatives in the U.S.—Citrus Industry." RB.C.DS Research Report 137. Washington, DC: USDA.

USDA National Agricultural Statistics Service. 2017. "Cranberries—Operations with Area Grown." Data table. NASS—Quick Stats. https://quickstats.nass.usda.gov/. Accessed June 14, 2022.

UW Fruit Program. nd. "Cranberries." https://fruit.wisc.edu/cranberries/. Accessed December 20, 2022.

VacCAP. nd. https://www.vacciniumcap.org/. Accessed March 11, 2022.

Vernon, R. 1966. "International Investment and International Trade in the Product Cycle." *Quarterly Journal of Economics* 80 (2): 190–207.

Vorsa, Nicholi, and Jennifer Johnson-Cicalese. 2012. "American Cranberry. In *Plant Breeding*, vol. 8, *Handbook of Fruit Breeding*, edited by M. L. Badenes and D. H. Byrne, 191–223. New York: Springer.

Wall Street Journal. 1923. "Sun Maid Raisin Growers." *Wall Street Journal,* December 28. Pro-Quest Historical Newspapers. https://www.proquest.com/docview/13 0134357/733F1CCC8B4E4768PQ/1?accountid=13800.
Washington State Legislature. nd. "Title 16, Chapter 16-565, Washington State Cranberry Commission." https://apps.leg.wa.gov/WAC/default. aspx?cite=16-565. Accessed December 19, 2020.
Weber, Alfred. 1909. "Über den Standort der Industrien [*The Theory of the Location of Industries*]. Tübingen: J.C.B. Mohr/Chicago: Chicago University Press [1929].
Welch's. nd. http://www.welchs.com/products. Accessed October 18, 2019.
West, Melanie Grayce. 2018. "N.Y. Grape Growers, Squeezed by Low Demand, Look beyond Juice." *Wall Street Journal,* April 30.
Wisconsin Cranberry Research Station. nd. "About." https://www. wisconsincranberryresearchstation.org/about. Accessed December 28, 2022.
Woeste, Victoria Saker. 1993. "Cooperatives and Corporations: The Sun Maid Antitrust Case and the Legal Status of Agricultural Cooperation, 1890–1943." *Business and Economic History* 22 (1): 25–30.
Woeste, Victoria Saker. 1998. *The Farmer's Benevolent Trust: Law and Agricultural Cooperation in Industrial America, 1865–1945.* Chapel Hill: University of North Carolina Press.
WSCGA (Wisconsin State Cranberry Growers Association). nd. "About Cranberries." https://www.wiscran.org/cranberries/. Accessed December 20, 2022.
Xincainet. 2021. "Interview with the Chairmen of Honghai: Let the Chinese Eat Cranberries Produced in Their Own Country [Zhuanfang honghai zhiye dongshizhang: Rang zhongguoren chishang ziji guojia shengchan de manyuemei]." http://www.xincainet.com/index.php/news/view?id=233275. Accessed September 21, 2022.
Yang, G., and R. Stough. 2005. "A Preliminary Analysis of Functional and Spatial Clustering: The Case of the Baltimore Metropolitan Region." In *Industrial Clusters and Inter-firm Networks,* edited by C. Karlsson, B. Johannson, and R. Stough, 303–320. Northampton, MA: Edward Elgar.
Ye, Bihua, and Yana Dai. 2021. "Global Reserve of Frozen Cranberry Reaches Historical Lows [Quanqiu manyuemei dongguo chubeiliang dadao lishi didian]." 21st Century Global Economic Report. https://m.21jingji.com/article/20190927/herald/b11e13077148e2d68af26bc28d3874e6.html. Accessed September 21, 2021.
Zane, Edward. 1954. "Marketing the Cranberry Crop." MBA Thesis, Boston University College of Business Administration.
Zhang, Xiaobo Zhang, and Dinghuan Hu. 2014. "Overcoming Successive Bottlenecks: The Evolution of a Potato Cluster in China." *World Development* 63:102–112.
Zhao, S., H. Liu, and L. Gu. 2020. "American Cranberries and Health Benefits: An Evolving Story of 25 Years." *Journal of the Science of Food and Agriculture* 100 (14): 5111–5116.

APPENDIXES

Appendix A
Survey

NORTH AMERICAN CRANBERRY GROWERS SURVEY
Andy Hira
Updated: December 7, 2021

NB: The opening screen of the survey contained the following message, and the survey was formatted online with boxes to check and columns where indicated:

Intro to Survey

Thank you for agreeing to complete this 30 minute survey. Your responses are needed to better understand cranberry stakeholder perspectives, as part of a 3 year USDA-funded independent project studying the cranberry industry. The result will be a report that will provide a strategic overview of the industry and will be publicly available.

This survey is completely voluntary and confidential. Please note that there is a comments area after many sections. Every response is very important to us, so thank you for taking the time to fill this out. Please note that sixteen $50 Amazon gift cards will be selected at random with at least one per cluster once the surveys are complete, for those who fill out contact information on the last screen.

Questions

I. Identification

Please be assured all answers will be kept confidential. We only want to ensure that a key person from each institution fills out the survey so that we can understand the patterns across the industry.

1. Do you work for a larger company (that includes non-cranberry activities) or as an individual grower or handler? (*Choice: company/individual*)

2. How many acres of cranberry production do you have? Approximately how many barrels of cranberries do you produce per year? Please fill in the number or check the not applicable box if you are not a grower. Fill in box *(2 boxes, acres & barrels; non-applicable)*

3. Do you handle or sell some of your own cranberry production (directly to customers)? Y/N

4. How many barrels of cranberries do you handle/process per year? *(Fill in box for number, and put 0 if you don't process any.)*

5. In what state or province is your operation located? Please give us your zip or postal code.

6. The following states and provinces contain relatively large numbers of cranberry operations. Please select the one cranberry cluster with which you identify (your answer could be your own state/province or one nearby). If you do not feel that your operation is part of any of the clusters listed, select "none" and specify your location in the comments section after this question.
    a. British Columbia
    b. Massachusetts
    c. New Jersey
    d. Oregon
    e. Quebec
    f. Washington
    g. Wisconsin
    h. Michigan
    i. Maritime Provinces (Nova Scotia, New Brunswick, or PEI)
    j. Chile
    k. None of the above (please specify)
       Comments:

7. How many years have you been in the cranberry industry? *(Fill in box)*

8. How many years has your family been involved in the cranberry industry? *(Fill in box)*

9. How many full time and part time employees do you typically have in a year, including yourself? Please fill in the number for each one: *(box for FT; box for PT)*

10. Please check all the activities your company works in (choose as many as apply):
    i. cranberry grower
    ii. cranberry handler
    iii. retail sales (directly to the customer)
    iv. sales of a related service
    v. marketing
    vi. equipment sales, rental, or repair

11. Over the last 5 years, your company has been:
    xii. always profitable
    xiii. sometimes profitable
    xiv. not yet profitable

12. Are you a grower member of the Ocean Spray cooperative or an independent grower/handler? Check both boxes if you are both a member of both Ocean Spray and independent?
    (box for OS   box for independent)

13. Do you believe that the cranberry industry is in an oversupply situation where low prices will persist? Y/N
    a. If yes, is it a long-term (more than 5 years) issue? Y/N
    b. If yes, are you considering leaving the industry? Y/N

14. In a recent year, using the number of barrels sold for the percentages, please estimate the
    a. % of your cranberries do you sell directly to customers, and % to the Ocean Spray co-op or independent handler? *(3 boxes for each option)*
    b. What % of your cranberries do you sell in the following ways?
        i. I sell all my cranberries directly to Ocean Spray or a handler for processing *(check box)*
        ii. Fresh (%)

iii. Canned (%)
iv. Dried (%)
v. Juice (%)
vi. Frozen (%)
vii. Other (please specify) (%)
Comments:

II. Priorities for the Cranberry Industry

15. In your opinion, which of the following factors are the most important for success in your industry? On a scale of 0–10, in terms of level of importance (with 0 being completely unimportant, 5 somewhat important, and 10 being absolutely vital), please fill in each of the columns (state or national).
    a. Growing conditions (e.g., soil and climate)
    b. Proximity to densely-populated consumer markets
    c. Product price
    d. Product differentiation/new cranberry-based products
    e. Proprietary knowledge, including growing, processing, and retailing techniques
    f. New cranberry varieties
    g. Proximity to receiving stations (for freezing, making juice, or dried cranberries)
    h. Customer perceptions of cranberry health benefits
    i. Marketing and branding
    j. Distribution channels (competition among handlers)
    k. Size of cranberry industry/overall supply
    l. Shared strategic vision for the whole industry
    m. Partnership and coordination of academic, public and private sectors
    n. Access to new knowledge and technologies
    o. Access to national and global markets

16. How should oversupply issues be dealt with in the cranberry industry? Please rate on a 0–10 scale for each, with 0 being unimportant, 5 being somewhat important and 10 being absolutely vital.
    a. Take some of the acreage out of production
    b. Govt. purchases farms/beds for land conversion (e.g., to wetlands)

c. USDA marketing order; or supply management under provincial leadership
d. No limits—each grower/handler can sell as much as they want and let the price take its natural course
e. Increased quality standards
f. Limit imports of cranberries
g. Work on new cranberry-based products
h. Expand overseas markets

17. How important is research and development and marketing in the cranberry industry in the following categories, 0 as unimportant, 5 as somewhat important, and 10 as absolutely vital?
    a. New varieties
    b. Pest management (cultural and pesticide tools)
    c. Bed management (nutrition, canopy management, water)
    d. Stress management (cold, heat, drought, flood)
    e. Fruit quality (color, firmness, size, and keeping quality)
    f. Harvesting techniques
    g. Processing
    h. Transportation/Distribution
    i. Managing overall supply management
    j. Marketing—domestic
    k. Marketing—global
    l. Product innovation
    Comments:

III. Roles of Support Institutions in Your Industry

18. How important are the following in terms of the level of support they provide to you on a scale of 0–10, with 0 as unimportant, and 10 as absolutely vital:
    a. Fellow growers—local level (this means within your local community, such as within your county or neighbors)
    b. Fellow growers—state/provincial level
    c. Fellow growers—national level
    d. Government run agricultural extension or experimental station
    e. University run agricultural extension or experimental station
    f. Growers' organization at the state/provincial level

g. Growers' organization at the national level
h. Ocean Spray
i. Independent (other) handlers
j. Cranberry Marketing Committee
k. Cranberry Institute
l. USDA or AAFC
m. Retail (commercial) outlets, including grocery chains
n. Suppliers including consultants, equipment suppliers, chemical or seed vendors, IPM providers, etc.
o. Other (please specify)

19. How should the private sector be organized for coordination in the cranberry industry? Check the appropriate response. You can choose more than one.
    a. One global industry association with universal membership funded by a mandatory assessment
    b. One national industry association with universal membership and a mandatory assessment
    c. State or provincial industry associations with a mandatory assessment
    d. No mandatory industry association, only voluntary industry associations with voluntary contributions
    e. Continue with the status quo
    f. Other (please specify)

20. In your opinion, what roles do the (state/provincial or federal) government, universities, Ocean Spray, independent handlers, and Cranberry Marketing Committee/BC Cranberry Marketing Committee, and the Cranberry Institute currently play? Check any of the columns where the actors currently play a role. *(6 columns, 1 for each actor)*
    a. Provides strategic vision and leadership
    b. Sponsors conferences and other meetings
    c. Helps in marketing, promotion, and regional branding
    d. Helps with exports
    e. Regulates industry or influences regulation
    f. Disseminates new technologies and knowledge through the industry

g. Develops local suppliers and industries related to the cranberry industry
h. Training employees
i. Levies/Taxes
j. No significant role
k. Other (please specify)

21. In your opinion, what roles should the (state/provincial or federal) government, universities, Ocean Spray, independent handlers, and Cranberry Marketing Committee currently play? Check any of the columns where you would like to see the actors play a role.
(5 columns, 1 for each actor)
   a. Provides strategic vision and leadership
   b. Sponsors conferences and other meetings
   c. Helps in marketing, promotion, and regional branding
   d. Helps with exports
   e. Regulates industry or influences regulation
   f. Disseminates new technologies and knowledge through the industry
   g. Develops local suppliers and industries related to the cranberry industry
   h. Training employees
   i. Levies/Taxes
   j. No significant role
   k. Other (please specify)

22. How do new techniques, such as new ways to manage pests, reach the industry? Rate each in terms of importance, with 0 as unimportant, 5 as somewhat important, and 10 as absolutely vital.
   a. Internet
   b. Word of mouth, informal communication
   c. Industry journals or newsletters
   d. Industry conferences
   e. Contacts with other industries
   f. Consultants (including handler agents)
   g. Equipment suppliers
   h. Industry association outreach
   i. Public sector outreach- such as state commissions
   j. Agricultural extension by local universities

k. Other (please specify)

23. In your opinion, how should and does knowledge about new growing or selling practices spread throughout your industry to reach growers *(2 columns for should and does)*? Choose as many of the options that fit your vision of how the cranberry industry shares knowledge.
    a. Public research labs produce new knowledge. The knowledge then is developed for the fields and spread by extension and commercial agents.
    b. Producers solve problems on their own and share that knowledge when they meet at the local level.
    c. Producers work with vendors/consultants to solve problems and then share the knowledge.
    d. Producers work together informally at the local level to share knowledge.
    e. Producers work through grower associations at the state level to share knowledge.
    f. Producers work with their supply chain partners (handlers and retailers) to share knowledge.
    g. Producers approach public support institutions to help them solve problems as they come across them.
    h. Industry associations take the lead
    i. Other (please specify)
    Comments:

24. How often per year do you meet personnel from support institutions? Choose any that apply and if so check one column for frequency (daily, weekly, monthly, semi-annually, quarterly, or annually) and one column for level of importance 1 as unimportant, 2 as slightly important, 3 as important, and 4 as very important.
    a. Regulators
    b. Agricultural extension agents from universities
    c. Agricultural extension agents from Ocean Spray
    d. Agricultural extension agent from an independent (not Ocean Spray) handler
    e. Growers association(s) at the state or provincial level
    f. Industry association(s), such as CMC, Cranberry Institute, and CETAQ

g. Individual growers for informal assistance with common problems
h. University researchers
i. Other (please specify)
Comments

25. When you interact with other growers on a regular basis, are they local (in your community), within the state, regional, or national, and how often *(column: daily, weekly, monthly, semi-annually, quarterly, or annually)*. Choose all that apply.
    a. Local
    b. Within the state/province
    c. Regional (multi-state/province)
    d. National
    e. International
    f. Growers from other industries

26. When you talk to fellow growers informally, what kinds of knowledge do you share? Choose all that apply.
    a. Personal experiences in the industry
    b. New techniques
    c. Industry issues
    d. Marketing and pricing information

27. How would you rate the importance of geographical proximity to other farms, handlers, and industry support institutions? (Choose a number between 1 and 10 with 0 as unimportant and 10 as absolutely vital.)

28. Some growers in your industry have reported that they are beginning to see the effects of climate change—for example, changes in the start and end dates of the growing season.
    a. Have you personally noticed any agronomic changes (growing season, yield, product quality, pest damage, etc.) that you would attribute to climate change? (Answer Yes/No/Not Applicable)
    b. If you answered Yes to question 28a, do you currently regard these changes as a threat or an opportunity to your business? (Answer on a 10-point scale with 0 standing for a significant threat, 5 as neutral and 10 standing for a significant opportunity.)
    Comments:

29. Let us know if you have any other issues or comments on the cranberry industry that we should consider, including the effects of covid.
Comments:

Closing

Thank you very much for your input! Please encourage your fellow growers to fill in the survey as well. It will help us to better understand policies to help the cranberry industry. If you would like to participate in the random draw for the Amazon gift cards, please fill in the following contact information. Your information will not be tied to survey responses or shared with anyone.

Name
E-mail
Phone

You can contact Andy Hira, ahirsfu.ca for a copy of the public report that will result from this study. It should be available sometime in late 2022. You can also contact Andy if you would like to have a conversation to more fully express your views about the industry. All comments would be off the record.

Appendix B
Ethics (Confidentiality) Forms

CONSENT FORM AND E-MAIL SCRIPT FOR CRANBERRY CLUSTERS SURVEY

This e-mail will be forwarded by the US Cranberry Marketing Committee to all US growers and by the provincial growers' associations to Canadian growers in Dec. 2021.

Consent Form and e-mail script for Cranberry Clusters Survey
Andy Hira
Simon Fraser University, Department of Political Science
e-mail: ahira@sfu.ca
[*to be sent by e-mail*]

Dear colleague:

My name is Andy Hira and I am a Professor of Political Science at Simon Fraser University in Vancouver, Canada. I am part of a team led by Dr. Paul Gottlieb of Rutgers University and funded by the US Dept. of Agriculture to study what makes agricultural clusters successful. Our hope is to find lessons that governments and trade associations can use to develop more robust supply chains, knowledge dissemination, and local support institutions for particular agricultural commodities. As part of the study, I am conducting an in depth study of the cranberry industry throughout North America. I am asking you, as a participant in the industry, to voice your opinion by filling out an on-line or hard copy survey so we can better understand growers' and others' concerns. As a participant in the cranberry industry, you have a unique perspective that can help improve policies to promote these concerns.

Your responses will help me to complete a study that looks at long-term trends and strategy for the industry. The study will be made publicly available in 2022.

The survey should take about 30 minutes. If possible, I would also like to conduct a 20 minute follow up interview with you in person, or via skype, e-mail, or telephone at a mutually convenient time. Pls. note that only in person and skype are considered secure means of communication by the ethics board. I can send you the interview questions ahead of time if you prefer. You can also indicate your willingness to do the interview in the last question of the survey. As a participant in the cranberry industry, you have a unique and important perspective that can help inform and improve policies to promote them.

In recognition of the value of your time, we are going to randomly award 16 survey respondents a $50 Amazon gift card. We will select and send the cards to the winners after the surveys are in. If you would like to be considered for the award, we ask you to fill in your contact details (e-mail address) on the last screen. We will not use your address for any other purpose, and once the awards are given, we will destroy the identifiers from any subsequent use of the survey. To be clear, the addresses will not be identified or linked in any way to the survey results.

Your responses will be anonymous. You can find the link for the survey here: http://websurvey.sfu.ca/survey/370383696

Please note that the survey link may not work on the Firefox browser. It will work on Microsoft Edge or Google Chrome.

In accordance with Canadian standard ethics procedures I wish to inform you of the following. The survey is completely voluntary and you are free to not answer any questions. I would like to assure you that your responses will be kept confidential and will be reported anonymously unless you specifically give me permission to discuss your company. There is absolutely no risk to you. Since I am contacting you for your opinions as an individual, I have not requested permission from your organisation. However, I am happy to do so if need be. Refusal to participate or withdrawal/dropout after agreeing to participate cannot have any adverse effect or consequences on your employment. I am a researcher with no ties to or influence upon your company or any government, so my only motivation is to find the truth to create better policies.

The survey is run through Simon Fraser University and is secure; only I will have access to the results that identify participants. Once I finish with the research, I will download the data to a SFU Vault, a secure server that is password protected. Any hard copy surveys will be shredded. After the study is completed, upon request, I will make anonymized versions of the data available to you and other researchers upon request. If you have any doubts or questions, or would like a copy of the results, please contact me at ahira@sfu.ca. You can also contact the Principal Investigator for the whole project, Dr. Paul Gottlieb, by email. If you have any questions regarding ethics procedures, you may contact Dr. Jeff Toward, Director, Office of Research Ethics. The ethics file number for this study is 2017s0141.

Your agreement by e-mail to participate in the study will be taken as consent to the ethics procedures outlined here. You will see at the end of the survey the possibility to leave contact information in order to enter into the Amazon card sweepstakes.
Thank you very much for your time and consideration.

CRANBERRY CLUSTERS INTERVIEW FOR GROWERS (HIRA)

Dear colleague:

My name is Andy Hira and I am a Professor of Political Science at Simon Fraser University in Vancouver, Canada. I am part of a team led by Dr. Paul Gottlieb of Rutgers University and funded by the US Dept. of Agriculture to study what makes agricultural clusters successful. I will be conducting the interviews during 2019–21 for our case study, the cranberry industry. Our hope is to find policy lessons so that the US and other governments can promote the development of supply chains and local businesses around agricultural industries. As part of the clusters study, we are conducting an in depth national study of the cranberry industry.

I am writing to ask for your cooperation in participating in an approximately 45 minute interview with you in person, or via skype, e-mail, or telephone at a mutually convenient time. Pls. note that only in person and skype are considered secure means of communication. We will send you the interview questions ahead of time. As an important participant in the cranberry industry, you have a unique and important perspective that can help inform and improve policies to promote them.

I would prefer to do the interviews in person, however I am flexible. I will be visiting your growing area for approximately 2 weeks during Fall 2021, and would like to interview you at that time if it's convenient. I recognize that covid is a continuing concern. I have been double vaccinated. I will follow SFU's communicable disease protocols (https://www.sfu.ca/srs/work-research-safety/general-safety/cdp.html). I suggest we try to conduct the interview outside. I will wear a mask and maintain a distance of at least 2 meters. If we are inside, we can maintain the same distance. If you are uncomfortable with meeting in person, we can set up a time for a zoom or phone call at a time of your convenience.

Because I am asking for your opinions as an individual, I have not sought approval from your organization. However, if you think it necessary, I can ask for permission before we set up the interview.

If you are a cranberry grower (farmer), I will not list your name anywhere in the report. I will simply state in the beginning of the report, that I spoke to x # of growers in x state/province. In highly exceptional circumstances, I may ask your permission to attribute a quote to you, but only if you give me explicit permission first. It is important to note that that study is based on looking at broader patterns across the industry, not individual opinions. I will also send you an advanced copy of the report before it's publicly available, to raise any objections in regard to passages that might identify you. You will have 2 weeks to respond with any concerns, or longer if you request it. I will make modifications to the report before it's published if you raise them with me, to ensure your confidentiality in regard to the information in the report. Thus, the answers you provide will be amalgamated into a wider survey of cranberry clusters around the country, in which case all the answers you provide would be anonymized. In exceptional circumstances, we might want to use a direct quote from you. In that case, we would run it by you and ask for your permission before doing so.

In accordance with SFU/Canadian ethics standards, I would like to inform you of the following. The interview is completely voluntary and you are free to not answer any questions. We would like to assure you that your responses will be kept confidential and responses will be reported anonymously as outlined above. There is no foreseeable risk to you. Refusal to participate or withdrawal/dropout after agreeing to participate can not have any adverse effect or consequences on your employment. We are researchers with no ties to or influence upon your company or any government, so our only motivation is to attain information that may be used to create better policies.

The interview data will be kept by Andy Hira at Simon Fraser University on a secure SFU server (SFU Vault); only Hira will have access to the results that identify participants. For the interview, we will make some notes on our laptops, which can only be opened with a password. Once the research is completed and published, Hira will then place an anonymized version of the data in SFU's data depository, available on-line through the SFU library website, so it might be used by other researchers. No companies or individuals will be reported in the results unless we receive explicit permission from them first. After the study is completed, upon request, we will make anonymized versions of the data available to you and other researchers upon request. If you have any doubts or questions, or would like a copy of the results, please contact me at ahira@sfu.ca. You can also contact the Principal Investigator for the whole project, Dr. Paul Gottlieb, by e-mail. If you have any questions regarding ethics procedures, you may contact Dr. Jeff Toward, Director, Office of Research Ethics. The ethics file number for this study is 2017s0141.

Your agreement by e-mail to participate in the study will be taken as consent to the ethics procedures outlined here.

Thank you very much for your time and consideration.

CRANBERRY CLUSTERS INTERVIEW FOR EXPERTS (HIRA)

Dear colleague:

My name is Andy Hira and I am a Professor of Political Science at Simon Fraser University in Vancouver, Canada. I am part of a team led by Dr. Paul Gottlieb of Rutgers University and funded by the US Dept. of Agriculture to study what makes agricultural clusters successful. I will be conducting the interviews during 2019-21 for our case study, the cranberry industry. Our hope is to find policy lessons so that the US and other governments can promote the development of supply chains and local businesses around agricultural industries. As part of the clusters study, we are conducting an in-depth study of the cranberry industry in the U.S. and Canada.

I am writing to ask for your cooperation in participating in an approximately 45 minute interview with you in person, or via skype, e-mail, or telephone at a mutually convenient time. Pls. note that only in person and skype are considered secure means of communication. We will send you the interview questions ahead of time. As an important participant in the cranberry industry, you have a unique and important perspective that can help inform and improve policies to promote them.

I would prefer to do the interviews in person, however I am flexible. I will be visiting your growing area for approximately 2 weeks during Fall 2021, and would like to interview you at that time if it's convenient. I recognize that covid is a continuing concern. I have been double vaccinated. I will follow SFU's communicable disease protocols (https://www.sfu.ca/srs/work-research-safety/

general-safety/cdp.html). I suggest we try to conduct the interview outside. I will wear a mask and maintain a distance of at least 2 meters. If we are inside, we can maintain the same distance. If you are uncomfortable with meeting in person, we can set up a time for a zoom or phone call at a time of your convenience.

Because I am asking for your opinions as an individual, I have not sought approval from your organization. However, if you think it necessary, I can ask for permission before we set up the interview.

It is important for the credibility of this study to demonstrate an effort to collect the views of a diverse group of stakeholders across the cranberry industry. As a distinguished expert, I ask your permission to list your name at the top of the report as an interviewee. However, I will not link your name to any particular piece of information or quote, unless I first receive your explicit permission. You can also opt to go completely off the record if you prefer. It is important to note that that study is based on looking at broader patterns across the industry, not individual opinions. I will also send you an advanced copy of the report before it's publicly available, to raise any objections in regard to passages that might identify you. You will have 2 weeks to respond with any concerns, or longer if you request it. I will make modifications to the report before it's published if you raise them with me, to ensure your confidentiality in regard to the information in the report. Thus, the answers you provide will be amalgamated into a wider survey of cranberry clusters around the country, in which case all the answers you provide would be anonymized.

In accordance with SFU/Canadian ethics standards, I would like to inform you of the following. The interview is completely voluntary and you are free to not answer any questions. We would like to assure you that your responses will be kept confidential and responses will be reported anonymously as outlined above. There is no foreseeable risk to you. Refusal to participate or withdrawal/dropout after agreeing to participate can not have any adverse effect or consequences on your employment. We are researchers with no ties to or influence upon your company or any government, so our only motivation is to attain information that may be used to create better policies.

The interview data will be kept by Andy Hira at Simon Fraser University on a secure SFU server (SFU Vault); only Hira will have access to the results that identify participants. For the interview, we will make some notes on our laptops, which can only be opened with a password. Once the research is completed and published, Hira will then place an anonymized version of the data in SFU's data depository, available on-line through the SFU library website, so it might be used by other researchers. No companies or individuals will be reported in the results unless we receive explicit permission from them first.

After the study is completed, upon request, we will make anonymized versions of the data available to you and other researchers upon request. If you have any doubts or questions, or would like a copy of the results, please contact me at ahira@sfu.ca. You can also contact the Principal Investigator for the whole project, Dr. Paul Gottlieb, by e-mail. If you have any questions regarding ethics procedures, you may contact Dr. Jeff Toward, Director, Office of Research Ethics. The ethics file number for this study is 2017s0141.

Your agreement by e-mail to participate in the study will be taken as consent to the ethics procedures outlined here.

Thank you very much for your time and consideration.

Appendix C
Notes on GIS Maps

Notes: Only consolidated subdivisions (Canada) or counties (US) with five or more operations (farms) growing cranberries are included in the map. Each dot represents one operation that grows cranberries. Cranberries may not be the only crop grown or even the crop with the largest acreage at the operation. Dots are placed randomly inside the consolidated subdivision or county where an operation is located. Dark gray lines indicate provincial or state boundaries. Light gray lines represent consolidated subdivision or county boundaries.

Sources: Authors' visualization using Statistics Canada, Agriculture Division, 2016 Census of Agriculture; United States Department of Agriculture, National Agricultural Statistics Service, 2017 Census of Agriculture; and Authors' processing station data.

DATA SOURCES

USDA National Agricultural Statistics Service. 2017. Cranberries—Operations with Area Grown (data table). https://www.nass.usda.gov/Statistics_by_State/New_Jersey/Publications/Cranberry_Statistics/2016%20CRANBERRYSUM%209-2017.pdf.
NASS—Quick Stats. https://quickstats.nass.usda.gov/. Accessed June 14, 2022.
Statistics Canada. 2016. Table 32-10-0417-01: Fruits, Census of Agriculture, 2016 (data table). https://doi.org/10.25318/3210041701-eng.

About the Authors

ANIL HIRA

Anil (Andy) Hira is a full professor of political science at Simon Fraser University, the leading comprehensive university in Canada. He has published more than ninety books and articles, as well as numerous technical reports for agencies such as the UN and Global Affairs Canada. Hira is an expert on economic competitiveness, with an emphasis on the challenges facing developing countries. His publications include *What Makes Clusters Competitive? Cases from the Global Wine Industry* (McGill-Queen's University Press); "Mapping Out the Triple Helix: How Institutional Coordination Is Achieved in the Global Wine Industry" (*Prometheus: Journal of Innovation*, special edition, December 2013); several well-cited articles on biofuels; and a forthcoming book on socially responsible investment.

Hira is active in social media, on Twitter, Facebook, ResearchGate, and Academia.edu. He is planning to publicize this book through professional conferences, such as the industry and regional studies associations. He has also presented and will continue to publicize the work through the numerous stakeholder contacts made in the cranberry industry.

He can be reached by email at ahira@sfu.ca.

PAUL GOTTLIEB

Paul Gottleib is an associate professor in the Department of Agricultural, Food, and Resource Economics at Rutgers, State University of New Jersey. Besides heading up the USDA clusters grant ($490,000) of which this study is a part, Paul Gottlieb focuses on two main areas of research. The first is land use, where he studies the effects of large-lot zoning and purchase of development rights on raw land prices, rural preservation, and housing affordability. This work has appeared in such journals as *Land Use Policy*, the *Annals of the Association of American Geographers*, and the *Journal of Housing Economics*. His second current area of research consists of cost-benefit analyses of sustainability investments, especially irrigation systems that recycle water and community-scale anaerobic digestors.

The USDA project of which this book is a part grew out of Dr. Gottlieb's past research on economic development policy in urban settings, which he conducted at Case Western Reserve University's Center for Regional Economic Issues from 1993 to 2002. That work consisted of policy analyses of high-tech development for US states and metropolitan areas, paying special attention to industry clusters and their associated stocks of human capital. His economic development research has been published in *Economic Development Quarterly*, where he sits on the editorial board, as well as in *Urban Studies*, the *Journal of Urban Affairs*, and the *Journal of Regional Science*, among others. He has served on the board of the Council for Food, Agricultural, and Resource Economics and currently sits on the technical advisory committee for the USDA-funded Northeast Regional Center for Rural Development at Pennsylvania State University.

He can be reached by email at gottlieb@njaes.rutgers.edu.

NEIL REID

Neil Reid, PhD, is professor of geography in the Department of Geography and Planning at the University of Toledo. He is a regional scientist and industrial geographer, whose research interests focus on the dynamics of local economic development in cities located in old industrial regions of the United States. Some of his past work, funded by the US Department of Agriculture, focused on working with the northwest Ohio greenhouse industry. In particular, he helped the industry understand the benefits of cluster-based economic development and worked with them to establish the Maumee Valley Growers, a trade group focused on identifying areas where local greenhouses could collaborate to solve common industry-wide challenges. More recently, Professor Reid's work has focused on understanding the spatial dynamics of America's burgeoning craft brewing industry, particularly its contribution to local neighbourhood development. This research stream has also examined the impact of craft breweries on local hop production. As a recognized expert on the craft brewing industry, Professor Reid has contributed opinion pieces to the *Wall Street Journal*, *National Public Radio*, *Salon*, and the *Brewer Magazine*. Professor Reid's work has been published in a wide range of scholarly journals including *Economic Development Quarterly*, *Papers in Regional Science*, and the *Professional Geographer*. Professor Reid has served as chair of the International Geographical Union Commission on the Dynamics of Economic Spaces (2010–2014) and as executive director of the North American Regional Science Council (2013–2021). He currently serves as an associate editor for the journal *Regional Science Policy and Practice*, and as book review editor for *Economic Development Quarterly*, and he is on the editorial boards of the journals *Applied Geography* and the *Journal of Innovation and Entrepreneurship*. He can be reached by email at neil.reid@utoledo.edu.

STEPHAN GOETZ

Stephan Goetz is professor of agricultural and regional economics at Penn State University and the director of the Northeast Regional Center for Rural Development, where he provides leadership for economic and community development research and extension activities across thirteen states. Part of this responsibility includes linking state activities to national and regional initiatives. His research focuses on the determinants and effects of economic growth and development, with current applications of network science principles to economic growth, clustering, resilience, and innovation.

Dr. Goetz has published or presented more than two hundred professional papers, and he is the senior coeditor of four books, including *Targeting Regional Economic Development* (Routledge, 2009). He is the principal investigator on external grants valued at more than $15 million. Among other service roles, he is a member of the board of directors of the Center for Rural Pennsylvania (a legislative agency of the PA General Assembly) and the Council of Food, Agricultural and Resource Economics.

He can be reached by email at sgoetz@psu.edu.

ELIZABETH A. DOBIS

Elizabeth Dobis was a postdoctoral scholar in the area of regional economic growth and development with the Northeast Regional Center for Rural Development (NERCRD) at Penn State University from 2017 to 2020. Her research interest is spatial economic analysis, particularly pertaining to health, demography, and communities. Her health-related research has focused on topics such as health-care utilization of vulnerable populations, spatial variation in life expectancy, insurance coverage among the rural self-employed, and health-care supply and demand related to COVID-19. Her other research has included topics such as the evolution of the American urban hierarchy, the colocation of vineyards and wineries, and poverty and place. Dr. Dobis has published her work in journals such *Social Science and Medicine* and the *Journal of Economic Geography*. She contributed to this publication in her capacity as a NERCRD postdoctoral scholar.

Dr. Dobis joined the USDA Economic Research Service's Rural Economy Branch in March 2020, where she is a research agricultural economist with a focus on rural health in the United States. In October 2020, she was named to the board of directors for the North Central Regional Center for Rural Development, and in April 2022 she was elected to the executive council of the Southern Regional Science Association.

Index

A
agricultural extension, 12, 22–23, 26, 34–35, 39, 47, 49–54, 57, 68, 103, 105, 112, 114, 144, 148–149, 152, 163, 166, 172–175
agritourism in cranberry industry, 87, 104, 161
American Cranberry Exchange, 66–67, 69
APCQ (Québec Cranberry Growers' Association), 51, 81, 116–117, 120, 125–127, 147, 155
Atoka (cranberry company), 20, 41, 64, 117, 119, 120, 123, 128, 168
sale to Ocean Spray, 122

B
Bieler, Marc (Québec industry innovator), 47, 118–121
branding. *See* product differentiation
British Columbia (BC) cranberry industry, 33, 45, 47, 49–51, 81, 95, 101–115, 119, 122, 126, 128, 150, 152–158, 167, 171–172, 174
   BCCMC (marketing commission), 109–112, 112, 114, 147
   extension, 50, 112, 114
   IAF (Investment Agricultural Foundation), 113–114
   Production statistics, 97–100

C
Canada, production statistics, 97–100
Cape Cod Cranberry Growers' Association, 34, 59, 65–66, 103–104
Chaney, Arthur, 29, 65–66
Chile, cranberry industry, 24, 35, 39, 61, 72, 81–83, 102, 174
China, cranberry industry, 22, 39–40, 82–90, 117, 122, 128, 159–160, 163, 170
Citadelle (cranberry company), 41, 117, 119, 121, 125–126
climate change, effects on cranberry industry, 156–157, 164–165
cluster(s), boundaries, 16
   customer-driven, proximity to markets 1–2, 7–8, 39–40, 158
   decline ("lock in"), 12–14
   definition, **1, 8**
   and knowledge, 10–11, 35
   industrial districts, 1–3
   measurement of, 16–19
   to overcome commodity cycles, 25–26
   policies to promote, 3
   Porter theory, 8–9
   life cycles of, 12–15
   and technology, 6
   types of clusters, 15–16
   and supply chains, 6–9
commodification, 3
commodity cycles
   and clusters, 25
   definition, **4, 21**
   in the cranberry industry, 26–29, 61–64, 77–84, 90–106, 170–172
   lessons from cooperatives, 171
comparative advantage (law of), 6–7, 19–20
concentration of ownership, 20–21, 39, 46, 96, 102–106, 157–158
consolidation, in cranberry industry. *See* concentration of ownership
coopetition, definition, **22**
COVID-19, effects on the cranberry industry, 36, 76, 79, 93, 102, 109, 112, 124, 151
cranberry industry
   basic product categories, 36–37
   break even point, 92
   cooperation, origins of, 65
   costs of production, 92
   demand for, 77–81, 152
   economic value of, incl. by state, 24, 32
   entrepreneurship in, 47
   exports, 83–86, 89–90, 154–155, 159

cranberry industry (*continued*)
  geographic concentration of, 24
  global production by location, 81–82
  growing conditions, 31, 33
  harvesting methods, 38
  independent producers, 41–42, 73–76, 128–129, 151–152
  innovation and R&D, 39, 47–57, 165–167
  knowledge sharing across clusters, 50–51, 122
  marketing strategies, 165–167
  migrant/temporary workers, 110, 124
  organic cranberries, 54, 117
  origins of cranberries as a food crop, 31
  origins of industry, 58–60
  oversupply (potential), 28–29, 77–80, 156–157
  processing stations, 42–45
  productivity differences by cluster, 93–100
  quality attributes, 49
  supply chains, 36–38
  survey of growers, 147–149
  training, 50
  varietals, including new, 32, 48–50, 54–56, 103, 109, 157, 166, 175
  See also environmental regulation
Cranberry Institute (CI), 53, 149, 152–156, 164, 174
Cranberry Marketing Committee (CMC), 53, 68–69, 83, 90, 101–102, 120–121, 147–149, 152–153, 154–160, 163–164, 166, 168, 174
  origins in the cranberry industry, 64
Cranberry Research Foundation, 52–53

D
Decas (cranberry company), 40, 68, 174
Deming, Arthur, 3–4

E
Eck, Paul, 48, 51, 59, 61–63, 65–66, 69, 90
economic value (of the cranberry industry), 24
economies of scale, 7, 38–39
Emblème (cranberry company), 41, 117, 121, 124
endogenous growth theory (industry timing), 6

environmental regulation, 32–34, 126–127
extension. *See* agricultural extension

F
family farms. *See* concentration of ownership
firm-based (pecuniary) advantages, 6
Fordism, 3
Fruit d'Or (cranberry company), 20, 41, 68, 117, 119, 121–124, 126, 129, 174

G
Gardner, Michel, 119
Gereffi, Gary, 9–10
globalization (effects on clusters), 3
Global Production Networks (GPNs), 9–10
Global Value Chains (GVCs), 9–10

H
health benefits, of cranberries, 88, 162–163
  Helicobacter (H.) pylori, 88, 160, 162–163
  sugar concerns, 168–169

I
independent producers. *See* cranberry industry
information, role of. *See* knowledge
institutions, role in clusters, 10–11

J
juice, 20, 31, 41, 45, 64, 67, 113, 114, 117, 118, 121–122, 128
  100% cranberry juice markets, 63, 70, 102, 121–122, 142, 152, 162, 167
  in the Chinese market, 88–90
  and health concerns (about sugar), 56, 162–163, 167–169
  innovation in, 48, 62–64, 70–72
  juice concentrate (excess inventory), 102
  market trends, 79–81, 84, 90
  Ocean Spray production capacity of, 67
  Ocean Spray strategy around, 167–168, 175–176
  quality attributes, 106
  share of cranberry market, 77
  Sunkist, 130, 141–143
  Sun-Maid, 133
  supply chains for, 36–40, 42, 45, 48–49, 150
  and varietals, 56
  Welch's, 130, 133–137, 145

INDEX

K
knowledge (role in clusters), 10–11
  transfer of knowledge in cranberry industry, 118, 172
  tacit, 22–23, 35, 47
  See also cranberry industry
Krugman, Paul, 7, 37, 45, 171

L
land, costs of, effects on cranberry industry, 46
Land O' Lakes (cooperative), 137–139, 146
Larocque family, 118–120
Lassonde Pappas (juice company), 41, 63–68, 150
Laval, University of, 54
levies (for research and marketing), 53, 166–7
"lock in." *See* cluster decline

M
Makepeace (cranberry company), 35, 67, 69
Maine, cranberry industry, 34–35, 38, 42, 67, 68, 100, 172–174
MAPAQ (Government of Québec, Min. of Agriculture, Fisheries, and Food), 51, 119–121, 127
marketing order. *See* USDA
Markusen, Ann, 15–16
Martin and Sunley (cluster measurement), 18–19
Marshall, Alfred, 1–2
Massachusetts, cranberry industry, 24, 27, 31, 32–35, 40, 42–43, 46–49, 52, 56, 63, 65–67, 76, 81, 92–93, 98, 100–102, 112–113, 119, 150, 152, 161
  barriers to exit, 33, 103–104
  consolidation of cranberry industry in, 96
  and origins of cranberry industry, 58–62
  future of industry, 33, 103–106, 156–158, 165, 174
  as a source of knowledge, 118, 123
  state task force, 102–103, 156
  University of Massachusetts extension station, 33–34, 105, 163
  and Welch's 133–137
Michigan, cranberry industry, 33–35, 172–173
Minnesota, cranberry industry, 33–35, 173–174

N
NACREW (extension organization), 51, 167
National Cranberry Association, 69
New Jersey, cranberry industry, 33, 42, 45–49, 93, 96, 102, 150, 164
  agritourism, 161
  future of industry, 104–106, 156–158
  origins of cranberry industry, 58–61
  Rutgers University extension station, 105
New Zealand, cranberry industry, 21, 35, 39, 81–82
niche products. *See* product differentiation
Northland (fruit company), 63–64

O
Ocean Spray
  cranberry industry, role in 28–30, 67
  extension, role in, 47, 68, 75, 112, 152
  future role, 149–153
  and grapefruit market, 71
  history of, 67–69
  lite varieties, 168
  loyalty to, 72–76, 150
  market share in different clusters, 46–47
  and Nantucket Nectars, 71
  and Northland company, 63–64
  and PepsiCo., 71
  price premium to members, 92, 157–158
  purchase of Atoka, 122
  role in Québec, 120–121
  role in R&D and product development, 48, 62–63, 70–72, 112, 160–162
  See also cranberry industry, independent producers
OECD, 3
Oregon, cranberry industry, 39–42, 45–47, 54, 60, 62, 67, 89–90, 96, 104, 106, 112, 115, 157–158, 164, 175
  extension, 172

P
Pacific Coast Cranberry Research Foundation, 53–54
Painchaud, Jacques, 119, 127
Papadellis, Randy (former Ocean Spray CEO), 72, 160
Patten, Dr. Kim, 53–54, 111
Pelis, Joe, 118
PepsiCo., 63, 71, 171

Playfair, Susan, 51, 58, 60–62, 65–68, 82
product differentiation or diversification (marketing strategy), 4–5, 25–26, 73, 158, 160–162, 168
product life cycles, 12–15
Porter, Michael, 8–9, 17–18

Q
Québec, cranberry industry, 20, 46–47, 115–129
   CETAQ (Club Environnemental et Technique Atocas Québec), 125, 127
   environmental regulations, effect of, 33, 121
   extension, 39, 50, 54, 112, 123, 127, 129
   government policy to promote cranberry industry, 123–126
   growing areas, 41, 116
   and Laval University, 54
   origins of, 117–120
   MAPAQ (provincial agency, role of), 119
   production and export statistics, 97–100
   productivity increases, 93–96

R
Regional Systems of Innovation (RIS), 11
resource curse, 21
Rutgers University extension station, role in innovation, 32, 51, 55, 103, 105, 164–166, 175

S
Schumpeter, Joseph, 12–14
Scitovsky, Tibor, 6
SDCs (sweetened dried cranberries), **31**, 36–37, 38, 70, 79, 106, 150, 169
sectoral systems of innovation, 10–11
Sunkist (cooperative), 139–144, 145
Sun-Maid (cooperative), 131–133, 145
supply chains. See clusters; cranberry industry

T
technology (role in clusters). See clusters
training. See cranberry industry
transactions costs (for trade), 2
triple helix (innovation framework), 10–11

U
Urann, Marcus, 29, 67
USDA (US Department of Agriculture)
   extension, 52, 174
   fresh fruit standards, 36
   marketing order, 62, 101–102, 153

V
varietals. See cranberry industry
Vernon, Raymond, 14–15

W
Washington state cranberry industry, 23, 39–42, 45–47, 49, 56, 59–62, 73, 75–76, 96, 106, 157, 175
   extension, 51, 53–54, 172
   State Cranberry Commission, 53
Weber, Alfred, 7
Welch Foods Inc., 133–137, 145
wine clusters, 4, 11–12, 16, 22–23, 166
Wisconsin cranberry industry, 14, 20, 32–35, 37, 45–47, 49, 61–67, 69, 72, 75, 122, 129, 148, 155–159, 172–173
   Cranberry Board, 51–52, 147, 153, 174
   Cranberry Research and Education Foundation, 52
   and environmental regulations, 33
   extension and innovation, 32, 39, 51–56, 164–167
   growing areas, 40
   innovation in, 39, 48–51, 103, 175
   origins of cranberry industry in, 59–60
   productivity increases, 93–100